Praise for

BATTLING WHILE BLACK

"Major General Gravett has done a fantastic job telling these stories, which, without him, would certainly be lost to history."
—**Major General Laura Yeager,**
USA (Ret.), Former Army Division Commander, Former Commander of the California Army National Guard

"General Gravett provides a fascinating historical review of World War II from the Black perspective."
—**Major General James Delk,** USA (Ret.), Former Army Division Commander, Award-Winning Author of *The Fighting Fortieth in War and Peace; Fires & Furies: The L. A. Riots—What Really Happened*

"Major General Gravett's marvelous reflection on the many struggles, sacrifices, and contributions that so many unsung Black patriotic American men and women made throughout the history of our nation's military is commendable."
—**Dr. Kenneth Graham,** Lieutenant Colonel, USMC (Ret.)

"Superb writing remembering those who may have been lost to American history."
—**Edward Fitzgerald,** Military Historian

"Major General Gravett vividly showcases the unsung, heroic combat duty of four 'all-Negro' units . . . against the backdrop of pernicious racism, bigotry, and hypocrisy prevalent in the US military throughout WWII."
—**Captain Kelly Galvin,** USA (Ret.), Award-Winning Author of *PowerPoint Ranger: My Iraq War Log*s

"Army Major General Peter J. Gravett does a masterful job in his critique of the military in its treatment of African American soldiers throughout the history of the United States, with vivid details and descriptions of military policies, procedure, and protocols. His accounts are both stiring and soul searching and beg the question of fairness andequality of the African American men and women who put on a uniform in defense of America.
—**Felton C. Williams,** Ph.D., former President and Board Member, Long Beach Unified School District; former Chair, Council of the Great City Schools, former Dean, School of Business and Social Science, Long Beach City College.

General George S. Patton bestows the Silver Star on Private Ernest Jenkins of the 761st Tank Battalion. Photo courtesy of the U.S. Army.

BATTLING WHILE BLACK

General Patton's
Heroic African American
WWII Battalions

MAJOR GENERAL PETER J. GRAVETT, USA (RET)

VIRGINIA BEACH
CAPE CHARLES

Battling While Black
by Major General Peter J. Gravett, USA (Retired)

© Major General Peter J. Gravett, USA (Retired)

ISBN 979-8-88824-084-7

All rights reserved. No part of this publication may be reproduced,
stored in a retrieval system, or transmitted in any form or by any means—
electronic, mechanical, photocopy, recording, or any other—
except for brief quotations in printed reviews,
without the prior written permission of the author.

Published by

3705 Shore Drive
Virginia Beach, VA 23455

800-435-4811

*To my wife, Blanche McClure Gravett
Colonel, US Army (retired),
for her love, inspiration,
and assistance in this project.*

TABLE OF CONTENTS

Author's Note: My Father's Footsteps / 1

Introduction: The Mighty, Malicious Pen / 5

Part One: American's Secondary Airforce (320th Barrage Balloon Battalion) / 23

High Flight Poem / 27

Introduction / 29

Chapter 1: Sky's the Limit / 32

Chapter 2: Building More Segregation / 37

Chapter 3: Nothing Less Than Victory / 45

Chapter 4: The Beginning of the End / 53

Photographs / 56

★ ★ ★

Part Two: The Combat Arm of Decision (761st Tank Battalion) / 61

Introduction / 65

Chapter 1: Bitterly Opposed in the South / 70

Chapter 2: Come out Fighting / 73

Chapter 3: Lock and Load / 84

Chapter 4: Prelude to Battle / 91

Chapter 5: The Battle Is Born / 97

Chapter 6: From Victory to Victory / 104

Chapter 7: Calling All Negroes / 115

Chapter 8: Steel Coffins / 119

Chapter 9: Damn Good Soldiers / 128

Chapter 10: The War at Home / 140

Photographs / 144

★ ★ ★

Part Three: The King of Battle
(333rd Field Artillery Battalion) / 149

Introduction / 153

Chapter 1: Black Blood / 156

Chapter 2: Becoming the Weapon / 161

Chapter 3: Bullets, Balloons, and Bombs Away / 167

Chapter 4: Before the Bulge / 176

Chapter: 5: Battle of the Bulge / 182

Chapter 6: The Wereth Eleven / 187

Chapter 7: At War's End / 194

Photographs / 198

★ ★ ★

Part Four: We Deliver (6888th Central Postal / 201
       Directory Battalion)

Introduction / 205

Chapter 1: Women to the Rescue / 210

Chapter 2: The House Women Built / 218

Chapter 3: England: Mission Commenced / 225

Chapter 4: Mission Accomplished: Moving Forward / 232

Chapter 5: Home, Unsweet Home / 236

Photographs / 242

Postface: A Rear View of World War II / 245

★ ★ ★

Epilogue / 247

Acknowledgments / 252

Footnotes / 254

Index / 277

Major General (Retired) Peter J. Gravett with his father Clarence Gravett Sr.

Author's Note

In My Father's Footsteps

The genesis of this book dates back to the end of World War II—to when I was a child and can recall, for the only time, seeing my father, a private with the Tuskegee Airmen, in his Army uniform. I was too young to understand any context, or just how important his service proved, but I imagine he was dressed for his homecoming upon being honorably discharged from the Army. I recall his brown uniform, adorned in a waist-length jacket with a red and blue patch signifying his Army Air Corps unit. My dad removed his service hat and placed it on my small-in-comparison head; I pivoted and marched around the room, and at that moment, I was a soldier.

From then on, I was enamored with the military. My ambition in future decades, known by anyone who knew me, was to become a soldier like my father, who the Army had assigned to base operations ferrying pilots to and from their aircraft. And later, although brief, I picked his brain about his military service and what it was like to be a Black man in the segregated American Army. The older half of my siblings and I were raised in an integrated neighborhood in Southern California, where we attended a unified elementary school. I hadn't experienced the same, blatant discrimination as my father, who was born and raised in Jim Crow era Arkansas. I could hardly have fathomed his experience reporting to the local induction center, where he was processed into the Army, draft notice in hand, leaving behind a wife and eight children, all ten years old and younger.

My dad explained that, at this divisive time in our country's history, all soon-to-be soldiers were divided into two groups for separate training: Whites and Coloreds, which at that time included Asians, Native Americans, and Hispanics. During his basic training in the Colored unit, inductees from outside the South had a difficult time adjusting to segregation, this being their first exposure. To my father and his fellow Southerners, the separation felt like home. As I approached enlistment age, following in my father's footsteps, I wondered whether I would have to endure what he, and many Black soldiers, overcame. And, initially, I did.

My military career began in the late 1950s in the California Army National Guard in a segregated Negro unit that was, ironically, also made up of two Whites (both Jewish), two Asians (one Chinese and one Japanese)—all of whom had enlisted in the Negro unit by choice. Following the lead of the federal military, which had been mandated to integrate by presidential order in 1948, under Title 10 of the US Code, the National Guard in California and several other states began to voluntarily integrate. Prior to this, states followed Title 10 under the control of the president, but serving under Title 32, states would integrate under their appointed governor and, within a few years, see full integration within the National Guard.

I could have never imagined the experience and information I'd gain serving within that Negro unit. Stories from older soldiers who'd served in segregated Army service and combat units during World War II (some in the Korean War before the Army was fully integrated in 1948) merged with my father's military experiences and provided a rare glimpse into the isolated past of Black Army soldiers, only deepening my unique fascination with it all. Early in my career, I started gathering materials and histories of veterans, primarily from World War II combat units, and reminiscing with these men about their accomplishments and adversities.

Similar to all African American units, Colored soldiers were not initially trained for—and never expected to see—combat, as the Army deemed them only worthy to serve in support units; if they were deployed to combat areas, it was for the sole purpose of supporting White soldiers and appeasing the Black press of the day and Black leaders back home. However, all of this would change following three years of intense warfare; as the enemy advanced in the European Theater of Operations during WWII, the American Army would need all the combat power it could muster.

The disheartening events of this book are a mere snapshot of what four lesser known African American Army units endured during their service against Hitler's Army. The African American soldiers and sailors, men and women alike, played an integral part in America's segregated military during World War II. Much has been written about several of these units, such as the Air Corps's Tuskegee Airmen; the Army's 92nd Infantry Division, 555th Airborne Battalion, and the Red Ball Express; the Marine Corps's Montfort Point Marines; the Navy's Golden 13; plus highlighting exploits of individual Coast Guardsmen. The courageous men and women, ridiculed by their compatriots and leaders, were spread out among varying units—a barrage balloon battalion, tank battalion, field artillery battalion, and a postal directory battalion—but connected by the same segregation and treatment in America's military. Throughout, I have interchanged historic references to Blacks and African Americans, such as *Negro, Nigger, and Colored*, to accentuate the tone of the 1940s segregation.

At first, this book was simply a recounting of historical events that took place during WWII in America and Europe. Over time, it took shape as an emotionally triumphant but tragic journey through the early lives and service of African American men and women *and* a reflection about American history. These stories aren't intended as a complete record, but rather a fraction of a glimpse into a disturbing reality. The Black men and women of the 320th Barrage Balloon Battalion, 761st Tank Battalion, 333rd Field Artillery Battalion, and 6888th Central Postal Directory Battalion are chronicled in how critical they were to the success of General Patton, who led these US Army battalions to victory in the European Theater. I am proud to shed more light on these still mostly unknown Black heroes.

Lt. Col. Peter Gravett (Author), Commander 1st Battalion, 185th Armor Regiment, 40th Infantry Division (Mechanized), 1988. Photo courtesy of Peter Gravett.

INTRODUCTION

The Mighty, Malicious Pen

IN A POISONOUS EFFORT that aided the spread of fear and ignorance in post–WWI America, which only further encouraged racism and bigotry nationwide, the US Army War College wrote a 1925 report on African American soldiers. *The 1925 Army War College Report* or *The Study* was released seven years after World War I to "furnish a basis for the employment of the Negro in the next war." *The Study* became the bible that would perpetuate the misguided thoughts, actions, and policies of leaders in the United States Army fifteen years later in World War II. Prominent generals in the European Theater of Operations (ETO), including Eisenhower, Marshall, Patton, Clark, Bradley, Gerow, Ridgeway, Smith, Hodges, Simpson, Truscott, Krueger, Haislip, and Collins, were heavily influenced by this Army "Good Book," as it was the first-ever comprehensive study of the physical, mental, and psychological capacity of Black soldiers. This misguided doctrine undoubtedly shaped tactical and administrative policies, thinking, and actions toward the abilities of the Negro soldier for years to come.

The brainpower behind The Study belonged to White midgrade officers, some of whom actually saw combat in WWI as part of segregated White units, as many Black units were summarily dispatched to serve under a foreign French leadership. White officers had minimal, if any, previous interactions with African American soldiers in battle and zero knowledge that Colored men had patriotically and bravely served in every war since our nation's founding—from the time of the Boston Massacre in 1770, where Crispus Attucks, a Negro, was the first American killed. Since the American Revolutionary War, several Black soldiers had also been recipients of the coveted Medal of Honor, often referred to as the Congressional Medal of Honor, the nation's highest award, and the Croix de Guerre, the French Army equivalent. The Army's at-large ignorance meant the maligning of African American soldiers in wars to come, before a single Black man, or woman, had even stepped off the bus at basic training. Empirical evidence suggests this logic was later carried over into combat as senior Black NCOs (noncommissioned officers) were reduced to privates to fight as infantry soldiers, prohibited from holding any further leadership positions over Whites.

A staple in Army War College curriculum at the time, the "science" behind *The Study* was heavily weighted in physical tests (from fitness to brain measurements) and visual observations conducted by Army officers upon the Black stevedores' return from France after WWI in 1925. This gave trained White soldiers an unfair advantage in testing over Negroes, most of whom had spent their lives working cotton fields in the American South and had no experience handling cargo—it didn't matter to the Army, which specifically targeted "ignorant Negroes" to enlist as stevedores and helped by rejecting their applications to join the front lines. These segregated Black units were deployed to a foreign country, during a world war, without official Army uniforms, proper medical evaluation and care, or consistent nourishment, and the military still expected them to return home in the same physical condition as well-trained, well-fed Whites. If the study truly was "measured by the standards applied to the White man," as it claims (though it also simultaneously states "different standards were used in the physical examination of White and Negro draftees"), why didn't the Army consider its inconsistencies in training, housing, and nourishment across White and Black soldiers? This, alone, was enough to disrupt its theory that Blacks are an innately inferior species.

A NEW BIBLE

The 1925 report was commissioned by Gen. Peyton C. March, the WWI Army chief of staff, and conducted by Maj. Gen. H.E. Ely, then commandant of the US Army War College, a military educational institute opened in 1901, still relevant today. The study commenced with a prologue from Ely:

> I am enclosing a study on the employment of Negro Manpower in War, made by a committee of The Army WarCollege . . . . It is based on research by previous classes, by the Faculty, as well as on War Department experiences during the World War. It is believed to be of such value in lieu of further study by the General Staff, as to furnish a basis for the employment of the Negro in the next war. I recommend, unless and until a more complete study be made on the subject by the General Staff, that it be accepted as the War Department policy in handling this problem.[1]

The excerpts below from the November 10, 1925, *Memorandum of the Chief of Staff Regarding Employment of Negro Manpower in War*[2] include some of the US Army's conclusions about African Americans post–WWI.

Section IV. Opinion of the War College

1. In the process of evolution, the American Negro has not progressed as far as the other subspecies of the human family. As a race, he has not developed leadership qualities. His mental inferiority and the inherent weakness of his character are factors that must be considered with great care in the preparation of any plan for his employment in war.

2. In the past wars, the Negro has made a fair laborer, but an inferior technician. As a fighter he has been inferior to the White man even when led by White officers.

3. Negro soldiers as individuals should not be assigned to White units.

4. Negro officers should not be placed over White officers, noncommissioned officers, or soldiers.

5. Negro officer candidates should attend training camps with White candidates. They should have the same instructors, take the same tests, and meet the same requirements for appointment as officers as the White candidates. They should be sheltered, messed, and instructed separately from White candidates.

6. The eventual use of the Negro will be determined by his performance in combat training and service.

7. If the Negro makes good, the way is left open for him to go into combat eventually with all-Negro units.

Reference A: Analysis of Physical, Mental, Moral, and Psychological Qualities and Characteristics of the Negro

1. It is, generally, recognized that the pure-blood American Negro is inferior to our White population in mental capacity. Such Negroes as have shown marked mental attainments also show a heavy strain of White blood. The Negroes are descended from slaves imported from West Africa. Their characteristics, physically, were formerly "uniform" and show them to be very low in the seals of human evolution. The cranial cavity of the Negro is smaller than the White; his brain weighing thirty-five ounces contrasted with forty-five for the White.

2. As judged by White standards, the Negro is unmoral. His ideas with relation to honor and sex relations are not on the same plane as those of our White population. Petty thieving, lying, and promiscuity are much more common among Negroes than among Whites. Atrocities connected with White women have been the cause of considerable trouble among Negroes. Experience before and in the

World War showed that the Negro will protect his color in cases of emergency without regard to truth. The same lack of honesty was evident with reference to reports, the lack of information being supplied from an active imagination.

3. All (White) officers, without exception, agree that the Negro lacks initiative, displays little or no leadership, and cannot accept responsibility. Some point that these defects are greater in the Southern Negro.

4. Due to his susceptibility to "Crowd Psychology" a large mass of Negroes, e.g. a division, is very subject to panic. Experience had indicated that the Negroes produce better results in segregation and cause less trouble. Grouping in Negroes generally in the past has produced demands for equality, both during war and after demobilization.

5. An opinion held in common by practically all officers is that the Negro is a rank coward in the dark. His fear of the unknown and unseen will prevent him from ever operating as an individual scout with success. His lack of veracity causes unsatisfactory reports to be rendered, particularly on patrol duty.

6. One of the peculiarities of the Negro as a soldier is that he has no confidence in his Negro leaders, nor will he follow a Negro officer into battle, no matter how good the officer might be, with the same confidence and lack of fear that he will follow a White man. This last trait has been so universally reported by all commanders that it cannot be considered as a theory—the Negroes themselves recognize this as a fact.

7. The Negro needs trained leadership far more than the White man needs it, and above all they need leaders in whom they have confidence, and whose presence they can always feel and see.

8. On account of the inherent weakness in the Negro character, especially general lack of intelligence and initiative, it

> requires much longer time of preliminary training to bring a Negro organization up to the point of training where it is fit for combat, than it does in the case of White men. All theoretical training is beyond the grasp of the Negro—it must be intensely practical, supplemented by plain talks explaining the reasons for things in simple terms.

Not much had changed by April 1942, as Brigadier General R.W. Crawford, of the War Department's general staff, submitted to General Eisenhower a revealing memorandum, quoting from *The Study*: "Probably the most important consideration that confronts the War Department in the employment of the Colored officer is that of leadership qualifications. Although in certain instances Colored officers have been excellent leaders, enlisted men generally function more efficiently under White officers. Officers experienced with Colored troops lay this to the lack of confidence on the part of the Colored enlisted men in the Colored officer."[3]

The War College marked its 1925 study as secret, which, according to US security classification levels, implies the information could cause serious damage or disruption to national security at the time. The Army had to ensure the document never fell into the hands of American civilians, whose access to tailor-made news was in full swing in most states, and the biased report could further disrupt the segregated country.

Army leaders had *zero* confidence in the fighting spirit of Negro soldiers, and the chief of staff of the Army, Gen. George Marshall, in 1941 gave Blacks entering the Army a vote of no confidence, remarking:

> "The only place [Negroes] could be counted on to stand would be in Iceland, in summertime, where there was daylight for twenty-four hours."[4]

The same could be said a decade later with the conclusion of WWII, when the military, again whitewashed history into delusional depictions of an all-White fighting force that saved the day, the military mocking Black Army units as mere sideshows to major tactical and strategic military operations. Ignorance in the media also stretched to great lengths to ensure Negro combat units never garnered any news that suggested they were equal to, or more successful than, White soldiers. In reality, African American soldiers in WWII (men and women) never perceived themselves or each other as anything but capable—they were prepared for the main attraction as patriotic, highly skilled, and technically qualified soldiers, just as brave and willing to engage the enemy as any White American. Black Army battalions tackled every conflict that WWII, and the organization, threw their way, whether it was guiding tanks through treacherous enemy lines, working day and night to ensure troops received incoming letters from home (for soldiers, receiving mail was as critical and as nourishing as food), or living with the reality that their service, as minorities in segregated America, may never amount to anything in the public's eyes.

THE BEGINNINGS OF WWII

Germany, under dictatorial rule, had been preparing and massing for war since Hitler rose to power in 1933. Immediately, he embarked on a massive military buildup of arms and equipment, primarily tank and airplane production, in direct violation of provisions of the Treaty of Versailles, signed by nations after World War I. The treaty required Germany to disarm and *not* rebuild[5], but it did, and its expansion was never challenged by any other country. In the late 1930s, America stood on the sidelines to, hopefully, avoid the arms race Germany had initiated; isolationists in the US insisted entering the war would only antagonize its Nazi participants.

America was sympathetic to Britain, from afar, watching the

occupation of France in June 1940, just weeks after its invasion by Germany. Britain suffered a devasting and humiliating defeat at the French port city of Dunkirk the same year—that's when America moved to support Britain, quickly and indirectly, in signing the Lend-Lease Act to authorize borrowing military equipment, primarily naval ships, and replacing weaponry abandoned at Dunkirk, like rifles, machine guns, field artillery, and ammunition.[6] President Roosevelt deemed arming Britain equal to *rearming* the United States and believed that if the British Navy were to be defeated, Germany's next target would be North America with a possible invasion route through Newfoundland and the Gulf of Saint Lawrence, a sovereign territory of Canada.

All of this changed when Japan, in hopes of weakening the tenacity of the American people, launched a surprise attack on Pearl Harbor in the early morning of December 7, 1941. America declared war against Japan on December 8, and Germany launched warfare against the United States three days later.

Even Americans who had been isolationists—espousing that America should remain neutral and not engage in the war raging overseas—believed we should retaliate against Japan for its egregious aggression, knowing it would bring us into the European war. And it did. From the time America entered the war against Hitler's Germany, we knew defeating the Axis Powers (also known as the Rome-Berlin-Tokyo Axis) would require an extremely difficult cross-channel combat operation. Launching an attack from Great Britain into occupied France would be necessary to take the war to the Fatherland and dethrone its leader, Adolf Hitler, which would prove to be a tremendous challenge. America was woefully unprepared at the beginning, with a limited and unskilled fighting force of only 190,000[7] men. A major contributing factor for the existence of such national combat deficiencies was, in part, attributed to the significant demobilization of Blacks from military ranks at the end of World War I.

Note: By 1940, there were only 4,179 Black soldiers in the Army and five Black officers, three of whom were chaplains and, the remaining two, father and son, Benjamin O. Davis, Sr. and Benjamin O. Davis, Jr.[8] Senior Davis would become the nation's first African American general. His son worked his way to commander of the highly decorated Tuskegee Airmen, America's segregated Negro fighting squadron. By the end of WWII, more than one million Black men and women had served the United States Armed Services.[9]

BUILDING A SEGREGATED ARMY

Theorizing that Germany could invade the US from the north, through Canada, *and* from the south, through Brazil and Central America, President Roosevelt successfully petitioned Congress for funds to strengthen our military. Mobilization evolved to more than fifteen million men and women, from all parts of the country. It took Roosevelt eighteen months to mobilize industry to match Germany's aircraft, vehicles, weapons, and munitions. In summer 1940, as Congress debated the president's request for military expansion, which included a peacetime draft, Black leaders saw a prime opportunity to influence the agenda. After all, it was an election year, and the Black vote would yield clout like never before, as Roosevelt required these votes for a successful third term.

In formulating this legislation, Congress initially proposed a clause in the funding bill guaranteeing equal rights for all soldiers, something war planners opposed. Based on the 1925 War College Study,[10] they envisioned a limited role for Negro recruits. Military planners of the day had long believed that the Negro race was intellectually and physically inferior to Whites[11]—a consequence of ignorance collided with pseudoscience. This small-mindedness evolved with the US government's perpetuation of unmerited information, as seen in the War College Study, which declared African Americans merely a margin above sub-species and mentally incapable of operating complex technical or mechanical equipment, like tanks—just one of the dozens of mischaracterizations represented in research and the media at the time (for example, claiming all Blacks were afraid of the dark).[12]

Note: Black soldiers at the time (1925) were assigned to, and had expertly crewed, artillery weapons in the American Army for nearly 150 years. Every Black unit in WWII (take members of the African American 320th Barrage Balloon Battalion, for instance) endured physically and mentally grueling training and regimentation while having to also combat the ugliness of racism and segregation, as the US Army wouldn't integrate until 1948 under President Harry Truman. For those African American units stationed in Southern states, the tribulations of segregation were compounded, and for members of the 320th Battalion, and other Negro units, there was no respite from their separated existence in US Army camps.

Upon America's entrance into WWII, all recruits were given the Army standard qualification exam (wrongly referred to as an IQ test). This test didn't measure intelligence but, rather, knowledge gleaned from the educational and cultural experiences of Whites; 84 percent of Blacks tested in the lowest two categories, out of five, while 60 percent of Whites tested in the top two. Among poor Southern Blacks, the situation was far worse, with four out of five possessing only a fourth-grade education.[13] Why were Blacks so disadvantaged in the South? In parts of rural America, Negro schools were abysmal, many of the children illiterate and left by the wayside; many schools had no options beyond seventh grade, as White administrators believed additional schooling was unnecessary to would-be laborers. Usually, seventh grade was the end of formal education for children lucky enough to have made it that far. High schools (if any) charged Black families fees they couldn't afford and required transportation they couldn't provide. This meant that around age twelve was the end of the line of formal education for many future African American soldiers.

Note: Consider that this was only fifty-five years since the end of slavery. During that time Blacks in the South, and some parts of the Northeast, were prohibited from learning to read or write and often physically abused when caught doing so.

Before the Army literacy program's findings, in early 1942, Blacks from all over the country began receiving letters from local draft boards—orders to report for induction. In the South, draft boards were generally made up of appointed, local, influential (White) citizens from the area. During World War I (or the Great War) and again in World War II, draft boards were notorious for unfair treatment of Negro men, denying the same exemptions given to Whites in similar circumstances. Under pressure from Black leaders to equalize the draft, President Roosevelt appointed an African American, Dr. Paul B. Jersey, as assistant director of the Selective Service in 1941. But this resulted in little change. When a group of Black pastors appealed to the Tennessee governor to appoint minorities to that state's board, the governor refused, responding:

> "This is a White man's country . . . . Negroes had nothing to do with the settling of America."[14]

Had the governor forgotten Black slaves built our White House and US Capitol building, in Washington, DC, decades earlier? Had he never heard about the Black soldiers from the 9th and 10th cavalries (Buffalo Soldiers) who settled the West?

Finally, in 1943, an Army literacy program proved that, when given the same opportunity to learn, Colored recruits *excelled*. Out of one hundred fifty thousand soldiers who attained a functional standard of literacy, eighty-seven thousand were Black—and a larger percentage of Blacks completed the program than Whites.[15] Ignoring the vehement objections of Southern legislators, Congress approved a final draft bill that stated there would be no blatant discrimination against Negro soldiers, *provided* recruits met physical and mental standards, all the while knowing Blacks were not allotted the same opportunities as Whites. The bill lamented, with no timeline and in full support of segregation, that Negroes could not enlist until the Army had fully segregated its facilities. Just three years before the new bill, only 539 Blacks had been accepted into the US Army;[16] this would change, however, over the next five years, as more than one million African Americans would serve in the military.

A Red Cross field director reported draft boards were practicing a great injustice, enlisting African American soldiers who should have been excluded for reasons ranging from medical issues to having families who depended on them. One Negro soldier—a husband and father—was drafted, leaving behind a stay-at-home wife and eight children, ten and younger. His wife was left with no way to support their family, no car, no job, no phone, and no savings. The four oldest children (all boys) began to scour their neighborhood, offering to run errands, wash windows, and cut lawns for nickels and dimes. One even had a paper route to help keep his mother and siblings fed.[17]

That soldier and his housewife were my father and mother, Clarence and Alice Gravett, and those neighborhood-sweeping boys, my four older brothers.

SEPARATE BUT NOT EQUAL

Outside of patriotism, many African Americans during this era saw enlisting in the Army as an escape from their despondent circumstances of having no foreseeable future with lesser education, lack of a job title, and no money. With the draft bringing several *thousand* draftees into the force each month, coupled with thousands of volunteers, more than a half-million African American soldiers were in the US Army by December 1942.[18] Military bases, where basic training was held, sprung up throughout the country, mainly in the South, to supplement existing ones. Segregated basic training companies were formed, separating Negroes from Whites, with Mexican Americans and Native Americans assigned to White companies.[19]

From the beginning, and to no surprise, Negro training facilities on new military bases could never reach parity with those for Whites.

Black recruits were forbidden to use the main post exchange (PX), or Army store, on base and were directed to smaller PXs, which stocked minimal supplies (soap, toothpaste, cigarettes, and candy). Everyday essentials were scarce, leaving Negroes with fewer opportunities to purchase civilian clothing, postcards, stationery, books, magazines, and other necessities for tired, homesick soldiers. If a base had only one PX, it belonged to the Whites. Even base swimming pools were off-limits to Black soldiers.[20]

All discriminating customs, local traditions, and mores of the Jim Crow South were transferred over to the new, hastily erected bases, separating Whites and Coloreds at drinking fountains, NCO clubs, and in mess halls; in fact, Negro officers *had* no clubs because there were so few of them. Some chapels even listed religious services for Catholics, Protestants, Jews, and Negroes (as if Black were a religion), and the last rows in movie theaters and buses, on bases or in town, were reserved for Black soldiers, unless, of course, White soldiers needed additional seats. African Americans were required to relinquish their seats and leave, sometimes with no refund. Bus routes began on the White part of the base, and often all seats were filled by the time they arrived to pick up Black soldiers, forcing the men to tread on foot to their final destinations. And, adding insult to injury, it all took place on military bases in the South that were named after Civil War Confederate generals (the last such base is scheduled to be renamed in late 2023).

In cities and small towns surrounding the bases, local citizens were resistant to, and even outraged, at the idea of Negroes stationed nearby so *opposed* in fact, that Black soldiers riding on trains in segregated cars had to draw their window shades when passing through certain towns, as it wasn't rare for angry Dixie Whites to fire weapons at the men.[21] The majority of Whites in the South believed Negroes didn't belong in the military and seeing Black soldiers in uniform was an affront to Whites and what they considered to be American culture and tradition.

REFERENCE MAPS OF WORLD WAR II: EUROPEAN THEATER

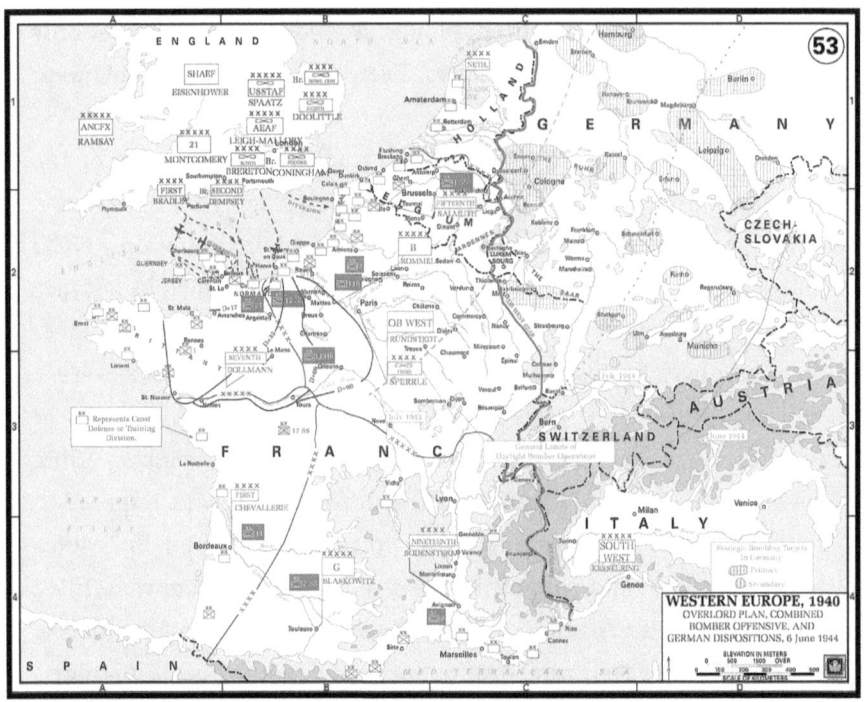

Western Europe, 1940. Overlord plan, combined bomber offensive, and German dispositions. June 6, 1944. Courtesy of the US Military Academy/Army.

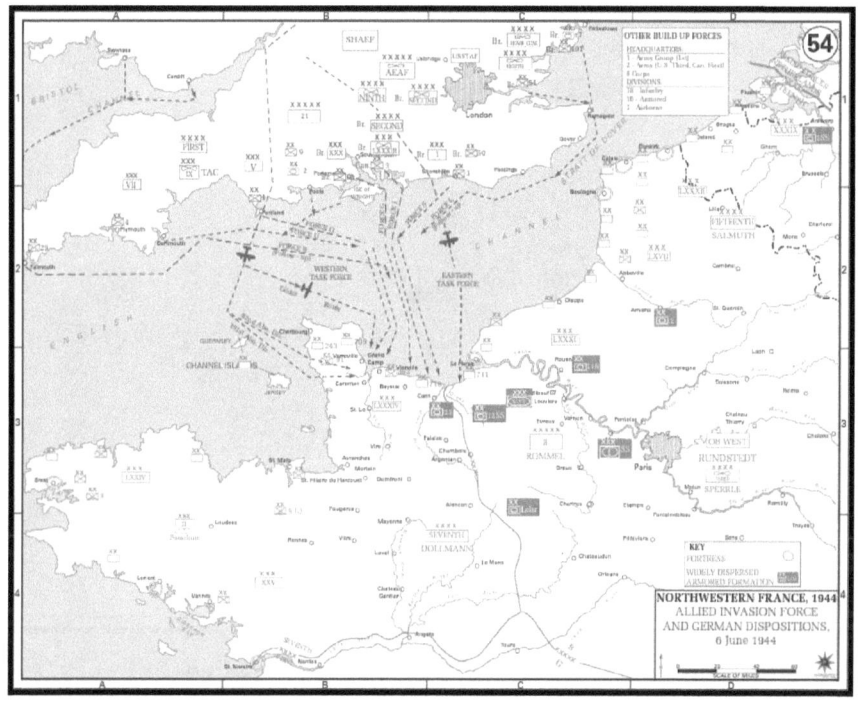

Northwestern France, 1944. Allied invasion force and German dispositions, June 6, 1944. Photo courtesy of the U.S. Military Academy/Army.

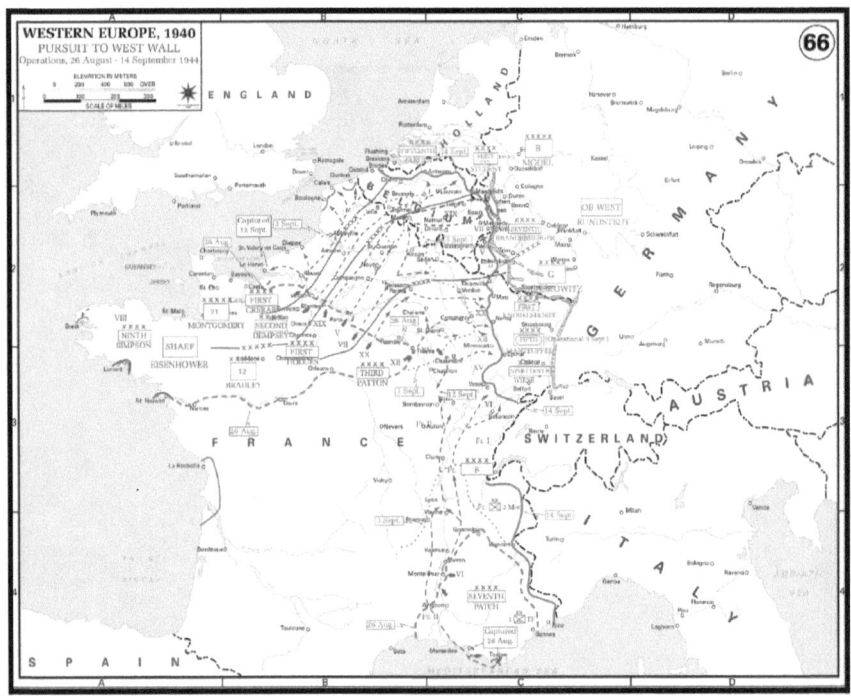

Western Europe, 1940. Pursuit to the West Wall. Operations, August 26–September 14, 1944. Courtesy of the US Military Academy/Army.

Europe 1944. Allied gains in Europe. June 6, 1944–December 15, 1944. Courtesy of the US Military Academy/Army.

(Left to right) PFC Arko Shaw, PFC Alvin Smith, Cpl. Jessie Sumlin, and Pvt. James Shrapshire towing a barrage balloon through treacherous, active minefields in France, 1944. Photo Courtesy of National Archives and Records Administration.

PART ONE

America's Secondary Air Force
The 320th Anti-Aircraft
Barrage Balloon Battalion

June 6, 1944 D-Day landing at Omaha Beach in Normandy, France. Photo courtesy of National Archives and Records Administration.

The conventional wisdom
of D-Day is that
there were no
Black soldiers who
landed on those beaches,
but the truth is
that there were almost
2,000 Black soldiers
who landed by
the end of the day
June 6, [1944].[1]

—Linda Hervieux,
*The Untold Story of D-Day's Black Heroes,
at Home and at War*

"High Flight"

By John Gillespie Magee, Jr.,
WWII Canadian Royal Air Force fighter pilot

Oh! I have slipped the surly bonds of Earth

And danced the skies on laughter-silvered wings;

Sunward I've climbed, and joined the tumbling mirth

of sun-split clouds, and done a hundred things

You have not dreamed of—wheeled and soared and swung

High in the sunlit silence. Hov'ring there,

I've chased the shouting wind along, and flung

My eager craft through footless halls of air…

Up, up the long, delirious burning blue

I've topped the wind-swept heights with easy grace

Where never lark, or ever eagle flew—

And, while with silent, lifting mind I've trod

The high untrespassed sanctity of space,

Put out my hand and touched the face of God.[2]

World War II soldiers. Photo courtesy of Peter Gravett.

INTRODUCTION

It's been sixty years, and I can still vividly picture my friend's mother frantically inflating bright, multi-color birthday balloons, using her own hurried breath, and pinning them to the weathered fence in their backyard. Fast forward to memories of high school dances, where the scent of latex still lingers in the gymnasium in my mind, as floating orbs descend onto the dance floor to signal the end of an unforgettable night.

My memory still strolls down balloon-lined lanes in Los Angeles (where my parents eventually located and I was raised), leading sightseers into small, beachside shopfronts. And, like a child, I still fit beneath the Goodyear blimp's historic shadow, the locally stationed sky giant soaring for nearly a century.

A lifetime of celebrations—and, yet, I would have never imagined balloons would go from birthday parties to battlefields, where they would play a significant role in our successful Allied D-Day landing on the Normandy Coast on June 6, 1944.

During the aftermath and recriminations of Japan's attack on Pearl Harbor, the War Department Investigative Board assembled to assess blame, noting intelligence failures, destruction, and partial sinking of our Pacific Fleet could have been minimized if we had only launched military barrage balloons to protect US ships; perhaps, this would have thwarted attacks by low-flying Japanese aircraft. After all, balloon defensive measures were a success in London and English industrial cities during the 1940–1941 German Blitz, as war balloons—oversized, tethered, kite balloons sometimes attached to explosives—were extremely instrumental in helping interdict lower-altitude enemy airplanes. These floating balloons with cables attached to highly explosive devices would often collide with attacking enemy aircraft wings, drawing up the tethered bomb and destroying the aircraft.

With this revelation, the US Army built and activated twenty barrage balloon battalions, numbered 301 through 321—the 320th Barrage Balloon Battalion being the *only* balloon unit and the *only* African American unit of any kind to deploy to Europe and land at Normandy on D-Day.

A BRIEF HISTORY

Vengeance began on June 6, 1944, the day with the highest half tide (when the tide is halfway between high and low water), at Utah Beach, the most westerly beach in Normandy, France, forty minutes after light broke and following a night with moonrise between 1:00 a.m. and 2:00 a.m. The *"D"* in D-Day represents one of the most significant *decisions* made in American history, when our Army had to swiftly determine whether it would unleash the largest armada the world had ever seen. *And it did.* The highest half tides in June 1944, ideal for the D-Day landing, would occur on June 5, 6, and 7 in 1944.[3] Crossing the one-hundred-mile-wide English Channel to capture Normandy's coast would be the first, massive step in liberating war-torn Europe. Unfortunately, beginning June 1, weather conditions deteriorated as meteorologists declared violent storms in the upcoming days. Mother Nature showed no mercy, as if to curse humanity for its wicked ways, which would make for a hectic cross-channel launch on June 5; any delays were serious, causing impenetrable congestion in the ports of Normandy. The only silver lining? Poor weather conditions have given the Germans a false sense of security.

Come morning on June 5, chief meteorologists announced an unexpected weather change for what would become D-Day—calmer seas, lesser winds, and stronger visibility one day later, June 6, 1944. General Dwight D. Eisenhower, Supreme Commander of Allied Forces, was situated in his command headquarters, at Southwick House, England, surrounded by his senior commanders who would play a major role in the invasion, including Gen. Omar Bradley, commander of US ground forces; British General Bernard Law Montgomery, commander of the 21st Army Group; Admiral Sir Bertram Ramsay, the naval commander who orchestrated evacuation from Dunkirk; British Air Chief Arthur Teddy; Air Chief Marshal Sir Trafford Leigh-Mallory, and Maj. Gen. Walter Bedell Smith, Eisenhower's chief of staff.

Finally, with calm skies and anxious, seasick assault troops, and after four years of war in Europe, Eisenhower's verdict on "Operation Overlord" was:

"Okay, we'll go . . ."[4]

The room was empty within seconds; the power behind three little words launched our task force into the European Theater of Operations. Now, June 6 would be the first day of the beginning of the end of World War II, forever known as D-Day. The assault armada was powerful with 195,000 soldiers (including 20,000 airborne troops) 3,958 heavy bombers, 1,284 light and medium bombers, 4,709 fighter aircraft, more than 7,000 ships and landing craft, and upward of 700,000 pieces of various other equipment.[5] When the Allied Secondary Air Force arrived, members of the Luftwaffe (or German Air Force) were present to greet the men of the 320th African American Anti-Aircraft Barrage Balloon Battalion.

CHAPTER ONE

---★---

Sky's the Limit

TWENTY BALLOON battalions were trained at Camp Tyson, Tennessee, during the war (1941–1945), including four African American units: the 318th, 319th, 320th, and 321st; White soldiers made up units 301 through 317. War balloons were first established under the command of the US Army Air Corps, one of the largest battalion-size organizations in the Army, each unit boasting an average of forty-two officers, one thousand enlisted men and fifty-four balloons.

Note: Initially, these units were "coast artillery barrage balloon battalions," but the first half was dropped on July 15, 1943, after antiaircraft command took over the balloon program, changing the name to antiaircraft barrage balloon battalions.[6]

The Army never intended to build and deploy Black battalions. And, although Blacks *would* go on to *successfully* serve overseas in battle after bloody battle, the military hardly recognized them as humans, let alone official combat units. African Americans were merely there to prove a "technical presence" in the Army—just something to quiet the loudening voices of Black leaders uniting to disrupt popular opinion that Coloreds had no right to fight for their country. Little did our military know, the men of the 320th Barrage Balloon Battalion would make ignorance-shattering history landing at Normandy on D-Day.

Barrage balloons, *big bags, air whales,* or *sky elephants,* however referenced, were seemingly simple, but incredibly effective, war machines. With two hundred years of military, commercial, and recreational uses, tracing back to eighteenth-century France, these blimp-sized, hydrogen-filled bags affixed to steel cables were sent out with orders to obstruct enemy attacks. They have been seen, and felt, worldwide.

Note: The first, short flight of an "unmanned" balloon—testing animals in place of humans—dates back to 1783 with a harrowing flight that unleashed future opportunities: transporting humans. Not long after, people were taking commercial and recreational balloon flights with in-flight food and beverage services.

The success and first application of combat aerial balloons dates as far back as the late eighteenth century. The first known military application of balloons was established by Napoleon Bonaparte in 1794, when he formed a brigade to spy on Austrian Army troops, which was, naturally, fearfully in awe of the new floating, fighting phenomenon. For Bonaparte, this was only the beginning. Eventually, he launched an entire balloon force, *la Compagnie d'a*érostiers (French Aerostatic Corps), and engaged Egypt, hoping to instill fear equal to that felt by the Austrians; but it didn't happen. British troops stationed in Egypt decimated Napoleon's balloon force upon arrival.

By 1784, England and Germany were experimenting with balloon warfare.[7] The trend then soared into developing America in 1784, first in Philadelphia. These aerial vehicles inspired a new age of flight possibilities, including cross-country travel. On the tactical side, during the American Civil War, Union forces launched big bags to spy on the Confederates, a capability not available to the Southerners due to the high cost of manpower and equipment. Even for Northern soldiers, employing balloons meant employing a substantial, logistical tail—barrage balloons varied in size, with the largest carrying thirty-two thousand cubic feet of gas and five passengers. Such operations required fifty ground-support soldiers and wagons loaded with supplies, towed by eight horses.[8] The Union experienced ups and downs as the first American forces to utilize balloon technology. At one point, one of its manned balloons was wind-blown onto the Southern Confederate battlefield, the Northern soldier trapped inside, temporarily held as a spy.⁹

When Europe entered the Balkan Wars in 1912, Germany dangled a measurable advantage over France and England with its superiorly equipped balloon corps. As soon as a German balloon, or drachen (dragon), named for its high inflammability and incredible roar during inflation, was captured by Allied forces, the technology was quickly replicated, the enemy's tethered kite design proving a more stable, higher-flying war machine.¹⁰ A few years later, the French designed an even more powerful and versatile lower-flying balloon that could tolerate wind gusts up to fifty miles per hour yet soar up to thirteen thousand feet if needed. It was only a matter of time before Germans took the idea and flew, improving on the French design with newer, higher-flying balloons. It wasn't long before Goodyear and other American companies designed and built similar models for the US Army.

With the realization that we would enter World War I, the United States scrambled to train a solid balloon corps, reopening the US Army's balloon school by 1916, which had been mothballed at Fort Omaha, Nebraska. The Army's big bags hadn't seen action in eighteen years, last used in Cuba during the Spanish American War in 1898—Gen. John J. "Blackjack" Pershing, commander of the American Expeditionary Forces in WWI Europe (and given the moniker "Blackjack" for having commanded Black units in the past) was determined to wake up and wage war with America's sleeping battle balloons. Fifty barrage balloon companies, and one brilliant, bloody battle later, Pershing ordered a final Allied inflatable to ascend on November 11, 1918, the day of the Armistice, which ended the fight.

Big bags proved most effective in protecting a contained area, unlike during the 1940-1941 London Blitz, which saw massive, high-altitude bombing over a *huge* swath of territory. But, come D-Day in Normandy, balloons would be the perfect defense mechanism.

Floating just above the beaches, the aerial vehicles forced enemy aircraft to fly higher, making it difficult for them to accurately drop bombs or strafe Allies below with machine-gun fire. As the enemy ascended, powerful antiaircraft artillery (AAA), at ground level, could clearly ready, aim, and fire at German planes.

> Even Germany, the enemy, reported admitting to a high-ranking US officer that, of all American units, the balloon companies were the "most efficient and effective."[11]

There were nearly seven thousand American balloonists in Europe by the end of WWI, the larger-than-life gas bags leaving their mark as intelligent, intimidating war machines. Those same battle-winning balloons retired postwar while recreational ballooning resumed to serve in aerial races, excursions, demonstrations, flyovers, and contests.[12]

Along came the 1920s and '30s, which thrust the world into the golden age of airships, with newer, lighter-than-air crafts called dirigibles (also popularly known as zeppelins or blimps). Entrepreneurs around the world were convinced airship design had been *perfected*, betting the colossal inflatables would quickly soar into a bright, brilliant future in air travel. But, on May 6, 1937, tragedy dimmed their balloon dreams with the violent fate of the infamous German airship, *Hindenburg*, one of the largest aerial ships ever built. She was scheduled to dock at Lakehurst Naval Station in New Jersey and would have completed her first transatlantic voyage that day, but, in her attempt to land, *Hindenburg*'s hydrogen reservoir caught fire, and the craft crashed to the ground, killing thirty-six of the ninety-seven passengers on board, plus, one crew member on the ground.[13]

The airship's demise is still cited as the worst air disaster accident of all time, but there were deadlier incidents in lighter-than-air history. The most fatal airship disaster occurred in April 1933, with the USS *Akron*, which resulted in seventy-three onboard deaths and two casualties from another airship, the J-2, which flew to *Akron*'s aid. With the lives lost on the USS *Akron* and those aboard the cavalry airship, it was deemed the most tragic airship accident in history. The demise of the *Hindenburg* and USS *Akron* came at the end of the golden age of airships—but, with America's eventual involvement in the Second World War, its balloon technology would resurface like never before. In modern warfare, balloons have been used as recently as the wars in Iraq and Afghanistan for reconnaissance purposes and are still employed today.

CHAPTER TWO

---★---

Hiring Away the Help

On AUGUST 15, 1941, the US Army revealed the future location of its official barrage balloon training center—Camp Tyson, named for Army Brig. Gen. Lawrence D. Tyson, located six miles from the small Southern town of Paris, Tennessee, home to only a few thousand people. Like most rural US towns in the area, Paris was proudly segregated with a small African American community living on nearby farms and on "the other side of the tracks."

Camp Tyson eventually expanded to nearly three thousand acres with more than four hundred structures, including barracks, PXs, post offices, chapels, garages, sawmills, and hospitals. Tyson required hundreds of workers to operate its facilities, and because of rampant segregation, the military duplicated areas like barracks and mess halls—one for Whites, one for Blacks. The approaching, massive construction project demanded workers from every field. Its labor force would boast skilled and unskilled craftsmen and general laborers (carpenters, plumbers, electricians, roofers, cement masons, and street pavers), requiring men to fill multiple positions, especially at the post's laundry facility, which would serve more than three thousand soldiers.

The Army began hiring and filling thousands of open positions at its future facility now that construction was completed. Just like many Southern towns, most African American women in Paris, currently employed as domestics, quit their housekeeping jobs to fill positions at the post laundry and in other administrative and logistic roles that didn't require specific skills. To nobody's surprise, many former White employers criticized the military for hiring away the "help"—though, the government job paid *three times* what the Negro women made as civil housekeepers, plus full benefits. The city of Tyson rapidly grew to more than eight thousand; a 25 percent growth in just a few months. Small businesses and restaurants began to flourish, but there was still the significant issue of employee housing, specifically for African American workers and later African American soldiers. Many Black employees and soldiers turned in wherever they could, often left come nightfall, without a sleeping quarter.

Note: In one lucky case, a Black family living on a farm outside town reluctantly took in a Cajun couple from Louisiana after the two came across the farm with no place to sleep. At first, the instant language barrier between thick Cajun tongue and Tennessee slang proved worrisome for the farmers, but over time, the family and the Louisiana couple grew to be friends. This was incredibly rare at that time and place in history.[14]

Overall, the Army had made zero provisions for housing soldiers (of *any* race) who were posted at Tyson before it opened in 1941, the few original, vacant apartments and houses onsite quickly claimed by incoming White workers. Town leaders, in an effort to support the US Army, implored Black *and* White townspeople to accommodate new workers—of whatever race—in their homes until the military could provide actual living quarters. So, Tyson citizens, regardless of race, welcomed workers into their homes, moving beds into living rooms and basements, screening and converting back porches, sectioning off attics, and other ingenious ways of expanding; some workers even bedded down in barns.[15]

Despite these complications, the US Army chose Camp Tyson, Tennessee, because of its remote location away from air routes, and variable weather ideal for training with big bags. Tyson would become the first base *specifically* built to train soldiers to fly, build, and repair war balloons.

TRAINING THE BIG BAGS

The US Army activated the all-Black 320th Barrage Balloon Battalion on December 10, 1942, under its (White) first commanding officer, Lt. Col. Leon Reed. The unit's totally Caucasian staff of cadre instructors hailed from multiple camps, including Fort Eustis, Virginia, with personnel from Camp Steward, Georgia, Fort Meade, Maryland, and Fort Bragg, North Carolina. The Army's newly established, racially mixed (yet, still segregated) balloon command in Tennessee burgeoned into a beehive of activity. Since most existing temporary balloon facilities were built for Whites only in racially discriminatory states like North Carolina, Texas, and Nebraska, the 320th Battalion would be the first Colored unit to disrupt the military's trend of ignorance and bigotry in the South.

As weapons training began, soldiers primarily worked with two balloon types: very high altitude (VHA) and very low altitude (VLA). Requiring the manpower of several men, VHA balloons called for forty-eight thousand cubic feet of hydrogen for initial inflation (for comparison, today's hot air balloons command more than double, at ninety thousand cubic feet of air) and a maximum altitude of fifteen thousand feet, equivalent to almost three miles. The Army's excessive need for more workers—a twelve-man squad per balloon—forced it to discontinue VHAs in May 1942 and convert all training to lower-altitude (VLA) models. With the amount of required hydrogen cut in half, accompanied by a maximum altitude of five thousand feet, handling and training of VLAs were proven to be less intensive, less expensive, and required only four men per weapon system.[16]

One year later, on February 11, 1943, the first war balloon ascended into the skies over Camp Tyson, flown by the first African Americans to ever man a war balloon—the 320th Battalion.

This called for a celebration, as it was the first of hundreds of sky elephants built for WWII. Training was organized by battalion, each provided a headquarters battery (which facilitated their ability to command and control, plus, bore all administrative and logistical functions, i.e., "beans and bullets"), and three lettered batteries—Alpha, Bravo, and Charlie, designators consistent with other similar Army infantry and artillery units. It took months of extensive, time-consuming training to develop the skills to become a balloonist, and every 320th officer and soldier had graduated within their specialty, all achieving noteworthy field tactical training prior to deploying.

The tactical and technical qualifying training of the newly established unit's personnel were required to undergo further proved to be quite interesting. With respect to the leadership training, the primary six-week officer course was designed to fully prepare leaders to perform duties unique to balloon units, mainly managing installations, inflation and deflation, repair, winch operations, meteorology, aerostatics, barrage control, gas operations and manufacturing, balloon inspections, and using tether devices.[17] To further solidify their new skill sets, officers were also required to take special advanced courses in equipment, engineering, gas, communications (each six weeks), and advanced meteorology (twelve weeks). Enlisted personnel were required to undergo similar, expedited six-week courses for balloon chiefs (the senior noncommissioned officer in charge of the company). Such training entailed inspecting balloons, communication protocols, gas service, rigging and fabric repair, winch operation and repair, auto mechanics, and teletyping (a printing device used to send and receive telephonic signals).[18]

Finally, prior to the unit's deployment to Europe, Army units were training for up to twenty-two weeks, preparing for Omaha Beach, Normandy, and any inclement weather they might experience overseas. Once soldiers completed basic and unit training, including mission-critical physical tests and tactical exercises (like boat training on the Tennessee River, where the men hoisted heavy war balloons above choppy waters), after seventeen weeks, they focused on solving any potential oversights and setbacks before officially entering World War II.

UP, UP, AND AWAY

The African American men of the 320th Barrage Balloon unit finally departed Camp Tyson by train on November 8, 1943, heading one thousand miles east to Camp Shanks, the Army's largest embarkation camp, situated about fifteen miles outside New York City. Dubbed by the troops as *Last Stop USA*, it represented the kickoff point for most military units prior to deploying overseas during World War II. Camp Shanks would become the unit's temporary home as the men learned how to work ground equipment and revisited boot camp training. Predeployment operations at Camp Shanks (named in honor of Maj. Gen. David C. Shanks, who once directed New York's Port of Embarkation during World War I) was quite intense, as one might imagine. As a final reality check, deploying soldiers were issued their tactical combat equipment and individual combat service weapons that would, hopefully, save their lives. Quartermaster personnel issued each soldier a fully functioning M-1 rifle with a bayonet, helmet, ammunition cartridge belt, and a tactical equipment field pack, which included essential combat items: a raincoat, half tent, canteen, toiletries, mess kit, and a first-aid kit.

Preparing to deploy to combat, however, wasn't *all* work—

Army troops made the most of their stay and caught the bus to the Big Apple on a twelve-hour pass and for a forty-five-cent roundtrip fare. Southern soldiers (including Whites, surprisingly) were excited to experience Harlem's nightlife, especially its nationally famed nightclub, the Savoy Ballroom, which had closed before, and opened again, after the Harlem race riot of 1943. New York lived up to its reputation, its nightlife keeping troops entertained with performances by era-popular musicians, comedians, and boxing greats, like World Heavyweight Champion Joe Louis, a Black man, who refereed amateur matches and fought exhibition rounds.

Camp Shanks never slept for reasons outside its proximity to New York City. As mentioned, it was also the Army's primary point of departure for Europe from the East Coast for various combat divisions and separate battalions, which eventually included four other history-making African American units: the 761st Tank, 333rd Field Artillery, and the 6888th Postal battalions.

Shank's busiest day was in October 1944, when nearly two divisions—27,626 men—departed its gates. Just one year before that grand exit, in November 1943, the African American 320th sailed from New York aboard the HMS Aquitania, arriving in Greenock, Scotland, six days later. Next, the unit filed into a plane headed to their official staging area (a zone reserved for the military to prepare for new missions or operations), in Checkendon, England, less than fifteen minutes by air from the German-held airfields in France.

> By now, it was clear to the Black ballooners that they would play a significant role in the invasion force crossing the English Channel into Europe.

During their brief staging deployment in England, the men were assigned a separate mission with instructions to fly a static barrage (to help inhibit enemy troops from moving and attacking) at Cardiff, South Wales. This assigned mission was designed primarily to assist in augmenting existing protection of critical Allied harbor installations. At the time of this assignment, a Royal Air Force (RAF) barrage balloon squadron was already flying a barrage at Cardiff, utilizing entirely different equipment than the Americans, and, needless to say, the 320th never received the equipment it needed to fulfill the mission. Come the new year, 1944, the battalion packed its bags for yet another relocation, this time to Bulwark Camp, Wales, where the unit was supplementally trained with hot-air (versus hydrogen) inflation and equipment—another skillset under their belts in case it was ever needed. Once trained in hot air, the Colored unit was finally headed to its permanent assignment in New Inn Camp, South Wales, where limited space permitted only thirty-two balloons in the air at a time, at an operational height of two hundred feet; this meant the US Army's final D-Day preparations wouldn't be as extensive as it had hoped and planned. Still, big-bag training at New Camp Inn was intense and proved more complicated in other ways. Army leaders knew they had to modify its organization and ballooning equipment, based on the fact that standard balloon winches were too bulky for amphibious operations, and these airships had to land ashore early in the assault phase with the lightest load possible. This meant one soldier from each four-man crew was dropped from the assault stage, along with his balloon, leaving three men behind to do the heavy lifting.

LOCKDOWN

By April, the 320th Battalion divided, yet again, into assault groups and residue, or *reserves*, according to the English. Residues remained at the camp, while 195 enlisted men and five officers from each alpha-designated battery moved into marshaling areas for maneuvers in Southern England. Batteries returned to their respective marshaling areas and were assigned invasion equipment, as preliminary exercises began May 4, 1944, on England's southern coast. Army camps were now closed and wrapped in barbed wire—no unauthorized personnel were allowed in, and soldiers weren't allowed out. Liberty passes were no longer issued or permitted, and the leaders forbade outside communication, including severing access to trains and other means of transportation; needless to say, these newly heightened security conditions took on the appearance and resembled a prison or POW facility, which no doubt was necessary for operational secrecy and security.

The soldiers were cut off. Isolated. Preparing for war.

Later that month in May of 1944, the tactical balloon unit was once again broken up, primarily to allow individual squads to join infantry combat teams for the assault invasion. To facilitate the invasion, 150 landing craft would ultimately transport the supporting battalion to France, along with teams of combat infantry units.

CHAPTER THREE

Nothing Less Than Victory

EISENHOWER ADDRESSED a D-Day message to the "Soldiers and Airmen of the Allied Expeditionary Force" on June 6, 1944:

> You are about to embark upon the Great Crusade, towards which we have striven these many months. The eyes of the world are upon you. The hopes and prayers of liberty-loving people everywhere march with you. In company with our brave Allies and brothers-in-arms on other Fronts, you will bring about the destruction of the German war machine, the elimination of Nazi tyranny over the oppressed peoples of Europe, and security for ourselves in a free world. Your task will not be an easy one. Your enemy is well trained, well-equipped, and battle-hardened. He will fight savagely. But this is the year 1944! Much has happened since the Nazi triumphs of 1940–41. The United Nations have inflicted upon the Germans great defeats, in open battle, man-to-man. Our air offensive has seriously reduced their strength in the air and their capacity to wage war on the ground. Our Home Fronts have given us an overwhelming superiority in weapons and munitions of war and placed at our disposal great reserves of trained fighting men. The tide has turned! The free men of the world are marching together to victory! I have full confidence in your courage and devotion to duty and skills in battle. We will accept nothing less than full victory! Good luck! And let us beseech the blessing of Almighty God upon this noble undertaking.
>
> Dwight D. Eisenhower[19]

Prior to their D-Day departure, Royal Air Force crews in England filled thousands of balloons, tethering them to ships and smaller craft for the battalion's journey to France. The airships, with a bird's-eye view of aquatic ships below, formed a miles-wide aerial curtain; this tactical strategy is how the 320th would aid in providing crucial aerial support to protect its fleet from German dive-bombers. Balloons flying as high as two thousand feet above the assaulting Allied fleet, and at least two hundred yards apart, made it virtually impossible for enemy aerial assaults. Once near the shore, the men were instructed to rush their balloons onto the beach, transferring the overarching and intimidating, protective veil onto land.

> A newspaper correspondent on Omaha Beach called the 320th Battalion's balloon curtain "one of the most important missions of the war."[20]

Upon landing on the beach, a majority of the 621 men assigned to the 320th assault force headed to a five-mile-long, crescent-shaped patch of sand once known as Beach 313. The Americans' tactical planners renamed it *Omaha*, and it was one of five designated assault beaches (Sword, Gold, Juno, Utah, and Omaha) seized by the Allies on June 6, in the seventeen hours of daylight available to them. War planners expected a bloodbath on Omaha Beach—the most challenging terrain whereby enemy defensive guns lie hidden in scrub-covered bluffs as tall as 170 feet. Omaha and Utah Beaches would, therefore, witness the first element of the 320th come ashore and make history as the only Negro battalion to land on D-Day. As expected, the amphibious assault was a massacre, with thousands of soldiers killed or wounded.

THE BEACH LANDING

The Germans defending Normandy beachheads on D-Day skillfully withheld their fire until the 320th landing crafts dropped their ramps. This was the enemy's signal to commence its attack. Nazi entrenched and well-aimed machine guns sprayed, their deadly bullets slaughtering countless invading soldiers, sometimes before landing troops were able to even disembark from their amphibious landing crafts. Intense indirect mortar shells rained down on boats, inflicting additional casualties upon the landing forces and setting ammunition afire. On the extreme flanks of Omaha Beach, German tactical gun defenses were far more forgiving, as many assaulting infantry platoons experienced no resistance and few casualties as they forged ashore. However, elsewhere on the beachhead, there was little less than human carnage. Nearly half of America's amphibious tanks, which were predesignated to supply defensive fire support to the beaches early on in the assault, were scuttled and set loose—far from shore, sinking in the tides and unfortunately, in many instances drowning their own crew. A few of those tanks that were fortunate enough to have made it to the beach were struck by enemy shells, causing their burning hulls to send up thick clouds of blinding, black smoke that obscured the scene of horror for the existing landing forces and to those wading ashore.

Along with battalion medics, who landed during the assault at 0600 hours (6:00 a.m.), some of the first beachside elements were combat engineers and demolition teams tasked with clearing obstacles to create pathways. The Americans were hard-pressed to perform their jobs, attempting to blow up barriers while boats loaded with arriving US infantry soldiers were nipping at the heels of the Army engineers, pushing them to quickly get the job done. Naturally, the ocean's tide caused various teams to land late, many straying far off target. With so many tanks out of commission, there was little protection. The main body of the 320th was slated to land midmorning, after the heaviest enemy fire, in order to create time and space to raise their balloons. But *nothing* went according to plan on D-Day. The Normandy operation may have been one of the most tightly synchronized battles ever—but it seems the intense planning and clockwork precision went awry from the start.

When the Allies had carried out their preinvasion bombing, no defensive craters had been left for the soldiers to use for cover on the beachhead upon landing—another miscalculation affording the landing assault troop little or no cover protection. Everywhere the men looked was a vast expanse of bloodstained sand, littered with pieces of wrecked radios, gas masks, ration tins, photographs, and guns, big and small, rifle barrels still shielded with rubber latex condoms to keep the corrosive salt water out. Tactical landing congestion was so cluttered on the 320th side of Omaha Beach, that commanders were forced to halt follow-on elements within their sectors from landings. The shore was scattered with troops from the initial assault element of the 320th, most of the assault elements landing *without* balloons, which were scheduled to follow in future transports, along with winches, cable reels, six thousand cylinders of hydrogen, and other important supplies. As part of the preplanned assault strategy, each balloon crew was *supposed* to have landed by evening on D-Day, however, such was not the case due to the continued confusion and calamity persisting for four more days after the initial assault.

For the better part of that historical day on June 6, the 320th Battalion was entirely on its own, lost without tactical directions and searching for its brothers and balloons, as was every other combat unit.[21] This unforeseen setback delayed men and their critical essential materials, much of which was lost to the sea, including two jeeps and a three-quarter-ton armed weapons-carrier vehicle, which sank unloading in unexpectedly deep waters. The unanticipated consequences of that day were not evident early on, but later, as the 320th commander attempted to round up his soldiers, he discovered the enemy had slain four of his men. The Germans had observed the tumultuous scene from varying heights, beaming with confidence in their apparent victory; they knew what was coming next. Nightfall would welcome the Luftwaffe, Germany's formidable air force, the largest in WWII Europe. American soldiers on the sands below became sitting ducks when Nazi planes hurdled out of the clouds, machine guns blazing and precisely aimed bombs falling to the earth, headed straight for America's mountain of supplies offloaded at the shoreline, even despite the defending balloon tethers.

Note: The Germans were so determined to knock out every last Army balloon, they developed a knife-edge cable cutter, called a *Kutonase*, installed at the leading edge of a plane's wing; although it wasn't a successful measure, they took it to ensure every last American soldier was dead.[22]

Fortunately, extra hours of daylight on June 6 worked to the advantage of the Allies. Come nightfall, fifty-seven thousand Americans and seventy-five thousand British and Canadian troops had safely landed on the beaches of Normandy[23] with a tremendous foothold along fifty-five miles of heavily defended coastline.

> By 11:15 p.m., on June 6, 1944, the first 320th Barrage balloon was flying over Omaha Beach.[24]

Accompanying their high hopes was the equally high possibility of the enemy destroying US balloons. And by the next morning, the dozen balloons that were, hours before, floating above Omaha Beach, were no longer airborne; the enemy had abolished our defense. Brilliant, and quick in their action, the 320th launched another set of more than thirty balloons over Omaha and Utah Beaches, though a third of them would be destroyed by enemy artillery fire in coming days—but not before the mighty sky elephants controlled by the all-Black 320th Barrage Balloon Battalion had downed several Luftwaffe planes, our airborne enemies colliding with balloon cables which drew the planes closer, triggering and detonating a soda-bottle-size bomb. The balloons destroyed German planes and their Nazi pilots.

HEROES IN THE SKY

The men of the 320th Battalion, in spite of numerous tactical setbacks during the Normandy landing, provided a valuable tactical asset to the Allied Forces and proved heroic in their steadfast combat performance. On June 7, the morning after the unit had conquered the skies despite all odds, one African American soldier, Staff Sergeant Waverly ("Woody") Woodson Jr., a medic, committed numerous acts of untold bravery on Omaha Beach. Woodson was a Philadelphia native and a university premed student at the time of joining the Army and deploying to combat as a medic during World War II. Although Woodson had scored high on the US Army Anti-Aircraft Artillery Officer Qualification Test and was subsequently allowed to attend and complete the officer course, he was denied an Army officer commission, as he was advised that the Army "had no positions for him due to his race." Undeterred and committed to serving his country, Woodson opted and was trained as a combat medic with the barrage balloons unit before deploying to combat in Europe. As part of the advanced landing assault element on Normandy Beach, Staff Sergeant Woodson made one of the most heroic decisions of his life.

While struggling against fatigue, combat exhaustion, and throbbing pain sustained from grave wounds, he made the decision to plunge into the surf and drag four drowning soldiers to safety. The survivors were "Tommies," or British soldiers, attempting to swim ashore with help from a guide rope extending from the beach to their landing craft, anchored in deep water. The rope had broken, and the men were floundering and certainly would have perished had it not been for his heroic actions. Woodson rescued and retrieved numerous other soldiers from the water and, quickly instructed other soldiers to do the same to save their brothers. Woodson eventually succumbed and collapsed later that afternoon from his exhaustion and was medically evacuated. Official Army records reported that he saved the lives of more than one hundred soldiers, pulling some of them from the surf to safety and administering medical aid to numerous others. He was subsequently transported to a supporting hospital ship, where Army nurses treated his shrapnel and bullet wounds. Three days later, he was determined to return to the beach to join the fight.

> Back in combat, he continued his medical mission for the 320th, and other units, still recovering from his serious wounds for which he would later receive the Purple Heart.

An Army Press Release lauded Woodson's heroism, stating he had ignored his wounds and worked for thirty hours. The *Stars and Stripes* military newspaper wrote that Woodson and the other medics, "covered themselves with glory on D-Day."[25] The Black press back home reported that he deserved the Congressional Medal of Honor, the ultimate symbol of valor and self-sacrifice. However, in the end Woodson's commanding officer would only recommend him for the Distinguished Service Cross, the nation's second-highest award. However, upon reviewing the story of his heroic actions, US Gen. John C. H. Lee, commanding general of the Communication Zone in Britain, believed Woodson deserved the Medal of Honor, so the official recommendation was properly upgraded to reflect the rightful award for his heroic actions.[26] Despite his unselfish and courageous act of heroism, and no doubt once again due to racial discrimination, War Department officials never awarded Woodson the Medal of Honor as recommended. For this reason, still vague today, Woodson was only awarded the Bronze Star, a far lesser award, generally granted for meritorious service.[27]

> This is just one instance of how Black units in midcentury wartime felt the fullest extent of racism, bigotry, and ignorance.

Overall, World War II would see 433 Medals of Honor awarded to White servicemembers, along with, ironic at the time, eight soldiers from the all-Japanese American 100th Infantry Battalion. Still, *none of the one million* African Americans within any branch of service, in any theater of that war, received a Medal of Honor for their heroic acts.[28] For their exemplary service during D-Day, over the next several weeks following the battle, commendations were issued to the battalion by Gen. Dwight D. Eisenhower, supreme commander, Allied Expeditionary Force; Gen. Courtney H. Hodges, commanding general, First US Army; Lt. Gen. Leonard H. Gerow, V Corps commander; Maj. Gen. Hoyt S. Vandenberg, Ninth Air Force commander; Brig. Gen. William L. Richardson, IX Air Defense command; and Brig. Gen. E.W. Timberlake, 49th Anti-Aircraft Artillery Brigade.[29]

At a special 2009 ceremony in Paris, France, commemorating the sixty-fifth anniversary of D-Day, 44th US President Barack Obama bestowed the French Legion of Honor upon the last surviving member of the 320th Barrage Balloon Battalion, Corporal William Garfield Dabney.[30] Although much deserved, it took sixty-five years to bestow this heroic, all-Black unit with recognition for their role in the Normandy D-Day landing.

CHAPTER FOUR

---★---

The Beginning of the End

By AUGUST 1944, the skies over Normandy were quiet, with Allied aviation assets now controlling the skies and with the Luftwaffe down to an estimated seventy-five fighters. By September, the once mighty German bomber air force was all but dead, and the 320th Barrage Balloon Battalion was redeployed to fulfill other tactical assignments throughout the country during its remaining 140 days in France. Later that year, two of the battalion's four batteries moved to the tip of the Cotentin Peninsula to fly a balloon barrage at Cherbourg—the key port city captured by Allies three weeks after D-Day. The remaining two batteries stayed on the beaches, their balloons soaring above Omaha and Utah until early October, when deteriorating weather prevented ships from landing.

On October 24, 1944, the Battalion received final orders to redeploy back to England, embarking aboard three landing crafts for their journey. Upon arriving in England, and after three weeks of inaction, the 320th was finally ordered to return back to the States in mid-November. The unit's twelve-day voyage back across the North Atlantic proved quite harrowing and eventful. Although there were no German U-boats to contend with, the ocean showed a violent side of its own, as the war-weary soldiers endured her treacherous, hurricanic waters for two weeks. After fourteen endless days aboard ship, the battalion finally arrived at Staten Island, New York, on November 25, 1944, and subsequently transported to Camp Kilmer,

New Jersey. Days later, the men were granted highly anticipated and much deserved and needed leave. The battalion regrouped and was shipped to Camp Stewart, Georgia, in December, back into the cradle of Southern racism and bigotry. According to an account provided by Staff Sergeant Woodson, the D-Day Bronze Star Medal recipient, the first words he heard from the mouth of a White soldier at Camp Stewart were:

> "Here come that Nigger group. Got all them medals over there in France. We're gonna make sure we take care of them while they're down here."[31]

ISLAND BOUND

Upon settling into their new home at Camp Stewart, the war-tested 320th, now experts in moving and fighting with a moment's notice, started intensive training—this time for a tropical jungle environment. All indications pointed to the likelihood of Hawaii. Brand-new balloons and supporting equipment were issued with each lettered battery assigned to fifteen balloons. On April 15, 1945, the unit embarked on a five-day journey to Fort Lawton, Washington, before boarding the USS *Aconcagua* and docking at Oahu, Hawaii, Camp Aiea, on May 6, 1945. The men were still unaware exactly what their new assignment would be, since the mission had begun before their arrival at Camp Aiea. The speculation was that they were slated to participate in the land invasion in Japan, Operation Olympic, but it did not come to fruition. The battalion ultimately spent the remaining months of WWII in Hawaii. The US dropped atomic bombs on Hiroshima and Nagasaki over two days in August 1945, which altered the course of the war. Japan surrendered shortly afterward, and the war was officially over on September 2, 1945, for the Allies and the fighting 320th:

THE ONLY AFRICAN AMERICAN COMBAT UNIT TO LAND AT NORMANDY ON D-DAY.

The unit's winning mission at the Normandy beaches helped cull the German air force, opening the skies for Allied air forces for weeks and months to come. The battalion and its big-bag balloons contributed to the success of the 761st Tank Battalion, the 333rd Field Artillery Battalion, and all ground combat units that came ashore after D-Day, becoming an integral part of WWII and General Patton's Third Army.

Barrage balloon recovery performed by battalion members. Photo courtesy of National Archives and Records Administration.

Barrage Balloon training in Camp Tyson, Tennessee. Photo courtesy of the Library of Congress, LC-USE6-D-008677.

Street view of Camp Tyson, Tennessee, Barrage Balloon Training Center. Photo courtesy of National Archives and Records Administration.

320th Barrage Balloons flying over Omaha Beach. Photo courtesy of National Archives and Records Administration

The American flag flies half-mast below barrage balloons on the beach that would become one of the first cemeteries for American soldiers lost at Omaha. Photo courtesy of Alamy..

General David Eisenhower, Supreme Allied Commander Europe.
Photo courtesy of National Archives and Records Administration

Corp. Carlton Chapman of the 761st Tank Battalion. Photo courtesy of National Archives and Records Administration.

PART TWO

The Combat Arm of Decision
761st Tank Battalion

Lieutenant General George S. Patton. Source: Courtesy of the Library of Congress.

A Colored soldier
cannot think
fast enough
to fight
in armor.[1]

—George S. Patton, Jr.
WWII General, United States Army

INTRODUCTION

Second World War Third Army Commander Gen. George S. Patton, Jr.—"Old Blood and Guts"—always had something to say to his men (and the rest of the world) and he said it with pride and conviction:

"Lead me, follow me, or get the hell out of my way."

"Say what you mean and mean what you say."

"If everybody is thinking alike, then somebody isn't thinking."

A product of the Old Army, with assignments in the Old South, Patton also made a ton of unfounded claims, specifically surrounding African Americans, especially when it came to deploying Blacks in the US Army.

"A colored soldier cannot think fast enough to fight in armor."

These words especially resonated with me, after spending most of my entire military career in mechanized tanks (or armor, the official US Army designation of tank corps), starting twenty years after WWII and, eventually, crossing over five decades. Upon examining the historical and heroic actions of Black mechanized combat units such as the 761st, Gen. Patton no doubt underestimated the will and determination of the Black soldier. During World War II, the 761st Tank Battalion was a segregated Black Army mechanized combat unit, which according to then War Department policies, was prohibited from fighting and serving alongside White American soldiers. And as a living testament, Patton's misguided and distorted comments proved incorrect about me, a determined Black soldier who ultimately rose through the ranks to become the first African American Army National Guard Division Commander in the 225-year history of the US National Guard, leading over 18,000 men and women soldiers.

Regardless of one's color, race or ethnicity, something all soldiers have in common is a primal desire to master the technical side of the weaponry of war. A desire to become both technically and tactically proficient with entrusted and assigned lethal equipment prior to deploying to the battlefield. This involves an incredible amount of time and dedication, all fueled by the desire to perform the assigned mission and successfully serve our country. Reflecting on my military training as a commissioned officer, my basic armor officer's course prepared me for tank-platoon leadership and armor-company command positions. In undergoing this specialty training, it was incumbent upon me to ensure, as commander, that my soldiers underwent extremely comprehensive technical training, including understanding all aspects of mechanized tank operations and their tactical deployment. Such tactical and technical training included but was not limited to systems mechanics, tactical deployment, defensive and offensive emplacements, gunnery target acquisition, meteorological impact on targeting, machine gun deployment, gun assembly and disassembly, round selection tank maneuvering techniques, and much more. As commander, the most distressing and technical part of my battalion's training was vehicle maintenance, which invariably required crew members to be technically proficient not only in system tactical deployment, but in mechanics. Additionally, the troops learned engine and transmission repair, radio operations and procedures, track-and-road wheel maintenance and repair—whatever was thrown their way. The unit toiled day and night because we understood from history that a disabled tank on the battlefield could mean certain death.

Masterfully, I studied these systems and combat tactics, though on more advanced, modern tanks, starting with the M-48 during my armor officer's advanced course, which prepared me for armor battalion command and later, armor brigade command, training on M-60 and M-1 Abrams Main Battle Tanks and the M-1A1. At the conclusion of my final mechanized armor training, my primary emphasis became focused on gunnery, tactics, large unit operations, and tactical offensive and defensive formations. In short, always going back to review the basics—an essential part of learning any trade. The culmination of such intense technical armor training and experience enabled me to closely monitor, with a trained, expert eye, the actions of my soldiers. My sporadic venture with tanks as a senior leader continued for the remainder of my career, even while serving as the commanding general of an armor-heavy mechanized infantry division (armor battalions outnumbering infantry battalions).

Though he may have been a brilliant combat tactician, and no doubt an integral figure attributing to both the Allied and America's success in WWII, Gen. Patton's racial attitude and unforgiving beliefs as to the abilities and capabilities of the Black soldier were in fact on an equal par to that of his fellow White GI. Patton would never have permitted, nor could he have possibly foreseen, my personal success as a Black man and two-star general in the US Army. Finally, it remains an understatement to say Patton was surprised by the accomplishments of his all-Black 761st Tank Battalion hailing from the Jim Crow South.

Bravery and battle balloons, coupled with a massive Allied fighter aircraft fleet, won the day against the Luftwaffe on June 6, 1944, making for an unforgettably devastating, but victorious, D-Day landing for the US at Normandy.

Uncertainty and doubt cast a dark shadow upon the overall planning—and ultimate success—of Decision Day early on, as the German Army entrenched itself in cliffs above the beaches of Normandy and had an initial advantage in the fight against assaulting Allied troops. Though Allied leadership had spent years planning for the imminent invasion of Europe through the French Coast, the exact invasion route was still a mystery to the Nazis. Allied strategic prospects included Normandy or Calais, the latter favored most US tactical planners (and highly suspected by the Germans) as the invasion landing point; Calais was closest to the European continent and had a direct access point located across the English Channel. Germany had battle plans tucked away for whichever landing became reality, with the lion's share of enemy resources and troops focused on Calais.

Hitler's military generals and forces were extremely skilled combat tacticians and no stranger to the game of strategic warfare. These were the same forces currently engaged on the Eastern Front and fighting losing battles against a stubborn Russian Army, after it foolishly opened combat against Allied and Russian armies at two separate, simultaneous fronts. The US Army knew Germany's strategy—these same tactics deployed in London during the 1940s Blitz, when England suffered saturated bombing by the Germans—which influenced America's plan to fly barrage balloons above the beaches to interdict attacking, low-flying, enemy aircraft. Three months later, the African American 761st Tank Battalion had an unopposed landing at Normandy, no doubt partially due to the success of that lone Black combat unit at Omaha Beach on D-Day, which is still widely unknown today.

As the 320th Barrage Balloon Battalion ascended to victory, the 761st Tank Battalion barreled into the war. The battle plan for Western Europe would include France, Belgium, Holland, Austria, Luxembourg, Czechoslovakia, and, finally, Germany. The 761st would travel up to three hundred miles at any given time, depending on their attachment to certain divisions, corps, or numbered armies upon relocation.

Note: When comparing Western Europe to the United States, consider that Germany is only the size of Oregon and Washington states combined, and Luxembourg is less than one-quarter the size of Los Angeles County.

From the time the 761st hit French soil, it was on the move. As a separate battalion, its mission called for constant, sometimes daily, mobility. These soldiers pursued the Germans from village to village, town to town, city to city, and, until the war's end, country to country.

CHAPTER ONE

———★———

Bitterly Opposed South

CALL IT A CALLING, a familial obligation, or an opportunity for adventure—whatever the motivation, today's young people entering the service have a luxury never afforded to servicemembers in the past. Today, they have a *choice*.

Before the creation of an organized draft lottery in 1969, military selective service was mandatory for most males through the involuntary draft. Young men, ages eighteen to twenty-five, either entered the active service, had a legitimate deferment, or found legal *and* illegal ways to avoid serving. Some claimed religious or familial obligation while others faked health conditions or fled to countries like Canada. The new, organized draft required all men of age to register for service and make themselves available for induction. It was the local draft board's duty to determine whether a man would serve or be deferred after meeting a series of qualitative exclusions. The lottery was a system whereby the Army assigned each day of the year a number in corresponding order—365 days, plus leap year and, when drawn, a male born on that given day could be drafted (usually into the Army but, sporadically, sent to the Navy and Marine Corps). The number of men drawn depended on the military's demands.

When the Army deferred a soldier from serving in the US military, it usually implied medical or mental disability, essential technical or scientific employment vital to the country, or, for a while, having a spouse. Women have always been excluded from mandatory military service, the theory being the American populace would never accept, or fathom, a ritual of young, female soldiers returning home from the battlefield in body bags, as the US ultimately witnessed in homecomings from Iraq and Afghanistan.

With the cessation of the draft in 1973, the military experienced a higher percentage of minorities serving in the total force. This was attributed to fewer White men entering the services as volunteers, tilting the scale toward minorities, who often viewed the military as an escape from a life of picking cotton in the South or better put, a way to secure a job in a now desegregated America that was still very much prejudicial in many places.

At the beginning of World War II, the US Army initially imposed limits on the number of Negroes eligible to enlist, or conscript into the military. The War Department, the precursor to the Department of Defense, believed Negroes weren't fit for combat and were only physically and mentally intelligent enough to serve in support units, so the volunteer induction of Blacks was kept to a case-by-case minimum. Based on the 1925 *Army War College Study*, the prevailing belief was that Blacks had no place serving in combat units for two reasons: first they lacked the courage to confront the enemy, and secondly, Blacks were mentally incapable of operating complex technical or mechanical combat equipment, like tanks, field artillery cannons, and other sophisticated machines.[2] Contrary to popular myths, Black soldiers during WWII were assigned to, and expertly crewed, artillery weapons in the American Army for nearly 150 years, dating as far back as the American Revolutionary War (1775–1783) and US Civil War (1861–1865). Opposition to Blacks serving in combat units existed long before *The Study* in 1925, as seen in a 1917 report commissioned by the National Association for the Advancement of Colored People (NAACP) Chairman Dr. J.E. Springarn, who argued:

> "The South does not want Colored men to get any kind of military training; nothing frightens it worse than the thought

of millions of Colored men with discipline, organizing power, and dangerous effectiveness. This is why it [the South] is so bitterly opposed to universal military training."[3]

As the gale winds of war blew across Europe, America's Black leadership and Black print media were desperately urging the government to fully open its military to Negroes without limitations or quotas. This naturally made sense since African American Army support units were already forming. Despite such reluctance on behalf of the Army, it nevertheless took compassionate and forceful intervention from then First Lady Eleanor Roosevelt and her close friend and Black activist, Mary McLeod-Bethune, to facilitate policy change. Such transformation was welcomed by the Black community, even though the Army *still* hadn't built the ground-combat support units. Of course, this would all change with the activation of the 761st Tank Battalion—or, as White soldiers would call these courageous warriors, "Elenore's Niggers and Patton's Pets."[4]

CHAPTER TWO

———★———

Come Out Fighting

THE SEGREGATED 761ST Tank Battalion, along with its White counterparts, was eventually activated in 1942, shortly after its men completed traditional basic training. The tank battalion, upon reorganization, would ultimately carry more than fifty crews of highly technically skilled and tactically trained Black tankers during their two years of intense and continuous training at Camp Claiborne, Louisiana, and later, Camp Hood, Texas.

Constructed in 1940, Camp Claiborne was a World War II tent camp, initially called Camp Evangeline and renamed for William C. C. Claiborne, the governor of the Territory of Orleans and the first governor of the State of Louisiana. It was also home to the largest wargames (drills) in American history, the 1941 Louisiana Maneuvers, in which the US Army split thousands of soldiers into two opposing forces, the *blue* and the *red*, using the camp's open terrain to test the feasibility of mechanized equipment (like tanks) in actual warfare with a focus on the war raging in Europe. This was especially important for two reasons: first, to test the feasibility of its armored tank units since Germany had struck multiple countries with a tank blitz, and second, to assist Army planners in determining whether horse cavalries were obsolete. One might think of the Louisiana Maneuvers as a football scrimmage with players on the same team going head-to-head with one another.

The maneuvers, also known as the *Big One*,[5] stretched into Texas military territory and caught the attention of Army chief of staff Gen. George Marshall and a then little-known Army lieutenant colonel by the name of Dwight D. Eisenhower. As part of its winning tactical objective designed by Eisenhower, the Blue Army defeated Lt. Col. George Patton's Red Army in what seemed like a "vast laboratory experiment to prove the worth of ideas, men, weapons, and equipment," Eisenhower later recalled. More than four hundred thousand men in two continental US Armies took part in the 1941 wargames, and the tactical value of the exercise, according to Eisenhower, was "incalculable".

Note: Three years later, Lt. Col. Eisenhower would become a four-star general serving as the supreme Allied commander in Europe, and Lt. Col. Patton would elevate to a three-star general serving under Eisenhower. Eisenhower would eventually be promoted to a five-star general and Patton, four stars.

After the six-week exercise, Army units reactivated as tank battalions to begin training in preparation for what would become World War II. The 761st Tank Battalion was among the combat vehicle units initiated on April 1, 1942. At this time, in a segregated military, recruited Black soldiers were led by a mixed cadre of senior White officers with junior Black officers. White battalion commander Lt. Col. Paul Bates and executive officer Capt. D.J. Williams would head the Negro tank battalion, this would be the only tank unit staffed by African American soldiers. Lt. Col. Paul Bates would later be known as the "White colonel" who refused to court-martial future Hall of Famer Jackie Robinson.

Although their senior battalion leadership was White, most junior officers in the unit, including lieutenants and captains, were Black, making it one of the few Army battalions to mix races at the time. The battalion's personnel strength consisted of six White officers and thirty Black officers, complemented by 676 enlisted men—all Black.[6] The soldiers of the 761st adopted the nickname "Black Panthers," a reference to a new name for battle tanks: Panthers—the wildcats native to African jungles, vicious and strong, characterized by swift, silent attacks without warning. It was symbolic, the quick strike, unexpected and unsuspecting, carrying missions to a decisive conclusion. The Army subsequently coalesced and designed a uniform shoulder patch honoring the attacking spirit of the Black Panther.

Their motto: *Come out fighting*[7]

Black officers were generally assigned to the battalion by choice, while Whites were assigned due to some leadership deficiencies in Caucasian companies, popularizing the 761st Battalion as a dumping ground for overage and incompetent White officers. It was never a mystery as to how Caucasian troops felt about integrating with African Americans; even something as innocent as a Christmas carol weaponized by White units—*"I'm dreaming of a White battalion."*[8]

BLACKS UNDER WHITE COMMAND

Lieutenant Col. Bates was one of a very few White officers who volunteered and *chose* to lead a Negro battalion, quickly garnering his soldiers' loyalty and respect. The White officers leading Black troops had one of the toughest assignments in the segregated Army—not only did they need to relate to their men, but they had to earn the respect of fellow White officers who looked down on them for working with men outside of their race.[9] Both Lt. Col. Bates and Capt. Williams would meet the challenge within the battalions.

Unlike many White, Southern officers were often *involuntarily* assigned to Black units—the US Army believed they knew how to "handle" soldiers of color—Bates's cultural and formative experience was from the progressive West Coast (Los Angeles). As a former, all-American football player from New Jersey's totally racially integrated Rutgers University, Bates had worked and played alongside African

American men before enlisting in the Army following graduation. He received a commission after graduating from officer candidate school and progressed from the armor officer basic and tank-gunnery courses, earning his armor training under Gen. George S. Patton, Jr.[10]

One lieutenant of the 761st was a newly commissioned Black officer, John Roosevelt Robinson, known by friends as Jackie. Initially, Second Lt. Robinson was trained as a cavalryman at Fort Riley, Kansas, and later transferred to Camp Claiborne, where the 761st was stationed, and had undergone training as a tank crewman over the past several months. Robinson attended Pasadena Junior College and the University of California at Los Angeles (UCLA). He was a quick study and, just as quickly, gained the respect of the 761st soldiers and became the unit's platoon leader.

Because of an old college football injury, coupled with a legal battle that threatened to end his fledgling military career, and in the interest of the Army, Robinson was transferred to the Black 758th Tank Destroyer Battalion after a highly controversial court-martial trial charged him with insubordination and disrespecting a White officer. The charges stemmed from his refusal to sit at the back of the bus at Camp Claiborne. At the time, the military practiced the same segregationist policies as White communities outside the gate; this meant civilian bus drivers had the power to enforce policy and were even armed with pistols, if "needed" to protect policy.[11] After reviewing his charges, Bates determined there was no basis for court action. So, to avoid determent and distraction, and for the good of the service, the Army transferred Robinson to the 758th, where his newly assigned battalion commander (also White) examined the trumped-up charges and ultimately found Robinson not guilty. With the hope of rejoining his original battalion, the 761st, Robinson watched the unit sail for Europe to fight in ongoing WWII, which he believed was his destiny. But months before the war's end, he was honorably discharged,[12] and Lt. John "Jackie" Roosevelt Robinson had a new destiny—making history as the first Black Major League Baseball player.

DIVERSITY–LIKE NEVER BEFORE

As Jackie Robinson battled legal issues, the 761st received orders for a permanent change of duty station, the location unknown at the time. After its departure and a few days of train travel, the unit arrived at Camp Shanks, New York (the same Camp Shank that had been occupied by the 320th Balloon Battalion less than a year earlier). Before tank training at Camp Claiborne, Louisiana, like all soldiers leaving civilian life for the Army, members of the 761st underwent basic training, theirs at Fort Knox, Kentucky. For the first time, soldiers of the battalion met one another and learned just how diverse a group they were, possibly the most talented and diverse group of people coming together for the first time in the US.

These proud and talented men hailed from all over the country—from northern cities, like Boston, New York City, Philadelphia, Chicago, and Detroit, and the South, from Oklahoma, Florida, Texas, Georgia, and South Carolina; of course, the South had greater disproportional demographical representation than any other region. Southerners were African Americans reflective of every conceivable social background and ethnic creed—some Louisiana Creoles, South Carolina "Geechees," Gullahs (Black Muslims) from the Georgia Coast, and Black Native Americans from Oklahoma and Florida.[13] Each came with their own dialect of the regionalized, American version of the King's English. Black Southerners, of course no strangers to racism and segregation, were somewhat guardedly optimistic through it all. It had been their experience day in and day out—something quite new to Northerners, though, covert racism had always existed in northern cities.

The autumn heat during the unit's redeployment to Louisiana would become an equal challenge, especially during long conditioning marches when exhausted troops climbed dusty hills carrying full field packs and other combat equipment. Perceived by all the White Southern drill sergeants as potential antagonists, Northern Black GIs felt they somehow were always singled out for punishments, such as additional drills, extra push-ups, and physically exhausting marches. All simply because of a biased belief that all "niggers" from New York were "uppity."

The 761st Tank Battalion quickly became a contrasting study between inductees from above the Mason-Dixon Line and those from below. Generally, most soldiers from the South were from rural farm communities, entering the Army having endured harsh living conditions, like battling harsh climates and toiling with farming machinery further coupled with insufferable segregated conditions and limited educational opportunities. On the contrary, Northern Blacks were far more socially progressive and educated, many with high-school diplomas and some with college experience and even degrees. In fact, a few of these individuals possessed professional specialty training and teaching backgrounds, though some had never experienced operating vehicles, let alone complex farm equipment. It seemed the only commonalities among these men, aside from their race, were their ages, ranging from late teens to early thirties, and the fact that most were single and had no children.

THE CONDITIONING

There were, of course, challenges, given the soldiers' diverse ages and geographical, cultural, and physical abilities. Those individuals who were fortunate enough to have participated in sports back home were in better physical condition, as were others who came from farms, where long hours and demanding work were the standard. Either way, the innate bond and will to succeed among these Black soldiers, of similar physical and cultural characteristics, appeared far greater in likeness than the evil forces of racism and segregation that sought to divide them. The rigorous basic field training at Fort Knox required intense, physical conditioning, weapons familiarization, rifle marksmanship, bivouac, hand-to-hand combat, first-aid training, enemy vehicle recognition, and many other essential survival subjects. After three months of initial training at Fort Knox, the troops boarded a train and were shipped to Camp Claiborne, passing through Kentucky, Tennessee, and Mississippi, bound for Louisiana—the first time in the Deep South for some.

Finally arriving at Claiborne and exhausted from their long journey, the unit disembarked from the train to discover its billeting quarters adjacent to the camp's sewer treatment plant—an unforgettably horrendous smell they were forced to endure, especially when the potent wind blew toward their barracks—where field tents rested upon the Louisiana mud, a substance foreign to many. White soldiers were, by contrast, billeted in the base's newly constructed barracks, built by local civilian Black carpenters. On one of the few bright sides, the African American men were excited upon receiving their newly issued combat weapons and equipment, the Stuart tank. Mechanized tank training began almost immediately, first with familiarization on the M-5 Stuart tank and later the M-4 Sherman tank, both war machines designed to hold four to five crewmen.

The initial training was confined to one-on-one for soldiers before learning together as a crew. Early on, the farm boys quickly proved they made the best tank drivers, having experienced maneuvering machinery and reading terrain; skills they had acquired as youngsters working the fields at home. The troops eventually trained as a larger tactical echelon, such as a mechanized platoon, then a company and finally, as a tank battalion. Army policies required each man to teach a class to his fellow tankers in gunnery, targets, small-arms weapons, map reading, maintenance, mine warfare, and aircraft recognition.

Making training even more strenuous, the men were required to learn and rehearse mounted actions drills, procedures for removing wounded crew members from the tank, equipment inspections, sight adjustments, and destruction of the tank and its components, if necessary. Additional training covered fire orders—the sequence of steps in which a tank commander directs the gunner to fire—and dismounting actions, whereby a crew is forced to abandon a disabled tank and fight as an infantry soldier under fire.

Every soldier was required to cross-train to become tactically and technical proficient in each of the four positions (driver, loader, gunner, and tank commander), learning to accurately sight and dry fire (without using live ammunition) the main gun in varying climates and tactical conditions. Additionally, soldiers were taught basic vehicle maintenance from the technical manuals, which entailed changing tracks, maintaining system air cleaners, and daily oil and fuel checks. Battalion commander Lt. Col. Bates always insisted his tanks to be in top condition—just like his soldiers, into whom he instilled the importance of preventative maintenance to avoid tank mechanical difficulties during combat deployments. Such preventable technical failures under intense combat conditions would no doubt result in certain doom if soldiers were forced to perform preventable repairs while under enemy fire. Finally, additional critical combat training included emergency vehicle escape procedures, loading and stowing ammunition, and remedial emergency actions to take in case of an onboard fire. Drills were performed so often, exactly the same each time, hundreds of times or more, until it became second nature. Troops were soon able to perform procedures flawlessly and with ease, reminded that such actions might one day save their lives or that of a fellow comrade in arms. The training doctrine Lt. Col. Bates always instilled in his men—to *train as you fight, and fight as you train*—is an Army motto that still remains today.

Of course, it was vital to learn how to zero in on static *and* moving targets, or *bracketing*, a taught targeting procedural of first firing too high (long), then firing too low (short), in order to find the perfect range. Tank commanders would spot targets through a telescope sight and give orders to the gunner beside him, who shot to estimate the target's distance, and, if the rounds were short, went up fifty yards; if the rounds were long, the gunner came down fifty yards, and the third round would be on-target. Even though African American soldiers were learning the rudiments of operating and firing tank cannons, they weren't allowed to fire live ammunition; instead, they were told to go through dry runs. White Army recruits, in contrast, fired live rounds throughout training.

Finally, during the last week of the unit's intense training, the Army commanded Negro troops to fire a single round of live ammunition and nothing more, evidence the Army never intended for them to see combat.

> The Army could not bear to waste ammunition if the 761st was never going to war. So, if called into war, the Black men of the 761st would enter in tanks, after having only fired one live round in more than two years of training—a sad sign of the times.

With their preliminary training completed, new orders arrived through the pipeline directing the entire battalion to move to Camp Hood, Texas, for the final weeks of training—advanced exercises with day-and-night company and battalion maneuvers. Upon arrival, US soldiers were, rightfully, outraged to witness German Nazi prisoners of war treated better than African Americans, as the Army assigned work to captured enemies, allowing Nazis to boss around Colored Americans. The War Department, ignoring the obvious issue of favoring enemy soldiers over its own men (as the US Army would continue to do to Blacks throughout WWII), simply assigned the American soldiers new weapons, handed over by enemy POWs, and a hypothetical slap on the back.

The US War Department eventually decided to upgrade the unit to M-4 Sherman medium tank, which was far more lethal than its M-5 predecessor. The M-4, at thirty-five tons, was twice the weight of the M-5 with a 75-mm short barrel, low-velocity cannon, .50-caliber machine gun, two .30-caliber machine guns, and a two-inch smoke mortar.[14] The tank's turret boasted four inches of armor at its thickest point and a top speed of forty-five miles per hour, on top of its eighteen-inch threads. The Army later decided to modify the M-4 by retrofitting it with a 76-mm cannon.

A SUPERIOR BATTALION

The proficiency high marks earned by the 761st Tank Battalion in training and combat maneuvers at Camp Hood didn't go unnoticed by the Army's higher command echelons. The commanding general of the tank-destroyer center, along with others, reported to Washington on the unit's training and addressed the battalion on occasion. The standard procedure was for both generals constantly monitoring training of all units at Camp Hood to report to Washington which units had successfully achieved combat readiness status. The 761st recorded the highest marks during every evaluation period since arriving at Camp Hood, but still, only White units were initially deployed overseas.

At the conclusion of his detailed inspection, the general ordered all officers and first sergeants of the 761st to step forward. Gen. Lear commended the men of the battalion by stating, "All the reports coming up to Washington about you have been of a superior nature, and we are expecting great things from your battalion in combat."[15] During this same occasion, the commander of one US tank-destroyer training center, Brig. Gen. Ernest J. Dawley, also paid the highest compliments to the unit in his address as the troops awaited deployment. World War I veteran Dawley spoke of wartime possibilities—what may, or may not, happen during battle—for which there would be no explanation; some experiences would be chalked up to "fog of war," meaning situational uncertainty, or unawareness, faced in times of war. However, due to his age, Dawley would avoid combat service this time around. Upon concluding his speech that day, the ole general asked the soldiers of the 761st to fire a shot in his name, to establish his vicarious presence among US troops: "When you get over there, put in an extra round of ammunition and fire it for General Dawley."[16]

CHAPTER THREE

Lock and Load

TWO YEARS of grueling, repetitive training had passed, and rumor had it (a disappointing one, as it proved to be unfounded) that the 761st Tank Battalion would mobilize, eventually departing Camp Hood. After initial fretting, the battalion soon discovered its fate—it would finally receive orders to lock and load. These words, heard on Army rifle ranges across the US, invariably signaled any soldier to lock the firing bolt on their service rifle, load a magazine of ammunition, and prepare to engage a predetermined practice target. However, this time the circumstance appeared somewhat different for the men of the 761st. It was a call to load all personnel and combat equipment in preparation for a permanent change of duty station. The destination remained a secret.

Hopes and expectations among the physically weary troops were heavily weighted in Europe, but after anxious speculation, the men were ordered to Camp Shanks in New York (home state of many of them), about fifteen miles north of Manhattan. A two-week stay at Camp Shanks was the last stop for units preparing for overseas movement to England and, ultimately throughout Europe. It was a massive undertaking for the 761st soldiers, having to undergo personnel, logistical, legal, and medical processing. The unit may have stayed at Shanks, were it not for the hedgerow country of Normandy, France—one of the greatest hindrances of Allied ground forces. Maneuvering beyond the Normandy beaches and into the French countryside meant many of our men would succumb, in death, to the land's ancient earthen banks.

Hedgerows, known as *bocage* in France, are waist-high, hedged fields matted at the roots, out of which grow weeds, bushes, and trees up to twenty feet high. German troops sat snipers in trees and dug deep trenches behind the hedgerows, covering them with timber so that it was almost impossible for Allied artillery to engage their defensive positions. Often, without ever having to leave their foxholes, defending soldiers attached strings to machine guns, positioning them high enough to trigger deadly fire at approaching Allied forces over the hedge. The enemy even cut out a section of hedges to hide large guns, *even tanks,* concealing their weapons in surrounding bushes. They tunneled underneath the bocage, from the back, constructing an opening on the forward side—just large enough to poke through a machine gun. Their main defense, though, was a heavy machine gun hidden at each end of the field with infantrymen disguised along the hedgerow, rifles and machine pistols in hand.[17]

Since the time of the Romans, the farmers had bordered their fields with hedgerows, the terrain's features posing substantial issues for the Allies of D-Day, as soldiers couldn't see beyond the next bocage. Germans defended each embankment as the US Army, in its Sherman tanks, attempted swift movements made impossible by the terrain. A few times, a small German unit with a few machine guns, supported by antitank guns, blocked earlier deploying tank battalions from advancing. Tanks could not climb the embankment without exposing their undersides to antitank fire, and Americans were blasted by German tanks, assault guns, or antitank guns. Those disabled tanks would sometimes block the road for following tanks—the Army's own machines working against them.[18]

Intense planning had obviously gone into the D-Day invasion offensive. However, in hindsight, it appeared that tactical oversight into terrain analysis beyond the beaches was indeed a disaster. Similarly, in the weeks following the invasion off the northern coast of France, the US Army suffered tragic losses attributed to hedgerow country. By July 16, in its attempt to push inland, the 3rd Armored Division alone had lost more than a third of its 232 tanks. Scores of armored personnel were killed or seriously injured. The hedgerow terrain was playing havoc on all the weaknesses of the M-4 General Sherman. By August 26, the 4th and 6th Armored Divisions, spearheading Patton's forces, had lost a total of 269 tanks.

By now, Patton was "Old Blood and Guts" (an endearing title he proudly held),[19] or as one Black soldier put it, "*our* blood and *his* guts."[20] At the time, it was well established that Patton had little (if any) serious regard for African American soldiers, his letters and private journals abound with racist stereotypes and rhetoric toward the Black race.[21] Patton was, however, and above all, a consummate pragmatist. When manpower fell critically short in Europe in the fall and winter of 1944, he became one of the first American generals to integrate his rifle units, albeit supporting Gen. Eisenhower's edict requiring African American, noncommissioned officers (NCO) to integrate fighting ranks. Of course, Blacks had to relinquish their stripes and once again become privates to volunteer to fight in the infantry—this owing to his belief that Black NCOs should never command over or outrank White soldiers.[22]

In October 1944, new operational offenses necessitated the need for all qualified, available, and skilled Sherman tank crews. Patton, for the sake of tactical expediency and his own success, was willing to forgo commonly perceived notions regarding the intellectual and fighting skills of the Black soldier. In an effort to spearhead his planned assault on the Siegfried Line, the German western defensive barrier, Patton requested from the US Military Department of the Interior an additional tank battalion. At the time, there were only two remaining battalions, both Black, that had yet to deploy to the European Theater—the 761st and another with lesser training. When the War Department informed Gen. Patton, his response was:

"Who the fuck asked for colors? I asked for tankers."[23]

And the 761st tankers got the call.

The tactical organizational structure for most fighting battalions is organic to a brigade or regiment in a division and fight as part of that larger organizational force. An independent battalion, however, like the Black 761st, wasn't part of a structure, as it was independently assigned to a higher organization, providing the unit the ability to be moved around the battlefield as needed (an independent, or separate battalion, is a floating entity designed for temporary assignment to either corps, anchoring them to one division for a specific operation). In the case of the 761st, it was Patton's Third Army—the senior headquarters for the XII Corps and XX Corps. Patton was fully aware that this would make the tank battalion the first armored, African American unit to deploy into battle. The majority of the Army's brain trust believed their deployment would be a waste of equipment, but Patton was running out of options. The battalion would become an independent unit in Patton's Third Army. Had anyone of lesser stature called for the battalion, the Black men of the 761st may have never deployed into war.

ROLLING INTO WAR

The troops made the best of their stay near New York City. Like their 320th Balloon Battalion counterparts, the nightlife in Harlem helped the soldiers escape their everyday lives, specifically, the Savoy Ballroom, which at that time was the most famous nightclub in America for Blacks. The Savoy was a must-see, with appearances by notable Colored entertainers such as Louis Armstrong, Count Basie, Ella Fitzgerald, and Duke Ellington and his orchestra. Lionel Hampton's orchestra even played a goodbye concert on the docks of New York to bid the battalion adieu,[24] as it boarded the ship for embarkation, following what had unexpectedly been time off for carousing, interspersed with training. The battalion debarked in England on September 8, 1944.

Upon reaching land in England, assimilating overseas was difficult for American soldiers fighting the same war with a common adjective. Both Whites and Blacks were now confronted to accept a new norm that both races could equally patronize local businesses, as England neither promoted nor shared America's racist segregationist policies. Negro soldiers from the South were shocked to learn they had equal access to sidewalks, drinking fountains, and restrooms (or loos, as the English say). Even so, the US Army made zero concessions for the men and attempted to maintain strict segregation between the Black and White soldiers.[25] English policies caused considerable consternation among White US soldiers, especially as they observed their African American counterparts comingling with White English society, even more so when Blacks associated with English women, even when the women initiated interactions, as often happened.

> The most alarming thing for Southern White soldiers? Watching Black men dance with "their" women in nightclubs—with no retribution. In most Southern states, at the least Blacks would be beaten and jailed, in extreme instances, lynched.

The unit's stay in England was short-lived, as it was in New York; the men were locked and loaded, packed and ready to go with personal and unit equipment. New tanks were issued two weeks later, on October 7, their original tanks having been manufactured for training only. These incoming machines were designed for war. Their new and improved M-4 Sherman tanks came furnished with an array of equipment, or BII—basic issue items—including fire extinguishers, blackout lamps, goggles, safety belts, helmets, a canvas bucket, a tarpaulin, a crank, an ax, a crowbar, a pick, a shovel, a sledgehammer, a track wrench, a track jack and fixtures, a radio, six periscopes, flexible nozzles, and more, including the soldiers' automatic weapons.[26] Crossing the English Channel required LSTs (landing ship tanks, or "large, slow targets," according to Navy and Coast Guard crews): two-deck, flat-bottom vessels designed to keep the men and their equipment together. This type of landing craft allowed the soldiers to directly pull up onto the beach.[27]

Before departing England, the 761st Battalion was relieved from the Ninth Army, a temporary assignment for their overseas movement, and assigned to Patton's Third Army. Lt. Col. Bates received a letter of instruction from Patton, issued to all separate battalion commanders in the Third Army, regarding leadership:

> "Each, in his appropriate sphere, will lead in person. Any commander who fails to obtain his objective, and is not dead or seriously wounded, has not done his full duty!"[28]

As expected by higher-level Allied commanders, the Americans' crossing went unchallenged by the Germans, as this was a full four months after the D-Day landing along the Normandy Coast, and the Allies had firmly established a beachhead on land secured beyond the beach. Though secure in its approach, the Army needed to prepare for harsh channel weather; that, coupled with flat-bottom boats, made for a daunting crossing. The boats, rather than cutting through the water, rolled with the current, and many soldiers had never seen a choppy channel before, let alone crossed one.

At their landing location on October 10, 1944,[29] at what had been deemed Omaha Beach on D-Day, all casualties were cleared—but, for the first time, the US Army had a visual of the destruction and havoc wreaked on June 6; the soldiers could still see tangles of barbed wire, remnants of destroyed tanks, and other burned-out vehicles of all calibers strewn along the shore. Their first order of business was moving to a preplanned staging area near the town of Les Pieux, France, thirty-five miles away. Along the way, 761st soldiers followed a path of destroyed buildings, pulverized by the retreating enemy. Conditions worsened as they neared the front. Huge, iron teeth appeared to have mangled the land. Burst sewers, broken gas mains, and slain people and animals left an overpowering stench in their wake. Shattered glass paved the streets. Electrical and telephone lines dangled, broken and netted together. Women and small children sorted through the rubble of collapsed buildings, while outside, wrecked trucks and trolleys, buses and tanks, half-tracks, self-propelled guns, and dead horses littered the sides of the highway.[30]

As Black soldiers trekked through ruins of vehicles and entire towns, onlooking White soldiers could only assume the 761st was busy delivering tanks to White units.[31]-*Why else would Black men be anywhere near the battlefield?* But the tank crew knew exactly why they were there; the war had reached them, and they were more aware than ever that they were remarkably close to becoming a vital part of history.

CHAPTER FOUR

---★---

Prelude to Battle

WHILE IN THE FIELD at Les Pieux, Bates received the soldiers' first assignment for combat—to fight alongside the 26th Infantry Division as part of the XII Corps in Patton's Third Army, which they had heard so much about. The Third Army's long-range mission, then, was to penetrate and destroy Germany's Siegfried Line (West wall), according to the enemy—a heavily constructed barrier of fortification that stretched four hundred miles from the Netherlands to Switzerland, conforming to Germany's western border.

The 761st would personally encounter the Siegfried Line fortifications specifically designed to impede attacks by tank, using cement "dragon tooth" spikes, land mines, fallen trees, and wide and deep trenches too vast for tanks to cross. The most formidable defenses were pillboxes, or warehouse-sized, cement-block houses with portholes perfect for firing at incoming intruders.[32] Foreign forces went as far as camouflaging pillboxes as unsuspecting structures, like barns and old houses, in which, in place of hay or furniture, stood an outward-facing, 88-mm gun fixed to a nine-foot-thick concrete wall;[33] the death contraptions intermingled with civilian towns and villages[34] running alongside the entire West Wall, the most "heavily defended barrier in the Theater."[35] The Maginot Line was the French version of the Siegfried, which had began construction in 1930 to prevent another incursion by the Germans, as seen in WWI. The Maginot, another zone heavy with war fortifications, aligned with France's eastern border.

THE INFANTRY

The Third Army, consisting of the XII and XX Corps, was a massive collection of platoons (30 soldiers each), companies (189 soldiers), battalions (500 or more soldiers), regiments (3,000), divisions (15,000), and corps (100,000),[36] and a numbered army arrayed with a table of organization (TO) with nearly 300,000 soldiers combined; the largest WWII configuration was General Omar Bradley's XII Army Group with a headcount of 1.3 million—the largest force ever put under the operational control of an American commander.[37]

Two types of American armored units fought in WWII: the separate tank battalion, including the 761st, with fifty-six medium tanks and seventeen light tanks, and the armored division. Armored divisions were vast organizations containing between two hundred fifty and four hundred tanks with supporting artillery, engineers, ordnance, and quartermasters, or logistical elements, with their squads and platoons of infantry. Division commanders knew Sherman tanks inside and out and had trained alongside infantry units. By contrast, *infantry* division commanders knew next to nothing about tanks or how to deploy and maneuver them alongside infantry forces. For this reason, they were coupled with the 761st commander, and all of the men were advised to learn to work together while actively engaging in combat.

Patton's staff had questions regarding the Black tank outfit and how it would perform in combat. Would they fight alongside Whites? Many did not believe Blacks *could* or *would*. Patton clarified:

> "If you give those Niggers the best equipment you've got, give 'em good food, I'll take 'em."[38]

On October 22, the men left camp at Les Pieux for a six-day, four-hundred-mile trek to the town of St. Nicolas-de-Port in the French province of Lorraine. Upon arrival a week later, the Army commanded its soldiers to wait for further orders. Armed and ready to face battle for the first time, the Americans were dismayed to learn their battalion would be separated by platoons and companies and disposed to fight alongside separate elements of the 26th Infantry Division. This was a direct contradiction to how they had trained for two years—these soldiers were conditioned for combat together, as a single unit. However, that wouldn't be the usual case for the all-Black 761st. The 26th Infantry Division had intended all along to break up in the coming assault to help deliver dispersed firepower and fill holes wherever the Army felt necessary.[39]

All the soldiers could do was nod and move on, as Bates had warned them many times that plans could change without a moment's notice or consideration for anyone's feelings; this was war. The battalion would use the organizational disruption as an opportunity to demonstrate its flexibility and success in unpredictable times and with a change of mission and structure.

While performing tank and equipment maintenance on October 31, the routine was suddenly interrupted when the entire battalion was called to form in a semicircle and stand at attention around Lt. Col. Bates, as jeeps manned with military police (MP) escorts, armed with .50-caliber machine guns, approached the scene. Patton approached, and Bates gave a sharp salute. The general was high up on the hood of a half-track, an armored vehicle with front wheels and rear metal tank tracks. History notes Patton wasn't wearing rain gear, and the men could clearly see his two trademark ivory-handle pistols.

Trezzvant Anderson, an embedded 761st reporter from the *Pittsburgh Currier Newspaper*, a Negro publication, recorded his words:

> Men, you're the first Negro tankers to fight in the American Army. I would never have asked for you if you were not good. I have nothing but the best in my army. I do not care what color you are if you go up there and kill those Kraut sonsofbitches. Everyone has their eyes on you.

> Most of all, your race is looking to your success. Do not let them down, and damn you, do not let me down! They say it is patriotic to die for your country. Well, let us see how many patriots we can make out of those German sonsofbitches.[40]

He continued:

> This is war. I want you to start shooting and keep shooting. Shoot everything you see. Whenever you see a German, if it's male or female, eight to eighty years old, you kill them, because they'll kill you."[41]

Though his words were powerful and moving, much like a football coach building up his team in the locker room before taking the field, Patton's exhortation to his soldiers was never authentic. Later that day, back in his personal quarters, Patton wrote in a letter to his wife: "They gave a good first impression, but I have no faith in the inherent fighting ability of the race."[42] Further on in his diary, the general lamented:

> "Individually, they were good soldiers, but I expressed my belief at the time and have never found the necessity of changing it—that a colored soldier cannot think fast enough to fight in Armour."[43]

Though an unfortunate false front, the commander's words were spirit-lifting and instilled unshakable confidence in his men. They were honored by the visit from a three-star general, and still invigorated by his (seemingly) well wishes in war, many soldiers of the 761st felt immensely proud to be the only unit personally requested by Patton. This was only because the battalion wrongfully believed Patton had heard of its remarkable training back in the States and specifically requested the men for duty. In sad reality, the Black unit was simply the last fully trained tank battalion available to fight.

THE ARRIVAL

After four hundred miles, seventy thousand gallons of gasoline, and seven hundred gallons of oil, the men neared St. Nicolas-de-Port and could hear sounds of artillery in the far distance. Whether friendly or enemy fire was uncertain. What was certain—the soldiers knew they were entering the main event. Upon their arrival on November 8, 1944, boasting a compliment of six White officers, thirty Black officers, and 676 Black servicemen,[44] the battalion linked with the 26th Division command. Waiting for them was Maj. Gen. Willard S. Paul:

> "I am damn glad to have you with us. We have been expecting you for a long time, and I am sure you are going to give a good account of yourselves. I've got a big hill up there that I want you to take, and I believe that you are going to do a great job of it."[45]

Now, all that was left was war and the battalion's opportunity to realize its own valor amidst the hushed, but very real, skepticism surrounding them, despite Patton and Paul's seemingly encouraging words. As planned, the Colored 761st was convinced it was not only needed but wanted. Its first mission was laid out, with the highest-regarded armored commander (and now, the 26th Infantry Division commander) expecting only the best. The men were to capture the "big hill"—Hill 253.

Previously, a small group from a battalion within the 4th Armored Division, had been short ammunition and supplies, failing its vital mission to take the hill[46] and exterminate the Nazi forces that occupied it. Now, the responsibility belonged to the men of the 761st. Eliminating the enemies on Hill 253 was essential, as it was a strategic observation post in the 26th Division's area of operation. The battle was on, and it was intense. On November 8, 1944, the

African American unit not only conquered the hill—it liberated the adjacent towns of Bezange-la-Petite and Bezange-la-Grande.[47] St. Nicolas-De-Port would forever be entrenched in the battalion's mind, as its hard, fast rain and deep mud reminded them of home. Training at Camp Claiborne had prepared them for every bloody, muddy battle ahead.

CHAPTER FIVE

───★───

From Victory to Victory

IN THE COMING WEEKS and months, the 761st was singled out by different headquarters and the Negro media back home in newspapers and magazines for unit battle effectiveness and individual heroism against a determined enemy. Between October 1944 and April 1945 at different times the battalion attached to other divisions and groups in addition to the 26th, including the 17th Airborne Division, of which the commander, Major General William Miley, remarked:

> "During the Ardennes Operation, we had very little armored unit support, but of that we did have, the 761st was by far the most effective and helpful."[48]

The Black unit was also, eventually, attached to seven more Infantry Divisions: 71st, 87th, 17th, 79th, 95th, 103rd, and the 17th Armored Group. They met the enemy head-on in cities and towns including Tillet, Dieuze, Morville-lès-Vic, Birkenhardt, Neider-Schlettenbach, Erlenbach, Bollenborn Guébling, Bourgaltroff, Honskirch, Serre Union, Geimont, Silz, Vic-sur-Seille, among others, some as modest as hamlets (or small settlements). They fought the war as much as they did the weather, which the men described as cold and wet with blowing snow and, often, in sub-zero temperatures; warmth was sought but never promised.

Additionally, in mid-November 1944 during a fight in the vicinity of Moyenvic and Vic-sur-Seille, and while supporting the 26th Division, Lt. Col. Bates was wounded—a leg wound so serious, he was evacuated to the rear by 761st medics to a field medical facility.

His diagnosis was a broken leg bone, shattered by a single bullet. Unlike many wounded White soldiers, Bates didn't object to medical treatment by African Americans, which was especially important, as this was about the time when White nurses refused to treat the wounds or bathe any seriously wounded Black soldiers.[49] The lieutenant colonel's medical evacuation meant that the battalion's executive officer, Maj. Charles Wingo, a White soldier, should have immediately assumed command; however, the major suddenly disappeared, later showing up in the rear area suffering battle fatigue.[50] The next White senior officer, Capt. David J. Williams (or Capt. D.J. to soldiers) would assume his position as acting commander and quickly earn his men's deep respect and trust because of his keen leadership under fire and genuine respect for their race. Captain Williams was a Californian by birth, a product of the progressive West Coast, and a Yale University graduate who harbored no prejudices against Blacks.

Come November 9, with the battalion fighting in and around Vic-sur-Seille, artillery rounds rained forward on tanks and at the rear medical station. Capt. Adamson, medical doctor for the battalion, and his medics, though challenged by the incoming artillery fire, miraculously performed aid to wounded tankers who had been evacuated. One medic, Private Clifford Adams, was performing life-saving treatment on a wounded Panther when one of the German artillery shells exploded overhead, mortally wounding the medic. He became the first member of the battalion killed in combat—and he, certainly, wouldn't be the last.

Note: The Geneva Convention of 1864, and the Hague Regulations, ratified in 1907, defined rules for international warfare, protecting medical and religious personnel from direct attack. However, these treaties did not rule out artillery rounds fired on the battlefield, which could result in collateral injury or death to medical and religious personnel.[51]

On the same day Pvt. Adams was killed, Lt. Col. Hollis Hunt, from the 17th Armored Group, arrived and replaced the injured Bates as battalion commander. Hunt was accompanied by Maj. John George, who became the replacement battalion operations officer (S-3). From the beginning, it was apparent to Capt. Williams, and to the soldiers, that Lt. Col. Hunt had little or no respect for African Americans. He directed Williams to court-martial a junior officer for dereliction of duty after showing signs of battle fatigue from days of intense, heavy fighting in an area where the officer had watched his men die. Williams refused the order, stating legal action was never directed against Major Wingo, who had suffered battle fatigue *before the first shot had ever been fired* (Wingo had, in fact, deserted his men). Williams believed that the commander wanted legal action because the lieutenant was Black. He felt Lt. Col. Hunt had arrived at the battalion with preconceived opinions of Black soldiers—all negative.[52]

GAINS AND LOSSES

Patton hoped to crack the Siegfried Line by November 11, 1944, his birthday,[53] a wish that would go ungranted, as progress was slow along the Third Army Front. Sherman tanks of the 4th Armored Division held back until the 26th Division and the 761st Tank Battalion broke the tight German hold over Morville-lèes-Vic on November 12. The same day, two separate battalion platoons repulsed an enemy counterattack at Wuisse, destroying two enemy tanks. The next day one platoon, attached to the 2nd Battalion, 104th Infantry Division, counterattacked through its own initiative, took Wuisse in the afternoon, and defended the town throughout the night.

At Guébling, France, days later and after engineers completed a bridge, hastily constructed under artillery and small-arms fire, 761st tanks crossed into town to provide additional support to the infantry.

They encountered heavy minefields and took a horrific beating, which prevented the continuation of support. Of the five tanks in Guébling, three were lost to antitank fire and one to mines. Shortly after, Sgt. Ruben Rivers, a Negro staff sergeant, distinguished himself through actions above and beyond the call of duty, earning the Medal of Honor, albeit approved and awarded fifty years after the war. Rivers, though seriously wounded days earlier, refused medical evacuation and continued leading his tank into combat; the same spirit men had hoped leaders like Major Wingo would have shown. In excruciating pain, and still performing duties as a tank commander, Rivers exited the safety of his tank, facing a deluge of small-arms fire, to clear a roadblock. He attached a cable from his tank to a tree that had been felled by Germans and stalled the unit's advance. In the process, he was mortally wounded, his tank destroyed by enemy fire. Had Rivers not risked his own life, several tanks would have been destroyed and soldiers killed, as described in his award recommendation.

Rivers's accolade preceded a special review of his actions by an Army panel reviewing Black World War II soldiers serving in the segregated army deserving of such an award, but the Army denied Rivers recognition because of the rampant prejudice of the times. No Black soldiers, in those days, were authorized to receive any award higher than the Silver Star, no matter their efforts or actions.[54] Drafted by former President Bill Clinton, Sgt. Rivers's eventual award read:

> For extraordinary heroism in action during 15–19 November 1944, toward Guébling, France. Though severely wounded, Sergeant Rivers refused medical treatment and evacuation, took command of another tank, and advanced with his company in Guébling the next day. Repeatedly refusing evacuation, Sergeant Rivers continued to direct his tank's fire at enemy positions through the morning of 19 November 1944. At dawn, Company A's tanks began to advance towards Bougaktroff but were stopped by enemy fire. Sergeant

Rivers, joined by another tank, opened fire on the enemy tanks, covering Company A as they withdrew. While doing so, Sergeant Rivers's tank was hit, killing him, and wounding the crew. Staff Sergeant Rivers's fighting spirit and daring leadership were an inspiration to his unit and exemplify the highest traditions of military service.[55]

The supported infantry also suffered heavy losses of wounded and killed, including one soldier who died providing cover fire so his brothers in war could escape from a ditch, and later an entire infantry company was nearly annihilated. Infantry casualties were taken from the battlefield and evacuated to the rear, under the cover of darkness. Seven manned tanks were destroyed. One tank, showing no visible or physical damage, sat immobile on the battlefield, and, after an interior inspection, was found containing four dead 761st crew members, likely killed by the concussion of an artillery round bursting directly overhead; each man seated in his assigned battle position with no evidence of physical injuries[56]. There was death and destruction everywhere as the remaining 761st successfully destroyed German tanks and killed its supporting infantry.

On November 21, 1944, a day after the 761st fired assault guns on and cleared the town of Kerprich, France, Capt. Williams was asked to attend an impromptu memorial service arranged by the US soldiers in an ancient stone church. It was a call to pay personal respects to their fallen brothers, coming together to remember those who had given their lives in the fight for America. In the following days, the town of Morville-lès-Vic was liberated, but only after a bitter battle replete with heroism from American Negro tankers staking their claim that men of color could be just as successful in combat as White units.

By now, the 761st felt it had the right to its own motto:
Come out fighting.[57]

Through it all, Black Capt. Garland "Doc" Adamson, MD, the 761st Tank Battalion medical officer, fled the safety of the aid station on foot, through an artillery barrage, to assist wounded tankers with lifesaving medical treatment; he acted in total disregard for his own safety. For his strong devotion to duty, courage, and solicitude for his wounded comrades, the US awarded Adamson the Bronze Star.

"Doc" was around fifty years old, at the time, and the unit's eldest member. Before joining the Army, he had taught obstetrics and gynecology at Meharry Medical School in Tennessee.[58] Popular opinion among Black officers was that a White officer performing the same actions as Doc, a noncombatant, would have received the Silver Star as a minimum. And they were right.

Elements of the 761st entered Torchville unopposed in late November. They drove through Bois-de-Hessling to the western edge of Munster, a key objective, and occupied the town that evening, controlling one part with Germans controlling the other. For two days, the battalion stayed in Munster, firing on enemy snipers and mortar positions while the infantry fought house-to-house, room-to-room, in a bloody battle. The men cleared the town. Next fight—Dieuze. Their assault guns were so accurate that Maj. Gen. Paul, the 26th Division commander, remarked he had never seen such precise firing. And although the battalion held the lion's share of fighting causing the downfall of Dieuze, the military newspaper *Stars and Stripes* gave credit to the follow-on White company from the 4th Armored Division.[59] It was standard for Black units in combat to hardly receive positive press coverage.

One 761st soldier, evacuated to the battalion's aid station, recalled a degrading incident at the 100th General Hospital unit. While in treatment and bandaged for serious wounds, unable to sit or stand, a two-star general walked the ward to greet wounded White soldiers, asking about their wounds, treatment, and even their families. When the general approached the only Colored soldier in the ward, he asked if he was there to be treated for the "clap" (chlamydia), a venereal disease. A nearby White soldier, also recovering from serious wounds in a near full-body cast, joined in, joking with the general, "If he got it, he got it from your mother. Send me back to the front!"[60] This kind of disrespect and humiliation was woven into the war's already harsh reality for Blacks, whose experience was challenging enough within the segregated Army without added scrutiny.

CHAPTER SIX

---★---

Battle after Battle

Two days after Thanksgiving (which was anything but traditional), on November 25, 1945, the Black battalion was on a mission to serve as a spearhead for the 328th Infantry Regiment and attack the town of Honskirch, France. But, because of major flooding by the Dieuze Dam earlier, the area was thick with mud and impossible for tanks, leaving only the option to approach the town by the main road—as if part of their own morbid Macy's Thanksgiving Day Parade.

Ordered to lead the assault was one company from the 761st Battalion, armed with five staffed tanks in column, under the cover of darkness just before dawn. With reconnaissance in their mission, the company commander reported to the 328th regimental commander that the Germans were "dug in," their enemy tanks shielded under haystacks. A battle and tank veteran, and knowing how deadly they could be, he advised that performing a frontal attack as initially directed would be suicide for his M-4 Sherman tankers. Nonetheless, the regimental commander ordered the attack and their mission commenced, but only after the company commander purposely delayed it by hours, awaiting daylight.

As the assault force neared the town of Honskirch, enemy fire quickly and unassumingly struck lead and rear tanks from cleverly piled haystacks, destroying them, wounding several men, and killing one US soldier. The remaining tanks in the column fought a defensive battle but were ultimately destroyed. Surviving soldiers were rescued and relocated to the assembly area. Finally, days later the town of

Honskirch was taken. When Gen. Patton questioned why so many tanks had been lost so quickly, he learned the 328th regimental commander was actually a finance officer, had never been in combat, and didn't understand how combat units were employed. He was relieved of command and shipped back to the States, his on-the-job training costing a soldier his life.

Note: Both company commander and general should have known, and probably did, of the warfighting principles of Sun Tzu, two thousand years earlier, and Carl von Clausewitz, two hundred years earlier—it is never a smart battle tactic to conduct a frontal attack when the enemy has defensive advantage of the terrain on his own territory.[61] Even Commander J. Colin, of the French War School, noted that a frontal attack was useless.[62] One would've hoped that the finance colonel understood the commonsense fact that you cannot apply accounting principles to a raid against German Panzer Tanks. Apparently, he didn't.

Casualties, in men and tanks, were heavy in November 1944—twenty-two men killed in action, two dead from previous wounds, eighty-one wounded, forty-four nonbattle casualties, fourteen tanks lost, and twenty damaged. The war was taking its toll on the battalion. Tanks could be recovered and repaired, but the 761st, like most other Negro combat units, had difficulty replacing casualties due to Army policies. The battalion was short 113 men, and, by March of 1945, it would be short another eighty-nine.

Entering December 1945, the 761st, with infantry assistance, cleared another French town, Sarre Union (which had fallen to the onslaught of the German's Panzer force), only to have the Germans conduct a counterattack. For the next two days, the Black battalion fought viciously, the Americans prevailing and the Germans withdrawing to the fortified Maginot Line. Both suffered mass casualties. The Maginot Line was a defensive barrier, like Germany's West Wall, built by the French to separate themselves from Germany. Construction had begun in 1930 with bunkers and tunnels as an attempt to deny incursion by Germany through Switzerland and Belgium, as it had accomplished in the Great War. The French line still had not been completed by the beginning of World War II, so the Germans simply conducted a blitzkrieg around the unfinished portions; ironically, it was taken and used by the Germans as their own defensive barrier.

Unable to crack the daunting line with shells from 761st M-4 tanks, the US Army Air Corps obliterated portions of it with five-hundred-pound bombs, allowing the Panthers, and elements of the 26th Infantry Division they were now supporting, to crash through. On December 11, 1945, the 87th Golden Acorn Infantry Division arrived to relieve the 26th Division. In reality, there was no relief for the tankers. Three days later, the 761st Tank Battalion crossed the Blies River and rolled into Germany with the 87th. A communiqué from SHAEF (Supreme Headquarters Allied Expeditionary Forces) reported:

> "Lt. Gen. George S. Patton's Third Army, Infantry and Armor, slammed into German territory at a new point after crossing the Blies River."[63]

LOST IN TRANSLATION

The US troops, however, were unidentifiable by numerical designation, in keeping with the War Department's policy to never provide any positive press to Black units. Even days before, on December 9, the commanding general of XII Corps had written a letter of commendation for the 761st Battalion, but the Army never shared the impressive letter with the press. The recommendation read:

> I consider the 761st Tank Battalion to have entered combat with such conspicuous success as to warrant a special commendation.

The speed with which they adapted themselves to the front line under the most adverse weather conditions, the gallantry with which they faced some of Germany's finest troops, and the confident spirit with which they emerged from their recent engagements in the vicinity of Dieuze, Morville-lès-Vic, and Gruebling entitle them surely to consider themselves the veteran 761st.[64]

The commanding general of the 26th Infantry Division, Maj. Gen. Willard S. Paul, forwarded the letter of commendation to the 761st Tank Battalion with the following endorsement:

It is with extreme gratification that the corps commander's commendation is forwarded to you. Your battalion has supported this division with great bravery under the most adverse weather and terrain conditions. You have my sincere wish that success may continue to follow your endeavors.[65]

That same day, Patton directed all Army chaplains to pray. He published a prayer with a Christmas greeting on the back and sent it to all members of the command, including 761st Tank Battalion:[66]

Almighty and merciful Father, we humbly beseech Thee, of Thy great goodness, to restrain these immoderate rains with which we have had to contend. Grant us fair weather for battle. Gracious harken to us as soldiers who call upon Thee that, armed with Thy power, we may advance from victory to victory, and crush the oppression and wickedness of our enemies, and establish Thy justice among men and nations. Amen.

Reverse side:

To each officer and soldier of the Third United States Army, I wish a Merry Christmas. I have full confidence in your courage, devotion to duty, and skill in battle. We march in our might to complete victory. May God's blessing rest upon each of you this Christmas Day.

> G.S. Patton, Jr., Lieutenant General, Commanding, Third United States Army[67]

The 761st company commanders distributed the holiday prayer and greeting cards to each member of his company, and as a "personal touch" from General Patton, the cards were read aloud in unison.

THE BATTLE OF THE BULGE

That December, meteorologists recorded Europe's coldest month in more than fifty years with record-breaking, sub-zero temperatures. The German Army, reeling from a series of major strategic losses, used the weather as a cover to mount a major counterattack through Belgium's Ardennes Forest against unsuspecting allies. This incursion was later referred to as the Battle of the Bulge, as it created a bulge penetrating the front lines of the Allies. This would become the greatest intelligence blunder for the allies of the war. The Battle of the Bulge would also become the largest battle of the war in Europe. One point of the attack was in a sector positioned by the newly arrived 106th Infantry Division made up of raw recruits who had never seen combat. The unsuspecting Allies fell victim to the bold, foul-weather strike of the Germans, resulting in the enemy's initial success. With the weather as devastating as it was, blowing snow and heavy fog, the first days favored the advantaged attackers.

The intense battle resulted in captured prisoners on both sides, wounding and killing both enemy and ally. Disgracing the Geneva Convention—the core of international humanitarian law—American soldiers of the 106th Infantry were murdered by Germans at the town of Malmedy, rather than placed in captivity. The village of Wereth saw the same fate, along with several US soldiers from the Colored 333rd Field Artillery Battalion who had taken refuge there. The American media widely reported on the Malmedy incident, while the slayings in Wereth, discovered more than two months later, were kept silent by the Army so as to not offend German Americans back home. Sadly, the same concern was not extended to the families of the murdered soldiers.

America, a country of immigrants, had sizable number of new arrivals from Germany prior to the war. Many of them were concentrated in various cities, which often is the case with new arrivals. Some German immigrants were very vocal in their support for their fatherland and its leader, and this was known by our government. As segregated as our country was, tacit favor was given to White immigrants in the form of not reporting atrocities committed by German soldiers upon our own Black soldiers, so as not to antagonize them.

To blunt the Bulge threat, Gen. Eisenhower, Supreme Allied Commander in Europe, redirected Gen. Patton and his Third Army to engage the Germans. The 761st also played a role. Their mission? To support elements of the 87th Infantry Division in recapturing the town of Tillet, which was a few miles west of Bastogne, the village in which the 101st Airborne Division was surrounded, running low on food, ammunition, and medical supplies, unable to reach assistance because of the extreme winter. Tillet was critical to secure—the Germans just might mount a supporting attack. With Patton's 26th and 80th Infantry Divisions, plus, the 4th Armored Division, rushing to the aid of the 101st, the tank battalion was assigned to the 87th Infantry Division with initial orders to guard the southern sector of the Ardennes. However, in another change of plans, the men redirected toward Tillet, where another unit had already surrounded the Belgium city of Schönberg. Seven thousand American soldiers of the 106th Infantry Division had surrendered, which is why it was so important to relieve the 101st Airborne Division at Bastogne.

By December 21, three divisions from the German XLVII (47th) Panzer Corps had surrounded ten thousand American soldiers of the 101st Airborne Division in a perimeter around Bastogne. The next day, German corps commander Gen. George Heinrich Freiherr von Lüttwitz sent a note through the lines demanding the surrender of American forces in Bastogne, threatening to "annihilate" them, should they refuse. When the note reached Brig. Gen. Anthony McAuliffe, assistant division commander, he replied succinctly:

To the German Commander: N U T S!

The American Commander[68]

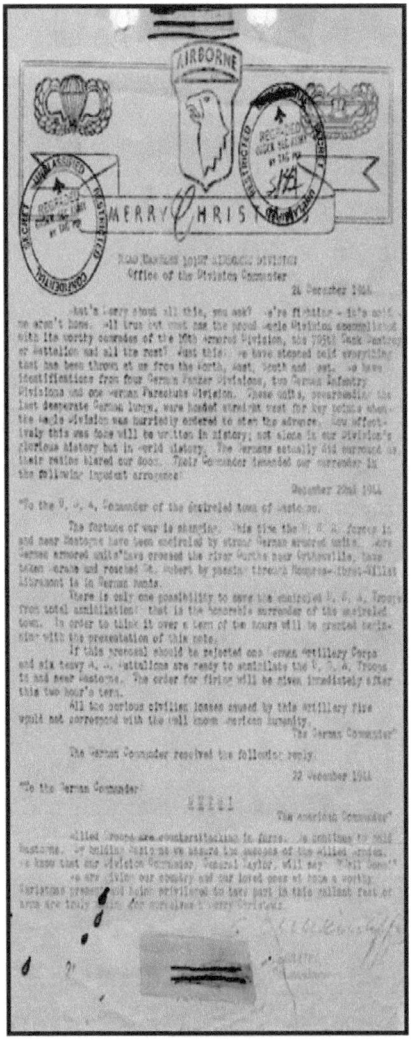

America's written reply to German Gen. Lüttwitz—N U T S! Photo courtesy of National Archives and Records Administration.[69]

There would be no surrender this time. The 761st Tank Battalion assisted with the rescue of the 101st Division, which went on to fight another day.

For five days, Tillet proved to be one of the battalion's most brutal battles. Defended by the Führer Begleit Brigade, a German armored brigade, some of its tankers had earned a reputation at the Russian front, the brigade having served as Hitler's personal palace guard. The Führer Begleit was an exceptionally large brigade, equipped with seventy-one tanks, assault guns, and an array of artillery—unknown by the American 761st at the time. By now, attached to the 87th Infantry Division, the American tank unit was part of the planned combined arms assault which would result in one of the bloodiest battles at the Bulge. The Germans defended as furiously as the 87th attacked with brave backing by the 761st. Day one of the brutal battle was a bloody stalemate, with both sides suffering a great loss of men and machines. The tank crew quickly fell in numbers, its soldiers killed and wounded in action.

The battle was fought under record-breaking weather conditions—generally, always below zero and, if not raining, freezing cold. Literally. The US was firing on all cylinders to focus on the enemy in front of them and the climate surrounding them, with tank blankets and sleeping bags offering minimal warmth. Most times, the harsh climate meant no air support for the soldiers.

THE VOICE OF VICTORY

Amidst the battle for Tillet, American tank crews discovered their communications had been cleverly scrambled by the Germans, who were ready to pull "Axis Sally" from their back pocket. In wartime, Sally was the generic name for women, who, in perfect

US English, broadcasted German propaganda with the intent to psychologically impair the Allies. Sally's voice came through soothing yet sadistic, speaking directly to the men of the Black Panther Battalion:

"Good morning, Negro soldiers of the 761st. I am sorry that you will die today in Tillet. Our fight is not with the Negroes in America, and your fight is not with us. Your fellow Negroes are rioting in Cleveland. Your commander is White and is leading you to death and destruction. He is not one of you. Leave your tanks now and return home to Cleveland where you are needed, and you will not be killed."

She continued over the loudspeaker, playing, "I Can't Give You Anything but Love" by Louis Armstrong[70]—a Black man's musical declaration of love made sinister. Against German hopes, Sally's words only gave the soldiers of the 761st more determination to fight on and take down Hitler.

Up until receiving air support in the Battle of Tillet, once weather conditions allowed, each tank was fighting its own battle from ridge to ridge, street to street, and house to house. After days of warfare, conditions began to turn in America's favor with help from P-38 air support. Planes were in the air as soon as the weather cleared. This would stand as a crucial victory in their mission to take Tillet. The Germans began to fall back and disengage; it had been such a savage and costly fight for the Americans that their success did not bring any real sense of triumph, as they'd lost many men and just as much equipment. On January 9, 1945, Tillet finally fell.[71]

After the Bastogne operation, and the battle for the town of Tillet a week later, the battalion received orders to proceed to Severne, France, to assist in the breakthrough of the Siegfried Line—the Third Army's overall objective. Its mission was to serve as the spearhead of Task Force Rhine, which later, in March 1945, would prove a major challenge. The 761st took to cities, towns, and villages from late December 1944 through mid-January 1945, staying mostly within Belgium and Luxembourg, later engaging in a major battle at Vic-sur-Seille, France. As conflicts closed in on the Americans, the men watched their team diminish with the loss of wounded and slain brothers. These losses, however, were significantly fewer than German injuries and fatalities inflicted by US troops, even with the enemy's upper hand in replacing downed soldiers.

The Nazis were in retrograde and continuing to fight in their retreat, the more losses, the further the retreat. The attacking 761st was in an offensive all-hands-on-deck approach in whatever firepower and manpower they could muster, though they wouldn't receive backup from incoming African American tankers because *there were none.* The willing and available Black soldiers were never trained as tankers, and replacement by White soldiers was out of the question. The US Army was not about to integrate tank crews, even at the cost of losing battles and, worse, American soldiers.

In late January, Brig. Gen. John Whitelaw, assistant division commander of the 17th Airborne Division, visited the 761st Battalion to award a Bronze Star to Capt. Williams and battlefield commissions, to the rank of second lieutenant, to two Black noncommissioned officers. The rule, however, was not as definitive as it seemed. The captain's award was based on his past performance while attached to another division, of which Gen. Whitelaw had minimal, if any, knowledge. The presentation of battlefield commissions to the Negro noncommissioned officers were for *leadership under fire* while attached to a previous command, another instance about which Whitelaw knew nothing.

Williams was concerned that no Black soldiers would see commendations for their valor (can history blame him?). So, upon receiving the Bronze Star Medal from Whitelaw, Williams made it clear he was accepting the award on behalf of his Black soldiers, assuring the general that each man, in his own right, had earned the commendations for his history-making actions in previous battles, including any tanker brothers killed in action (KIA). As common rule dictates, a commander would never authorize an award on behalf of a previous commander, especially not knowing specifics, and for this reason, there is significant chance nothing ever came of Williams's noble request.

CHAPTER SEVEN

Calling All Negroes

UNWELCOMED, like the frigid cold, early December 1944 saw growing shortages of infantry riflemen replacements and tank-fighting armor soldiers in the European Theater. This wasn't a new trend, as the Theater had experienced riflemen shortages since July, and its Ground Force Replacement Command (GFRC) had engaged in a training program to convert basic privates from other arms and services to infantry.[72]

The forecasted shortage came rapidly, as the US supply of replacements continued to diminish, man by man. One week before the German counterattack in the Ardennes, further fueling the shortage, the Theater estimated there would be an overall deficiency of more than twenty-three thousand riflemen by the end of the month;[73] a loss of this magnitude would curtail plans for pressing the attack against Germany. Once the Ardennes attack commenced, so did the Theater's plan to convert any physically fit Black servicemen to infantrymen, even though service units were never specifically trained for direct combat roles. Positions like truck drivers, suppliers, ammunition transporters, and stevedores, as well as jobs in graves registration and maintenance repair, were the only roles Negroes were expected to perform. Sure, these men had successfully completed preliminary infantry training during basic back in the US—but now, they were training for the real thing, for which the Army never completely prepared them. And later, it would turn around to bite them.

With recruits from new divisions flowing into infantry battalions within veteran divisions, which were already part of the fight, Lt. Gen.

Lee, Communications Zone commander, planned to release and train twenty thousand additional infantry riflemen from his "COMMZ" units. After consulting with Gen. Eisenhower and Army commanders, Lee proposed adding even more men, assigning soldiers from his COMMZ Negro units. And everyone agreed. He also consulted with Brig. Gen. Henry Matchett, commander of the GFRC, and Brig. Gen. Benjamin O. Davis, Sr., the highest-ranking African American officer in the European Theater, who was then special advisor and coordinator to the Theater commander on Negro troops. And again, everyone agreed. On Christmas Day, 1944, Matchett and Davis, and the GFRC G-1 (personnel officer) drew up a plan to train Negro volunteers as individual infantry replacements. The plan read:

1. The Supreme Commander desires to destroy the enemy forces and end hostilities in the Theater without delay. Every available weapon at our disposal must be brought to bear upon the enemy. To this end the commanding general, COMMZ, is happy to offer a limited number of colored troops who have had infantry training the privilege of joining our veteran units at the front to deliver the knockout blow. The men selected are to be in the grades of Private First Class and Private. Non-commissioned officers may accept a reduction to take advantage of this opportunity. The men selected are to be given a refresher course with emphasis on weapon training.

2. The commanding general makes an appeal to you. It is planned to assign you without regard to color or race to the units where assistance is most needed and give you the opportunity of fighting shoulder to shoulder with White soldiers to bring about victory. Your White comrades at the front are anxious to share the glory of victory with you. Your relatives and friends everywhere have been urging that you be granted this privilege. The Supreme

Commander, your commanding general, and other veteran officers who have served with you are confident that many of you will take advantage of this opportunity and carry on in keeping with the glorious record of our colored troops in our former wars.

3. This letter is to be read confidentially to the troops immediately upon its receipt and made available in Orderly Rooms. Every assistance must be promptly given to qualified men to volunteer for this service.[74]

Though the letter was later edited to ensure Negro troops weren't assigned to White units right away (thus abrogating the segregationist policy of the Army), the intent was clear—the Army was perfectly intent on keeping the fighting force segregated, with Negroes only allowed to serve in service units (of course, until circumstances turned for the worse). Under another new and, somehow, even more demeaning proposal amendment, select Black noncommissioned soldiers, including corporals and sergeants who had been in the Army for years, were demoted to private and private first-class for the "opportunity" to serve in infantry units with their White "brothers." In reality, the Negro soldiers were stripped of their hard-earned ranks and put on the front lines of war.[75] This was just another incident of blatant racism in the guise of brotherhood and country.

The commanding general of COMMZ knew the Theater had long been concerned with replacements for its Negro artillery, tank, and tank destroyer units. Existing orders stated no Colored soldiers were available from the United States, as they were never trained for combat, and the last of the Colored tank units, the 758th Tank Destroyer Battalion, was already active in the Theater. If the Army was going to retain Negro volunteers for combat, the greatest immediate need was in units like the 761st Tank and 333rd Field Artillery Battalions, whose losses, without replacements, threatened combat efficiency and, in the case of the 333rd, their existence. So, the units were commanded to establish a training program for replacements while on the move.

Note: Flash forward forty-eight years later to a 1992 interview with Lewis Weinstein, who served as chief of the liaison section of General Eisenhower's wartime staff, where he stated:

> We had Black volunteers—2,600 of them. They did nobly. Gen. Patton refused to accept any of the thirty-seven volunteer African American rifle platoons in his Third Army. In Bastogne, there were some Colored artillery (333rd Field Artillery Battalion); the quartermaster men provided themselves well with rifles and fought very well. They won medals. Purple Hearts, Silver Stars, Bronze Stars. They were brave. A number of them died. They were killed in action. Nobody could have been braver than those volunteers. If it were not for those soldiers, heaven knows what would have happened with the Bulge. Finally, after the Bulge was blunted, these soldiers—who had done their job brilliantly, side by side with Whites—went back to their segregated units, and these brave, heroic infantrymen, became cooks and dishwashers and truck drivers as privates all over again.[76]

CHAPTER EIGHT

Steel Coffins

ON NEW YEAR'S EVE, while the Western world welcomed 1945, surely wishing for war's end, the sky was bright with gunfire at Huem, Holland, as the Americans fought and demolished three machine gun nests and a 75-mm assault gun. Later in January, a 761st company, in support of the 194th Glider Infantry Regiment, entered Luxembourg against a German rearguard (someone who protects a unit from attack from behind) whose mission was to delay the Allies. The US claimed thirty enemy soldiers as the battalion knocked out an antitank gun and a machine gun nest.

The 87th Infantry Division relieved the 17th Airborne Division two days later, which went into strategic reserve—but there was no rest for the Panthers. On January 27, the brave Black battalion fought a battle at Kriegberg and Gruflange, Germany, under their new division. Together, the men eliminated small pockets of resistance while under small-arms fire. The Battle of the Bulge was over by January 28, 1945, the German incursion having failed. United States Civil War Gen. William Tecumseh Sherman is often credited with saying, "War is Hell,"[77] which is especially true when fought on three simultaneous fronts, just as the 761st Tank Battalion did in the European Theater during World War II. It was not enough to simply *fight* the Germans—like other US African American Army units, at that time and place, these men not only fought for their lives and America's freedom, but battled harsh, unforgiving weather and (just as unforgiving) racial discrimination, all at once. As part of the then segregated Army, the 761st was one of the few Negro combat units to deploy overseas and the *very first* tank battalion, the theory being that Blacks were too frightened to face and fight the enemy and were incapable of mastering the technicalities of mechanized equipment like the tank.[78] The 761st pushed to prove the Army's theories wrong time and again.

Beginning in October 1944, when the unit first entered combat, the weather was quickly becoming inclement and continuously worsened over the next weeks and months, well into late spring of 1945; you could say the 761st fought against "cold steel" in every way. As the environment worsened with extreme cold, it had a doubling effect, with temperatures inside the steel tanks even colder than the exterior.

> With piping-hot guns in frozen hands, the soldiers continued to fight from within freezing steel machines. When the opportunity arose, the frigid men sought comfort in houses, barns, and partially destroyed structures like churches and schools, cellars of deserted houses, or on the still-warm engines of their battle tanks.

Unimaginably, they continued. Engaged in a firefight, men on both sides witnessed extreme numbers of severely wounded and dead soldiers; nine of these fatalities were American tank crew members killed in a single day, during one battle. German ingenuity of establishing roadblocks played a key role in many of its successful skirmishes, placing herds of animals on roads, felling surrounding trees, and digging tank ditches.

The American soldiers—some still inside their tanks and others with feet on the ground (in cases where tanks were abandoned because of interoperability, damage, or destruction)—kept complete courage under fire. The 761st pulled fellow men from burning tanks, carrying the wounded and seeking cover while still engaging the enemy with small arms (possibly a short-stock .45-caliber grease gun strapped to their chests), sacrificing themselves in order to secure life-saving medical treatment for the fallen, each action worthy of honorable decoration. On January 28 and 29, the US soldiers moved toward Saint Vith, Belgium, and relieved elements of the 7th Armored Division and XVIII Corps. By the end of January, the battalion suffered five killed in action, fourteen wounded, and twenty-two nonbattle injuries, such as frostbite and maintenance accidents. Seventeen tanks were lost to enemy fire and sixteen required repairing.[79]

BURYING THE TRUTH

The War Department was particularly interested in how well the "experiment" with Negro armored troops was playing out. It sent observers into battle areas to question White officers about their opinions and observations of the Black men, who were initially deemed unfit to serve their country in combat. Lt. Col. Hunt was questioned about his brief command time with the 761st, a period during which the battalion saw continuous combat, liberated multiple towns and villages, and killed or routed several hundred German soldiers. They had suffered dozens of losses with men killed in action or wounded. During it all, men like Staff Sergeant Reuben Rivers demonstrated valor, and Black company commanders exhibited superb leadership under fire. Yet, Hunt's responses to the observation board had nothing positive to say about the battalion, his words mirroring comments from the Army's 1925 survey of Black soldiers. As if he were reading from the survey itself, he reported:

> "The Negro officers showed poor initiative, poor responsibility, and instances of fear and cowardice. Companies led by White officers showed more control while under fire than those led by Black officers and only about 15 percent of the soldiers measured up well."[80]

Hunt continued, his lies sharper: "No Negro captains were of field-grade (major) material and one officer had deserted . . ." (There was no mention of the officer being White, leaving the impression that a Black officer had abandoned his men in a time of need.) The Negro soldiers, he reported, did a poor job maintaining equipment, even though their vehicle operational rate was the same as other combat tank battalions.[81] Hunt poorly rated the overall performance of the battalion, though senior White officers, who were attached to the Black units in various operations, gave the men glowing remarks, as did Whites who had temporarily served beside them. Hunt, not knowing this, published more derogatory opinions of the Negro battalion.[82] He even failed to mention three soldiers under his command who had received battlefield promotions to lieutenant.

His tenure in the battalion only lasted a few weeks, but he observed his men successfully fighting in Belgium, Luxembourg, and France. His career, no doubt, was on the line, based on his reports to the War Department—and he was not about to render a positive review of a Negro battalion. Lt. Col. Hunt also refused to endorse the Medal of Honor recommendation for Reuben Rivers, citing that the 761st had the letter N (for Negro) following their numerical designation, and no soldier from a Negro unit would be recommended for such a significant award. Hunt wasn't alone in his erroneous assessment of Colored soldiers. Many of the top brass in the military, assuming Black inferiority, still felt Negroes were not fit for combat duty. The stereotype of the untrustworthy, indolent, thieving Negro who ran at the first shot fired persisted. Yet Patton's Panthers of the 761st remained determined to prove they were warriors equal, if not superior, to their White comrades in arms.[83]

THE REALITY OF IT ALL

Though outnumbered most times, the 761st smartly and accurately placed its few, precious rounds of tank and machine gun fire wherever the enemy hid; this could have been in forests, behind concrete bunkers, or camouflaged beside or inside buildings. In most cases, their tanks were no match against the German's superior 88-mm main gun cannon, compared to the smaller Sherman or Stuart tank. Why does the lethality (mm) of a tank matter? Because a first-round hit on an enemy tank is crucial to disable and destroy it. Since Germany's main battle tanks carried a larger main gun, it was vital that the 761st, and all other American tanks, executed a first-round hit with the intent to disarm or demolish the opposing enemy. Secondarily, the intent was to destroy the treads and road wheels; these two, successful hits would render the German Panzer tank inoperable, unable to move, shoot, or even communicate.

The next day, on January 30, the unit initiated its attack on Huem. A single company remained in position, in the vicinity of Herresbach, awaiting engineers to complete bridging operations, while another company assaulted Schönberg from a different direction in a long-range firefight, necessary with poor trafficability and road conditions. The battalion traveled 140 miles to Hermès, Belgium, in early February and established a forward command post in nearby Jabeek, Holland, where they were assigned to the 95th Infantry Division. This is where the battalion ran an intensive, two-week training course for the soldiers they had gained from service units weeks earlier—the untrained Black soldiers who were stripped of their higher rankings. While in active combat, the unit trained its new soldiers, focusing on bow gunnery and cannon fire and less on the technical side.

Three months after sustaining his battle injury, on February 17, 1945, Lt. Col. Bates returned to the battalion and resumed command.[84] This was a morale boost for the men, who had successfully fought under his initial command. With his return, the unit received new orders to continue supporting the 103rd Infantry Division in attacking the Siegfried Line.[85] As the lead of Task Force Rhine and, along with air support, the 761st was off to pierce the vaunted barrier separating France and Germany. The Siegfried Line was constructed to deny Allied Forces an incursion into Germany. From the time of the D-Day landing months earlier, the Americans knew that in order to achieve victory over Hitler's Army, they must breach the Line. On paper, the plan was simple: British General Bernard Montgomery's 21st Army Group would attack in the north with Gen. Jacob Devers's 6th Army Group occupying the south. The 761st would become Gen. George Patton's 3rd Army contribution to the 12th Army Group, which would hit the Siegfried Line around Metz, spearheaded by Task Force Rhine.

Come March 1945, the newly formed Task Force (TF) Rhine intimidatingly boasted the 761st Tank Battalion, 2nd Battalion, 209th Infantry Regiment, a reconnaissance platoon from a tank-destroyer unit that served as the eyes and ears of TF, the 103rd Signal Company, and a detachment of engineers to blow tank and antipersonnel mines—a total of eighteen hundred men led by task force commander Lt. Col. Bates. These soldiers already knew their objective: breach the treacherous Line, advance to the Rhine River, and cross unnoticed into Germany. If successful, the men would be the first in history to accomplish the harrowing feat. Fighting would be fierce on all fronts, as the Germans remained heavily entrenched in every crevice in their promise to protect the Fatherland.

IN THE LINE OF FIRE

War arrived in the late afternoon, as the US moved closer to Reisdorf, Bavaria, having successfully penetrated German defenses and losing a tank to *panzerfaust* antitank weaponry in an hours-long battle. Finally, with help from friendly artillery, Reisdorf was liberated, and TF Rhine continued to fight in, and free, the towns of Nieder-Schlettenbach and Erlendbach, clearing formidable pillboxes and machine gun nests, wounding and killing enemy soldiers, and capturing sixty-four defenders who surrendered with minimal resistance. With all of its success, and as part of a measured operational tactic, Lt. Col. Bates split his force into two separate elements; one element was sent northeast, toward Birkenhard, and the other east to Bollenborn.

The northern element, supported by TF Rhine artillery, smashed into the city, dodging small arms and antitank fire, to discover the devastation and sad realities of war—dead enemy bodies, decimated animals, and pulverized structures. The Bollenborn element, down south, faced an even deadlier challenge in confronting concrete-reinforced dragon-teeth tank barriers (imagine hundreds of miniature concrete pyramids spaced out across the land). The obstacle was expertly neutralized by a 761st tank bulldozer that covered them in dirt, enabling US tanks to safely cross the barriers. Bates's southern force lost two tanks to open fire by a concealed enemy 75-mm antitank gun, both American crews managing to escape the ambush. With the triumphant taking of Reisdorf and Birkenhard, the TF Rhine consolidated and advanced to its final objective in Klingenmunster, where the enemy heavily resisted its attempt to clear the city—but to no avail. The 761st and supporting units secured the bloody battle, freed Klingenmunster, and cleared the barricaded passage to the Rhine River. The 14th Armor Division, following the spearhead, rolled through the treacherous Siegfried Line, followed by the 761st. After months of intense fighting, the Americans were now postured to cross the Rhine River and officially enter Germany.

During the third week of battle, in March 1945, from Reisdorf to Klingenmunster and surrounding Siegfried Line villages, the 761st

Tank Battalion captured more than four hundred enemy vehicles and more than eighty heavy weapons (mainly German artillery), corralled -plus horses used by enemy forces to transport logistics, like supplies, food, ammunition, tank-repair parts, and engineering equipment, and several thousand small arms: machineguns, rifles, and pistols.[86] The Americans inflicted more than 4,000 casualties on the German regime with every dead enemy soldier assigned to an element within one of fourteen divisions. At the hands of the 761st Tank Battalion, the Germans suffered a fifteen-mile stretch of death and destruction with dead soldiers plastered across fields and upon hills, littered throughout towns and villages, most having been killed by allied artillery. The body count was so enormous that it was impossible, at first glance, to estimate how many enemy lives had been lost that week.[87]

PATTON'S PANTHERS

When the battalion first arrived in Europe, they were disappointed to learn they would not be fighting as a cohesive unit. Over the course of weeks and months, the Army attached the unit, piecemeal, to other commands. This operational tactic had an unexpected positive outcome in the war, as their elements were dispersed all over the battlefield in almost every operation. Shocked by the tenacity and daring spirits of the Colored tank troops, many German soldiers surrendered their weapons, fearing annihilation by the *schwarze soldaten*, or African American tankers, which they had heard so much about; one German rumor boasted that Black soldiers slaughtered all prisoners.[88] This kind of thinking was handed down from World War I, when soldiers from the African country of Senegal, a former colony of France fighting for France, purportedly butchered their captive Germans.[89]

The Germans, who continually map-plotted enemy locations, could not have imagined how so many Panthers could be in so many places. One captured German officer asked, "How many Black Panzer Divisions are there?"[90] They weren't expecting elements of the 761st battalion to be broken up and attached out—it gave the Germans a distorted picture, causing them to believe the American Army had *several* Black armored divisions. This played havoc on their morale; German soldiers were seeing Black tank units all over the battlefield, in most engagements.

CHAPTER NINE

---★---

Damn Good Soldiers

WITH EACH BATTLE, the US Army's big-picture objective was always to breach the Siegfried Line and cross the Rhine River that separated France from Germany. More confident than ever, the 761st could almost taste the inevitable trek—blood, mud, sweat, and tears. But this mission required multiple forces; it was too big a job for the tank battalion alone. That was why the Army formed Task Force Rhine in the first place.

In the end, many Colored soldiers went on to receive accolades from commanding officers—a surprise to many, you can be sure. XII Corps commander, Maj. Gen. Eddy, published a positive review of the unit's performance, and in a message to the 761st commander from Major General Paul of the 26th, the soldiers were finally granted some of the respect and attention they deserved:

> "Your battalion has supported this division with great bravery and under the most adverse weather and terrain conditions. You have my sincere wish that success may continue to follow you in all your endeavors."[91]

Finally, following the now infamous Battle of the Bulge, the unit experienced its first moment in the public spotlight. Gen. Patton was quoted in *Stars and Stripes*, saying, "The Negro Battalion attached to my command fought bravely in the Battle of Bastogne," and that, "its soldiers were damn good soldiers."[92] Even so, nearing his accidental death in December 1945, there was no concrete evidence that Patton had actually changed his unjustifiable judgments of African Americans in combat.

ALL OVER THE MAP

During the entire month of March 1945, the battalion fired more than three hundred tons of ammunition and consumed fifty thousand gallons of V-80 gasoline, losing only five tanks in the process. One officer was KIA, and six enlisted soldiers were WIA.[93] At the completion of TF Rhine, Major General Anthony A. McAuliffe, now commanding the 103rd Cactus Infantry Division, sent a congratulatory note to the battalion: "The first stage of our operation has been brilliantly completed. You broke through the famous Siegfried defenses and then boldly exploited your success. You have taken more than 4,700 prisoners. You have fought gallantly and intelligently, and you have led the way. I congratulate you."[94]

The United States Army's 761st Tank Battalion was no longer the sideshow to the main event; the men, hailing from diverse backgrounds but from the same, segregated homeland, worked endlessly to become showstoppers in war. It was, indeed, an independent tank battalion. In just four months, from December 1944 to March 1945, the African American unit had been attached to seven divisions (and went the same amount of time without an official bath or shower). With many changes in senior headquarters, the battalion had garnered the moniker, "Bastard Battalion,"[95] its companies and platoons supporting numerous organizations, losing command and control of the 761st. It was truly a lone-wolf team of men.

Now, with the Allies closing in on Berlin from three directions, the German Army's days were numbered. Gen. Eisenhower's armies were approaching from France on the west and Austria on the south, with Russian armies from Czechoslovakia on the east. On April 14, 1945, the American tank battalion, accompanied by the 71st Infantry Division (or "The Red Circle," formed mid–WWII) attacked the town of Kulmbach, Bavaria. In a fierce fight, battalion elements obliterated one armored car, fifteen machine gun nests, and nineteen enemy vehicles, and killed more than 225 enemy soldiers, capturing two battalions of 200-plus defending men. Before the battle's end, the 761st found and freed two captured American officers and one enlisted man.

War was in full motion, and there was no stopping the still underrated, underrespected tank battalion. Later, in another Bavarian battle near Bayreuth, while supporting another infantry regiment, the battalion engaged enemy armor elements that were protecting the town entrance. It destroyed one Panzer tank, which forced the Germans to scuttle four of their own tanks to avoid capture by the Americans. The end game saw seventy-five enemy deaths and two hundred surrenders. The captured soldiers were passed to the rear area into POW holding companies, where wounded enemy soldiers were taken to aid stations solely staffed by African American nurses, whose primary overseas mission was to treat the enemy. Still, Black nurses were not permitted to treat wounded White American soldiers.[96]

Bayreuth was now surrounded on three sides by the 11th Armored Division, 65th Infantry Division, and 71st Infantry Division, with the 761st Tank Battalion at the gate. Firing in unison, they pummeled German defenses with devastating results. After two days of shelling, the Germans could no longer withstand the barrage, and their commander surrendered to the 14th Infantry Regiment. On April 16, the US soldiers were a spearhead for yet another task force—this time, TF Weidenmark. With a mission to push to the Czechoslovakian border, they encountered minimal enemy opposition and were, to their surprise, greeted by white flags waving from the windows of homes, the freed Russian prisoners too emaciated to receive the Americans, as most were near death.

Days later, two US tank platoons supported elements of the 66th Infantry Regiment in assaulting Neuhaus and Velden, the site of Luftwaffe Chief Hermann Goring's Veldenstein castle, where he stored stolen, priceless artwork, artifacts, exquisite furniture, and other items looted from various countries. As the Americans approached, the enemy abandoned the castle and retreated to the Veldensteiner Forest for an unsuccessful, last-ditch stand, where they were either killed, wounded, or captured. The next clearing was the city of Amberg, where a battalion company, with pieces of the 14th Infantry, captured seventy-five enemy soldiers on April 22 without taking any casualties or losing a single piece of equipment. The next day, another battalion company element supporting another infantry unit cleared German soldiers out of nearby woods and placed them in captivity.

The Americans moved on to the city of Regensburg, Bavaria, where Gen. Patton planned to stage his forward command post. After the enemy rejected a surrender ultimatum, assault rained down on the city, at the far side of the Danube River. The battalion now with all its companies consolidated, pounded the city with every bit of its firepower, all of this supported by 155-mm Long Toms and eight-inch cannons that saturated enemy fortifications. Following the barrage, infantry units crossed the Danube on assault boats and stormed the city in a house-to-house, street-to-street battle. Regensburg fell on April 26, 1945, and thanks in part to his 761st men, Gen. Patton had his forward command post.

The unit rolled right into its next mission with no rest, leading the 71st Infantry Division, which helped liberated thousands from concentration subcamps in WWII with support from the 761st. In the final days of April, the African American tank battalion freed satellite POW camps at Buchenwald and Dachau, which had held and exterminated displaced Jews, gypsies, homosexuals, Jehovah's Witnesses, unionists, communists, and anyone who failed to fit the "ideal Aryan mold."[97] During WWII, populations in these facilities fluctuated between twenty-two thousand and thirty thousand[98]— three times their intended capacity, the Nazis having zero regard for anyone who wasn't on their side.

Before the war, Germany was home to colonies of Africans who had arrived in the Fatherland as students, tradesmen, entertainers, and former soldiers. Though frowned upon by tradition, German African unions formed as local women married foreign, Black men and had children, referred to as "Rhineland Bastards" and "mulattoes," who were first to be singled out for extermination.[99] Come 1945, Dachau's population had increased to 67,665 prisoners, including many Black Africans who were crammed into trucks and trains and transported to the camp. By the end of the war, the Nazis would exterminate more than six million people. Equally disheartening, especially coming from an American, Gen. George S. Patton, still celebrated for having led thousands of men (including the Negro tank battalion) in the war against Nazi Germany—and winning it—harshly criticized displaced people, as later discovered in his personal diary:

> *Everyone believes that the displaced person is a human being, which he is not, and that applies particularly to the Jews, who are lower than animals. Either the displaced persons never had a sense of decency or else they lost it during their period of internment by the Germans. My personal opinion is that no people could have sunk to the level of degradation these have reached in the short space of four years.[100]*

READ ALL ABOUT IT!

In a 1991 published letter to the editor of the *New York Times*,[101] Ben Bender, a Polish Jew, who was seventeen at the time of the war, refuted the legend that he and his inmates were freed by the Russian Red Army. He vividly recalled their liberation by the Black tankers of the 761st. Bender wrote:

> *The tankers from the 761st broke through the Buchenwald*

gates and, with their accompanying infantrymen, quickly ended the resistance from the SS guards. Black soldiers from the Third Army, tall and strong, crying like babies, carrying the emaciated bodies of the liberated prisoners. I was seventeen, and my life was almost extinguished. Forever, it was an instant awakening of life after a long darkness . . . . I was seeing black soldiers for the first time in my life, crying like babies, carrying the dead and the starved and trying to help everybody. That's the way it was.[102]

Johnny Stevens, a surviving member of the 761st, recalled in a 2003–2004 interview:

We were only there a little while, because, as tankers, we didn't stay anywhere long; we'd keep moving. We shot up the place and chased the guards out of there. It was a sight I never want to see again. I will tell you that. I jumped out of the tank, and there were people all over the place . . . they could hardly walk, and they're coming at you with their hands held halfway out, their eyes sunk in their heads; they were skin and bones, the women looking like something out of a horror movie . . . it was a horrible sight.[103]

Elie Wiesel, Nobel Laureate in Peace, stated this in his autobiography:

The most moving moment of my life was the day the Americans arrived. It was on the morning of April 11 [1945]. I will always remember with love a big Black soldier. He was crying like a child—tears of all the pain in the world and all the rage. Everyone who was there that day will forever feel a sentiment of gratitude to the American soldiers who liberated us.[104]

AMERICA! AMERICA!

The war was all but over—orders for the 761st Tank Battalion on May 6 read: "You will advance to the Enns River, and you will wait there for the Russians."[105] But, upon arriving late one afternoon, there were no Russians in sight, so the men established security and used the idle time to perform necessary maintenance on their tanks and garner some much-needed rest.

Note: Postbattle maintenance required "punching the tube," a procedure whereby a long pole was inserted into the end of the main gun barrel, with asbestos or a cloth ball at the end, and pulled back and forth to remove any black powder residue, which would build during each firefight. These required procedures came after every one-hundred hours of operation to protect from internal explosions within the gun barrel. Soldiers also had to remove small rocks from inside tank treads, check and tighten end-connectors, and clean and service machine guns. Other important requirements included lubrication, replenishing fuel and ammunition, and checking tracktension.

After waiting at the Enns River (famous today for whitewater rafting) in Steyer, Austria, to meet the Russians, who never showed their faces, the battalion assumed there had been a misinterpretation of orders—until Russian tanks rolled up on the far side of the river the next day, May 6. Not knowing what to expect, the US Army remained guarded until an intimidating, heavyset Russian soldier dismounted from the lead tank and strode across the bridge, straight for them. Only upon closer proximity did the 761st commander realize the Russian commander was a woman (the Russian Army having deployed tank units staffed by women, unknown to the Americans). This was the first time the unit had ever met a woman soldier, who turned out to be part of the Ukrainian Front of the Soviet Red Army.

> The Russian commander ran to greet the battalion, exclaiming, "America! America! America!"[106]

ESPRIT DE CORPS

After more than two thousand miles of combat, the US Army credited the 761st with four campaigns: Ardennes-Alsace, Northern France, Rhineland, and Central Europe.[107] The World War, and every tireless battle fought by the 761st, had come to an end, unlike their overseas deployment—at least for several more months. Warfighting ceased on May 6, 1945, and brought closure to what the American soldiers had so diligently worked and fought for over the past three years. They had lost men they loved on the way to achieving what most would still deem impossible. These men had realized their dreams. But there was no celebration—for what could they celebrate, other than acknowledging their brave win against almost-certain death, surely thankful they had lived through what many had died doing.

Victory in Europe Day (VE Day) arrived at 0241 hours on May 7, 1945. Gen. Alfred Jodl and Adm. Hans von Friedburg signed the official surrender document in Reims, France: "We, the undersigned, acting by the authority of the German High Command, hereby surrender unconditionally to the Supreme Commander, Allied Expeditionary Forces and simultaneously to the Soviet High Command all forces on land, sea, and in the air, who are, at this date, under German control."[108]

On May 9, Lt. Col. Bates sent a letter of commendation to the officers and enlisted men of his brave tank battalion:

> *It is with great pride that I review the accomplishments of the 761st Tank Battalion. You have more than lived up to the many indications of battle success recalled in your training in the United States and by the fine commendations received from the many officers who inspected you there. Your conduct in England, as you drew your equipment and made final preparations for the fighting ahead, was a model of the American soldier . . .*

.Equipment shortages and the great variety of equipment you received have called upon you to continually adapt yourselves and modify your concepts of the ability, limitations, and characteristics of weapons and vehicles . . .

Fighting in France, Belgium, Luxembourg, Holland, Germany, and Austria, with the Third, Seventh, and Ninth Armies, with the 17th Airborne, 26th, 71st, 79th, 87th, 95th, and 103rd Infantry Divisions, has required your adjusting yourselves to the requirement of a great number of different units . . . . The courage you have shown in your tanks has been magnificently matched by the truck drivers as they brought up supplies. The maintenance men have worked tirelessly to keep the armor going. They have gone without food and sleep and used every means possible to obtain spare parts . . . . The mess personnel, radio repairmen, clerks . . . all have performed their work in a superior manner.

At times, all have been called upon to lay down their regular work and use their guns . . . . The medical personnel followed fearlessly and always cared for us, regardless of enemy fire. You have met every type of equipment in the German Army, planes, V-Bombs, bazookas, panzerfausts, 88s, 75s, artillery, self-propelled guns, tanks, [and] mines. But all are behind you, useless, the German soldier defeated, his politician silent, and you are victorious! I salute you and look to your continued superior work in any assignment received, either as individuals or as a battalion.[109]

Note: Weeks earlier, Bates had a conversation with a professor from the University of Bonn in North Rhine-Westphalia, Germany. The scholar had a strong opinion of the Russians, believing that after the war they would occupy Germany, and he hoped for Allied control. The professor predicted a Russian occupation would destroy what remained of his nation and felt Americans should thank the Germans for preventing Russia from attacking our land. He also predicted the Germans and Americans would fight Russia, together, in the future.[110]

On May 9, 1945, the Army began to dismantle what had taken the 761st years to build, despite endless enemy fire, below-zero temperatures, and overwhelming racial inequality and segregation—a physically and mentally strong tank battalion staffed by African American soldiers. Most of the men arrived home by 1946 only to learn their nation had not changed as a result of their heroic service. America had forgotten them, and most Americans were unaware of their service on the battlefields of Europe. America had not changed, to their dismay, as Jim Crow was still alive and well, his shadow having accompanied them across the Atlantic Ocean to England and from the English Channel to Europe, and sailed home with them, greeting the brave as they debarked.

At the same time, Major Gen. Willard G. Wyman, commanding general of the 71st Infantry Division, sent a letter of commendation to the commanding officer of the 761st Tank Battalion, which acknowledged they had lived up to their motto, *Come out fighting:*

> *1. Now that the great war in Europe has been reached, it is appropriate that recognition be given to the superior manner in which you and members of your battalion have performed during the period of 29 March 1945 to 15 May 1945, the time you were closely affiliated with the 71st Infantry Division.*
>
> *2. The combat missions which were assigned to your battalion*

> *were performed magnificently, which unquestionably made possible the rapid advance of the entire division, and you share generously in the honors which are ours through the phenomenal progress which was made across Germany and Austria. The splendid way in which you and members of your command responded to the tasks assigned to you is worthy of high praise.*
>
> *3. The excellent combat record of your unit as veterans has been further sustained while operating closely with this command. Please, extend to all members of your battalion my congratulations and my sincerest thanks for a job well done."*[111]

The Distinguished Unit Citation (DUC) award was merited, the petition stating: "Because this unit has distinguished itself by extraordinary heroism in battle, and has exhibited great gallantry, determination, and esprit de corps in operation against the enemy, overcoming such hazardous conditions as adverse weather, mountainous terrain, and heavily fortified positions."[112]

Though Gen. Wyman could, and did, approve awards for individual honors, his powers could never authorize a Presidential Citation, the responsibility belonging to the providence of the commander of the US Forces in the European Theater. The Distinguish Unit Citation (DUC) included copies of every tribute awarded to the battalion by various US commands, including White Generals Patton, Eddy, Paul, McAuliffe, and Wyman. Upon receiving the DUC request, Gen. Eisenhower's office asked Patton's Third Army headquarters to review it. Headquarters replied:

> *After a careful study of the action of the 761st Tank Battalion ... it is considered that the action, while commendable, was not sufficiently outstanding to meet the requirements for a unit citation.*

Signed, For the General (George S. Patton) by Lt. Col. R.W. Hartman, Assistant Adjutant General.[113]

Patton, through his subordinate, Lt. Col. R.W. Hartman, had rejected his own request for a DUC, the theory being that history needed to reflect that neither Patton *nor* Eisenhower would affix their signatures to documents denying DUCs to the Black 761st Battalion—no matter the glorious victories the team had claimed for the United States. And, to this day, Gen. George S. Patton, Jr., is hailed as one of America's greatest leaders of World War II.

CHAPTER TEN

---★---

The War at Home

AFTER MONTHS of occupation duties near Teisendorf, Germany, in December 1945, the men of the 761st tank Battalion began the individual process of returning home to the US. The Army officially deactivated the battalion.

Black service members from all units were ill-treated upon homecoming, facing immediate scrutiny simply for returning to the US in their Army uniforms; some Whites in the South felt Black soldiers were unrightfully "uppity" for displaying their hard-earned combat ribbons. Negro soldiers from below the Mason-Dixon Line were, sadly and surprisingly, still second-class citizens (more like three-fifths of a human) with no rights to seats on buses or sips from drinking fountains—let alone the opportunity to vote. City sidewalks still gave priority to Whites, and lunch counters still came with bias. There would be no Black men serving on juries in most Southern states, and equal education remained a foreign concept; even with the GI Bill, White, four-year colleges and universities, public and private, were closed to Negroes in the South. Most government jobs went to Whites returning from war, and VA home loans were not honored for Blacks because of housing restrictions and *redlining*— White realtors refusing to finance Blacks to purchase houses in White neighborhoods.

Knowing what was going on at home, many US soldiers chose to reenlist, seeking a better life in the military than what home had to offer. Some accepted discharge and stayed in Europe, where racial segregation wasn't the norm.[114] The battalion had been singled out as one of the best in the European Theater but never received any official recognition, ostensibly because of race. Their war record exceeded similar battalions, in most cases, and some men received the Presidential Unit Citation (not from Patton, of course) and had statistics to prove it.

SUCCESS IN NUMBERS

The leaders of the 1925 Army War College Study must have felt baffled. Wronged. Shocked. These White minds had sworn that Black soldiers could not, and *would not,* fight for their country; Black men were afraid, even of the dark, and would never have the courage to defeat darkness.[115] But history says otherwise—in statistics and numbers. The African American 761st Tank Battalion spent 183 days in continuous combat, covering 2,197 miles. The men liberated thirty major towns and several satellite concentration camps aiding the 100th Infantry Regiment of Japanese American soldiers. The team freed 7 Siegfried towns, 4 airfields, and 3 ammunition supply dumps and destroyed 131 pillboxes, hundreds of machine gun emplacements, 34 tanks, 461 wheeled vehicles, 87 antitank guns, and 27 big guns. In defense of comrade and country, together, the battalion inflicted 129,640 casualties and captured more than 15,000 enemy soldiers— all results unmatched by any other similar unit.[116] Numbers don't lie; in fact, here, they prove wrong everything the United States Army had deemed true about Coloreds, before even giving them a chance.

Because war is hell for everyone involved, the 761st Tank Battalion lost seventy-one tanks to antitank fire, enemy mines, Panzerfausts, enemy artillery, and Panzers. They saw thirty-four men killed in action, 304 combat casualties (died later from wounds, suicide, fratricide, or other nonbattle reasons), and 201 noncombat casualties, who were killed by disease, illness, or environmental factors. These numbers accounted for an overall casualty rate of nearly 50 percent—

all while facing German divisions in four major Allied campaigns, attached to three separate American armies and seven divisions.[117] Eight 761st soldiers received battlefield commissions by the end of the war, and eleven were awarded the Silver Star, by order, the highest award possible for a Black soldier. Altogether, the men brought in sixty-nine Bronze Star medals, 296 Purple Hearts (eight with clusters signifying more than one award), the Presidential Unit Citation, and, fifty years later, a Medal of Honor.[118]

With urgency from members of Congress, in 1977 the secretary of the Army reopened the case. Empirical reviews determined that: "There were clear indications that racial discrimination . . . had been a factor in the disapproval, and the climate created by the Army commands could only have made it difficult to provide proper recognition for a Negro unit during the period 1944–1947."[119]

For DUCs, vital evidence was reexamined, along with information gathered, during several months of intense research, from the National Archives, the Library of Congress, the Office of the Chief of Military History, and the Eisenhower Library. Finally, the 761st Tank Battalion was presented the Presidential Unit Citation:

> The 761st Tank Battalion distinguished itself by extraordinary gallantry, courage and high esprit de corps displayed in the accomplishment of unusually difficult and hazardous operations in the European Theater of Operations from 31 October 1944 to 6 May 1945. Throughout this period of combat, the courageous and professional actions of the "Black Panther" Battalion, coupled with their indomitable fighting spirit and devotion to duty, reflect great credit on the 761st Tank Battalion and the United States Army and this Nation.[120]

President Jimmy Carter signed the award on January 24, 1978. His secretary of the Army, Clifford Alexander, invited survivors of the unit to Fort Myers, Virginia, on April 20 for an award presentation.

That afternoon, elite troops in uniforms of past wars presented their review while fighter planes roared overhead, accompanied by the United States Army band. Finally, its own country had recognized this brave battalion was anything but a sideshow in war.

On November 10, 2005—sixty years after the end of WWII—Fort Hood, Texas, became home to a historically significant monument dedicated to the 761st Battalion. The memorial was unveiled that day at a ceremony attended by surviving battalion veterans—a permanent tribute to the Black men who had gallantly served the United States against all odds. The monument showed four black granite tablets surrounding a life-size, marble sculpture of a 761st Tank Battalion fighter kneeled atop a granite pedestal, a tank at his front and a panther at his back.[121] In equal support, Killeen, Texas, named one of its main city streets *761st Tank Battalion Boulevard*.[122]

Armor corps tanks never fight alone. In most operations, tank teams receive support from indirect fire from the field artillery. As the 761st Tank Battalion maneuvered country to country, fighting as the spearhead of General Patton's Third Army, the all-Black 333rd Field Artillery Battalion, Long Tom guns in hand, had the backs of the 761st—both units making a name for themselves, despite everything—and everyone—in the way.

An African American soldier stands guard over a group of Nazi prisoners. Photo courtesy of Alamy.

The 761st Tank Battalion, photographed in England before shipping over to mainland Europe during WWII. Photo courtesy of National Archives and Records Administration.

Armor recovery vehicle assisting disabled tank. Photo courtesy of National Archives and Records Administration.

(Left to right) Capt. Ivan Harrison, Capt. Irvin McHenry, and 2nd Lt. James Lightfoot of the 761st Tank Battalion. Photo courtesy US Army.

Crews of 761st light tanks stand by awaiting call to clean out scattered Nazi machine gun nests in Coburg, Germany. Photo courtesy of National Archives and Records Administration.

Private Eugene Hamilton of Huntington, Long Island, New York, guards 761st Battalion tanks. Photo courtesy of National Archives and Records Administration.

61st tank crossing Bailey Bridge in Vic-Sur-Seille, France, moving to a forward position in the combat zone. Photo courtesy of National Archives and Records administration.

An M1 155-mm artillery piece in action, 1945. Courtesy of National Archives and Records Administration.

PART THREE

The King of Battle
333rd Field Artillery Battalion

369th African American Infantry, the Harlem Hellfighters, wearing French uniforms in the trenches during WWI. Photo courtesy of Alamy.

As fighting troops,
the Negro must be rated
as second-class material,
this primarily due
to his inferior intelligence
and lack of mental
and moral qualities.

—World War I commander,
1st Infantry Regiment, 93rd Division[1]

INTRODUCTION

Not only did General Patton believe, in 1944, that Blacks were not intelligent enough to fight in tanks, but thirty years later, many White officers still believed we weren't capable of operating field-artillery cannons, perpetuating the idea that even simple computations were too technical for dark-skinned soldiers.

Going through branching (choosing a preferred Army career field), along with 275 classmates, upon graduating from Officer Candidate School (OCS), I submitted three branches for consideration—field artillery, armor, and infantry, in that order. Policy dictates assignments depending on the Army's needs, but usually cadets are assigned first or second choice. But I wasn't allotted the option and was assigned to the Military Police Corps. One could argue it was because of my civilian law-enforcement background, but that was before an officer, who was part of the three-person branching panel composed of White officers, exclaimed something (to the extent of), "Field artillery requires experience with mathematical equations, which this cadet probably lacks." Had he reviewed my academic background before assuming my potential, he would've known I had earned a bachelor's degree with a major in criminalistics, a field that requires advanced math skills.

And had he not studied his history? African Americans—many with zero college experience and often little primary education—had been assigned to, and expertly crewed, cannons in the US Army since the Civil War. Blacks also commanded artillery units in World War I, World War II, the Korean War, and shortly after, Black officers would command artillery units in Vietnam. These men paved the path for my military career and were not simply capable but highly skilled, physically and mentally strong, and displayed more courage in a few moments than many of us do in an entire lifetime.

★ ★ ★

World War II was the first war in which, by informal gentlemen's agreement or binding treaty, the United States and its warring factions agreed to retract the routine standard of barbarically punishing foreign enemies. Even then, nations clashed on politics, governance, and borders, but would come together over the idea that human lives, on all sides of the equation, were valuable—the Divine creation above all others.

After the widespread mistreatment of prisoners, on all sides, during World War I, which ended in 1918, measures were instilled to ensure that during future international conflicts, captives of war would be protected from inhumane abuse by captors, something for which all warring nations were guilty. From this, the Geneva Convention was born.

Note: Drafted in 1929 in Geneva, Switzerland, the document specifically identified the "dos and don'ts" of the treatment of prisoners of war. Every warring nation in the world, except for one—the Soviet Union—cosigned the new agreement, and by 1931 every land had ratified the treaty. The rules clearly communicated that captives were never to be subjected to murder, physical abuse, or lack of shelter or food. Reports were to be submitted to the International Red Cross (and Red Crescent) regarding POW labor, wearing of uniforms, and numerous other procedures and rules that were designed to prohibit physical, mental, and medical abuses of the captives.

World War II, initiated in 1939 for European countries invaded by Germany that year, and joined by the United Kingdom in 1940 and the United States one year later, became the first international conflict under the new Geneva Convention.[2]

But the logic wasn't infallible, or global, apparently, as World War II witnessed some of the most unforgettable atrocities in the way of brutality and murder toward enemy soldiers. Part Three of this book series speaks to events, some tragic, involving the men assigned to America's 333rd Field Artillery Battalion, an all-Black unit of top-caliber soldiers fighting in Europe during the war. Upon activation, the 333rd Battalion was framed as most African American units in the US segregated Army—as space-fillers with no expectation of ever seeing the war. These men were the sideshow within an organization that believed the big top was destined for Whites alone. The 333rd Field Artillery Battalion would go beyond to prove otherwise.

> The violence and brutality Blacks faced from German soldiers in **WWII** wasn't the only Geneva violation committed, but it was the only case covered up by our own government. Upon discovering eleven massacred American bodies during the Battle of the Bulge, a confidential investigation was conducted, but its findings would remain top secret to appease German Americans in the United States, many of which held allegiance to the Fatherland and their ancestors. The greatest tragedy surrounding the 333rd massacre, outside of the event itself, was the fact that US soldiers were murdered, ditched, forgotten, and lost to time. Though their bodies were eventually found, the American media (within the military) concealed the soldiers' suffering at the behest of military leadership at the highest levels, serving as coconspirators. Yet, at the same time, another military massacre was making headlines worldwide: "Nazis Massacre Yanks"[4]—the massacre of more than three hundred White American soldiers near the town of Malmedy, Belgium, in an engagement that later became known as the Battle of the Bulge.[3]

CHAPTER ONE

Black Blood

WITH THE DECLARATION of World War II, in a segregated America, Black men streamed to draft boards and induction centers in a declaration of their own—to serve their country. Like any soldier, the Army could reject Colored soldiers for routine disqualifiers, including poor eyesight and flat feet, but also, because of blatant ignorance and racism unexperienced by Caucasians, the military worked to keep its ranks White. There was no logical reason to reject African Americans since they would only serve in support units, as the Army had deactivated Colored combat units following the end of World War I.

Not all African Americans supported the war; opposing voices were just as loud as those begging for US intervention. African Americans like George Schuyler, a noted columnist for the *Pittsburgh Courier*, wondered in an editorial piece:

> "Why should Negroes fight for democracy abroad when they are refused democracy in every American activity, except tax-paying?"[4]

African American writer C. L. R. James sympathized, retorting: "Why should I shed my blood for Roosevelt's America . . . for the whole Jim Crow, Negro-hating South, for the low-paid, dirty jobs for which Negroes have to fight, for the few dollars of relief and insults, discrimination, police brutality, and perpetual poverty to which Negroes are condemned even in the more liberal North?"

However, renowned Black leaders urged their communities to

join the world-war effort against Hitler's Germany, like labor leader Phillip Randolph, who argued in an article, "The Negro Has a Great Stake in This War," that "Japan has fired upon the United States, our country. We, all of us, Black and White, Jew, Gentile, Protestant, and Catholic, are at war, not only with Japan but with Hitler and the Axis powers. What shall the Negro do? There is only one answer. He must fight."[5]

James T. Taylor, dean of men at North Carolina College for Negroes (1926–1943), addressed a letter to the *New York Times*, voicing that Negroes *wanted* to win this war; Blacks were willing to work and were ready to fight for it. Taylor couldn't support silently standing on the sidelines while the enemy crucified democracy in the name of ignorance, prejudice, and self-servitude.[6] Echoing Taylor, in a telegram to President Roosevelt, was Edgar G. Brown, director of the National Negro Council and president of the United Government Employees. His telegram said, "Twelve-million American Negro citizens renewed, today, their pledge of one-hundred-percent loyalty to their country and our Commander in Chief, against Japan and all invaders. Negro youth await the call to serve in the Army and Navy, the Marines, the Coast Guard, and the Air Corps and National Defense."[7]

At the onset of World War II, summoned for land and sky, there were five Black officers in the US Army and about four-thousand enlisted soldiers.[8] Three officers were Army chaplains, having been ordained as ministers of the gospel before entering the service. The other two were father and son, Benjamin O. Davis, senior and junior, an instructor for the Reserve Officers Training Corps (ROTC) and a horse cavalry officer, respectively. One day, Davis senior would become the first Black general officer in the US Army, and his son would command the Tuskegee Airman, the famous Negro flying unit.[9]

Note: It's important to remember that this time in our nation's history shows Black soldiers primarily working labor and service jobs within the military, excluding a few remaining horse cavalry units—Buffalo Soldiers—constituted in 1866 and ranking for nearly eighty years, until the final horse cavalry unit was deactivated in 1944.

The Army's few labor and service units never officially trained for combat since our leaders were confident it was a waste of time and resources to employ Black soldiers on the battlefield. From an officer's perspective, these young men were capable only enough for careers in laundry and sanitation, water purification, chemical decontamination, maintenance, and graves registration, to name a few. Even African Americans in engineering units carried scarlet letters, forcibly identifying as "C" for Colored (and symbolic of engineers, who were assigned zero engineering missions and used as warehouse workers and longshoremen) or "N" for Negro later, when the Army formed tank units.[10]

Before the war against Hitler, Colored civilian men served as table waiters in officer messes, and when eventually drafted in large numbers, the Army considered creating kitchen police (KP) units staffed by Black soldiers. Their mission would be to continue serving White officers and carry out janitorial duties,[11] much as the Black women soldiers had done in the Women's Army Auxiliary Corps (WAAC), a precursor to the Women's Army Corps (WAC).[12] Eventually the idea of a Colored KP unit was discarded, fearing backlash from the Black press, but the Army's mindset was there. Still doting on the Army War College Study and Report released fifteen years earlier on the relevance of Negro soldiers in future wars,[13] Army leaders were determined to expand White units to meet any potential threat; this meant (to them, at least), that African Americans in noncombat roles would be relegated to provide even more supplies and services to support the growing number of White soldiers.

THEN, IT HIT

Following the Japanese surprise attack at Pearl Harbor in December 1941, Black leaders pushed for full participation of Colored soldiers in what was expected to be a second world war, just as they had done at the beginning of WWI. This was critical since the country had finally begun to recover from the mass effect of the Great Depression, which compounded for African Americans due to discrimination in employment and downsizing of Colored military units post–WWI. After having fought a war on foreign soil for the first time in World War I, Black leaders believed African American soldiers returning home had made their case for equality in America. Upon their return from World War II, however, it became abundantly clear that the social climate of de facto separatism and legalized discrimination in some parts of the country were still on full display.

Booming voices from leaders of Black organizations, like the National Association for the Advancement of Colored People (NAACP), the Negro press of the day (like the Pittsburgh Currier), and influential Black figures such as Mary McLeod-Bethune, a social activist and friend of First Lady Eleanor Roosevelt, pushed for African Americans to have the right to join the fight for their country. Loudly and boldly, she demanded social change—so much that it prompted FBI Director, J. Edgar Hoover to conclude:

"Mrs. Roosevelt must have Black blood!"[14]

With that, the First Lady became the most prominent White ally for social change within the military. Black and White voices alike were heeded, and the Army began building battalions of Negro men, though still, it had no intention of ever deploying them into battle.

The military expansion gave birth to the all-Black 92nd Infantry Division and several separate African American field artillery battalions, like the 333rd and 969th. These "new" arms of service had actually existed in federal Army and state militias for nearly one hundred years, deactivated after honorably and successfully serving in the Civil War and WWI.[15] Though never intended for combat, the 92nd Infantry Division battled in Italy as part of four-star General

Mark Clark's 15th Army Group; a unit of African American soldiers led mostly by White officers, as it was with the 761st Tank Battalion.[16] This trend of Whites managing Blacks bled into the 333rd Field Artillery Battalion with an all-White chain of command: Lt. Col. Harmon Kelsey, alongside executive officer (second in command) Capt. William McLeod. Given the divisive climate, Kelsey, like most of the military, had minimal confidence in Blacks, regardless of the shocking optimism held by McLeod, a confidence he had gained through positive past interactions with African Americans.[17] Kelsey resented his assignment to Negro soldiers, but to prove his own mettle and merit, he would "whip these boys" into shape to increase his stature, in hopes he would gain command over a White unit.

Even then, knowing field artillery was on the technical side of things, Kelsey's conceit had him convinced his "green, Colored boys, from the fields and streets"[18] would never satisfy Army requirements without *his* leadership. Eventually, Kelsey would make a name for himself in the eyes of the Caucasian-led government, although he had no personal experience with Negro soldiers. He too supported the popular, small-minded theory that Negroes were useless, stupid cowards.[19] Kelsey and McLeod had a double-edged sword to swallow—not only did they have an obligation to their men in the 333rd, but they still sought respect from fellow White officers,[20] who, across the board, felt working with Black men was a waste of their military careers.

CHAPTER TWO

Becoming the Weapon

ACTIVATION DAY arrived on August 5, 1942, eight months after the onslaught against Hawaii's Pearl Harbor. The new, all-Black 333rd Field Artillery unit and its 969th sister battalion,[21] were assigned as separate battalions and deployed to Camp Gruber, Oklahoma (west of Oklahoma City), for war training.

Note: Separate battalions are not organic, or part of a division commanded by a two-star major general. These units are assigned to the division's higher headquarters, the corps, generally commanded by a three-star lieutenant general or senior major general.

The purpose of the isolated 333rd was to allow the numbered army, like Patton's Third Army, or corps commander, such as VIII Corps (Eighth Corps), to attach to it as reinforcement at any given time, based on the demands of the current tactical situation. Once aligned with other corps and divisions, field artillerymen movements (or King of Battle,[22] according to Army parlance) were controlled on the battlefield like pawns in a chess match. The nine separate field artillery battalions would become vital to the corps' make up in WWII, with important checkmates made by Black artillerymen under Patton. Just like the corps, the 333rd would deploy to Europe, shifting from operation to operation and fight to fight. They were quickly battle-tested and approved—and the four, still-segregated Negro artillery group headquarters would eventually even gain some control over White artillery units.[23]

THE KING OF BATTLE

In WWII, each soldier entered the service with his or her own background and story. Some were high-school graduates, while others had never seen a junior-high-school blacktop; this was, especially, true for men from the rural South, their hometowns unbothered and lacking schools for Colored children. A handful of 333rd recruits had college experience and even fewer were graduates. With disparities in opportunities and education, learning and training together proved challenging for the battalion of Black brothers.

> And that's how they banded together—training and working together as brothers, sharing knowledge and experience—to destroy barriers.

Camp Gruber, Oklahoma, evolved into a dual site for 333rd soldiers in basic and artillery training. All recruits, White or Black, were required to attend basic training—age-old boot camp, where they learned practical skills in water purification, personal hygiene, and field sanitation, with the knowledge that, ironically, more soldiers are lost in combat to severe weather (heat stroke and frostbite) and disease (venereal, intestinal, and respiratory) over bloody battle injuries.[24] In basic small-weapons training, each soldier was handed a .30-caliber Springfield rifle and instructed to clean and care for it. The men learned their weapons like the backs of their hands, assembly, spare parts, accessories, safety measures, and all.[25] Marksmanship training taught the future frontliners how to aim and fire at moving targets on the ground, their antiaircraft training for those in the air. Daily, for fourteen weeks, their nine-to-five was drill tactics, first aid, code of conduct, Geneva Convention protocols, hand-to-hand combat, and physical and gas-attack training, not to mention training with a mammoth war weapon, the howitzer.[26]

The 155-mm howitzer, or "Long Tom" because of its incredible reach, boasted projectiles capable of traveling sixteen thousand yards, or nine miles,[27] an important weapon specification in fighting enemies long-range. Its lethal shells were grouped into three categories—explosive, chemical, or smoke—each projectile strategically selected depending on the target: defensive positions, enemy vehicles, or foot soldiers. At more than twenty-four feet long and eight feet high, operating the howitzer required a full crew with eleven men cross-training in each other's position. Even its training manual was massive at two-hundred pages of technical instruction. The goliath 333rd gun was an intimidating ally, and it took physical and mental strength to avoid injury—or worse, death by a friendly weapon.[28] These killer shells traveled at least eleven hundred feet per second[29] and, alone, weighed one hundred pounds, or more, justifying the heavy-duty Army trucks hauling them in tow, six-ton gun included. These two-tiered trucks rolled on battle-sized tires reinforced with up to sixty percent more rubber for maneuvering through rough weather and terrain.[30]

After weeks of training together with their 155-mm ally, the eleven-man gun crew defeated its original, twelve-minute gun-ready time, replacing it with an Army standard of five minutes. The exhausting preparation was soothed only by sounds of home, the men singing and humming old Negro spirituals you'd hear at a Black protestant church in that era; working the rudiments, improving with each repetition.[31] The 333rd mastering its process simply solidified second-in-command Capt. McLeod's confidence in the men, as Lt. Col. Kelsey considered creeping second thoughts; maybe, the Black battalion was just as capable as its light-skinned counterparts?

DEBARKATION

With a year and a half of tedious, uninterrupted training under their belts, and with preliminary preparation on the Long Tom, the soldiers were eager to deploy, especially as they watched White units enter the war with far less training—another sign of the segregated times. On February 2, 1944, after the 333rd finally had its heads-up for deployment, it prepared to depart Camp Gruber en route to its debarkation station. For security reasons, the men had no idea where they were headed, though rampant rumors insisted the final destination was somewhere on the East Coast (the same rumors, and fate, as their 320th aerial battalion and 761st tank battalion brothers before them). The soldiers, in the forms of fathers, husbands, sons, brothers, and friends, wrote final letters to their loved ones; some had been graced with family visits at Camp Gruber during training, and others had made new friends in their temporary community, who surely promised to keep in touch with their new, war-bound buddies.

The Black artillery unit was locked and loaded, ready to board buses and trains for its final destination at Camp Shanks, north of New York City, where they would spend a week in medical, legal, and logistical processing in preparation to set sail for the United Kingdom—their final stop and last chance for additional weapons training. They arrived in England seventeen days later, on February 19. This time, the men would cross-train on British artillery weapons, should the need ever arise to man the foreign guns. It was also here that the 333rd would later join the 969th all-Black Artillery Battalion as its sister unit. Between March and May 1944, after the arrival of the 969th, both groups of men were part of continuous combat training and field exercises with VIII Corps, to which they would eventually be assigned. The 333rd Field Artillery Group built a relationship with VIII Corps and the 969th that would last until the end of WWII.

PREPARING BRITS FOR BLACKS

Although East Coasters had routinely toured New York, New Jersey, Connecticut, and Pennsylvania, because of proximity and accessible transportation, most men from the South had never ventured outside their home state, let alone overseas. Upon arrival in the UK, our Southern soldiers had to anticipate discrimination from White Brits, because that's what Whites had enforced back in the States. Their "kind" was, surely, hated and segregated worldwide, right?

> **But the Black men were shocked when they were never met with the level of ignorance and hate they had experienced daily in some of their American hometowns.**

Most British citizens in the London suburbs hadn't encountered Black people, let alone Jim Crow laws, before the arrival of our soldiers. However, the White American soldiers did all they could to paint a distorted picture of Blacks before the minority group had ever reached European soil. Looking for ways to continue their ideals of segregation, military leaders encouraged unsuspecting British businesses to not serve Black soldiers and cautioned civilians to never extend invitations for a Negro man to enter their homes. Had our British friends across the Atlantic not heard? Blacks grow tails at midnight and bark at full moons.[32] Not to fear—the noble Whites were there to spread the word. Despite the hate-fueled rumors spread by fellow Americans (and minimal discrimination they did experience from the British), Black soldiers and local British women began connecting and dating, to the disdain and resentment of White soldiers. The Brits were treating African American soldiers as equals, openly friendly and accepting, which no American man, light- or dark-skinned, could fathom. The mindsets and attitudes of many White soldiers pushed Blacks to question:

> "Who are we over here to fight—the Germans or our own White soldiers?"[33]

One British farmer, with a mind and eyes of his own, agreed and was reported saying: "I love the Americans, but I do not like the White ones they brought with them."[34] British citizens in general held an unflattering opinion of the American GI: overpaid, oversexed,[35] and over here.

CHAPTER THREE

Bullets, Balloons, and Bombs Away

AFTER TIRELESS months of rehearsal and preparation, the US would soon carry out its invasion with the largest armada in the history of mankind. Although the 333rd Field Artillery Battalion would never see the incursion itself (as previously discussed), the Black 320th Anti-Aircraft Barrage Balloon Battalion would, making it the only African American unit to participate in D-Day.

On June 6, 1944, the Allies crossed the English Channel (the narrow arm of the channel separating England's southern coast from France's northern coast) and landed at France's Normandy coast, on the beaches of Omaha, Utah, Gold, Juno, and Sword. It was a scene to behold—from thousands of feet above, down to the coastal sands beneath their boots. The total American force was awesome with 176,000 men, 20,000 wheeled vehicles, 3,000 guns (artillery), 1,500 tanks, and 5,000 armored vehicles. Its fleet boasted 200 warships, supplemented by 500 smaller ships, frigates, corvettes, and patrol boats. An air force was formed, carrying 171 squadrons of fighters (2,100 planes) and 6,000 long-range bombers;[36] The soldiers of the 333rd crossed the English Channel on June 29, as part of the operational US Eighth Corps under command of Maj. Gen. Troy Middleton, senior of the generals of that rank. At the time, Eighth Corps was a subordinate command of the First US Corps, commanded by. Lt. Gen. Omar Bradley, a three-star general who would later pin on four and five stars.[37]

RISE OF THE FALLEN

A month following D-Day, the battalion's Omaha Beach landing remained unopposed, and the unit was already entering a new war. In its first fire mission in support of the 82nd Airborne Division,[38] on July 1, artillery rounds from the 333rd made a direct hit on a Nazi observation post (OP) sitting atop a church steeple nine miles away—a glorified sniper's nest—and the battalion was baptized by fire. Eliminating the German OP allowed our airborne division to continue its mission through town without enemy interception.

When the sun rose the next day, the Black 333rd received more orders to reinforce the 90th Infantry Division, all while still directly supporting its airborne brothers in arms. It was in this battle that the men realized their counterfire wouldn't be enough to hold off the enemy; this was where the battalion mourned its first casualties—teammates, now bonded after leaving their segregated home to train and fight alongside each other—injured or killed by German counter-battery fire. Days later, the band of Black soldiers shot down an enemy airplane, took their first Nazi war prisoners, and turned them over to the military police prisoner-of-war (POW) unit for processing and imprisonment.

Amidst the wins and losses of the bloody battles, the Allies joined together on July 4, at Normandy's Cotentin Peninsula, and fired a round of ammunition at the enemy to celebrate American Independence Day.[39] Hitler's army returned fire the next day but had no deaths or injuries to boast, as all US battalions had already been displaced into new positions. The 969th Artillery Battalion had arrived from *England to deliver general fire support to the 333rd troops—serving as a backup to their backup. With the addition of another field* artillery battalion, the two soldier elements were now part of the newly designated *333rd Field Artillery Group*, with a headquarters and all, with the 333rd and 969th as subordinate units. The group's first cooperation called for departure from Pont-L'Abbe, with new directions to head for La

Haye-du-Puits, in lower Normandy, to safeguard an important road junction.

On the outskirts of their destination, the soldiers met German artillery fire and were strafed by enemy airplanes; the American crews suffered numerous losses in the surprise attack. The slaying of their men, and their extensive training, fueled the battalion in shooting down a Nazi plane, the .50-caliber machine gun manned by a 333rd soldier. This was the African American battalion's first aerial takedown.[40] Although trained to shoot at low-flying enemy aircraft, this was their first kill. In the same breath, the 333rd was assigned another fire mission and scored a direct hit on an enemy tank camouflaged in a hedgerow at sixteen thousand yards.[41] Not long after, another counter hit sailed from hilltops surrounding the town, and enemy artillery rained on American military engineers clearing mines, repairing roads, and building bridges to keep the supply routes open; several brothers were killed on the spot.

> The battalion, grieving each devastating loss, would also witness its first fatality by friendly weapon, a 333rd soldier slain while operating their own 155-mm howitzer.[42]

The Negro unit's presence on the battlefield was short-lived, but the men finally garnered a fraction of the faith they deserved all along from Lt. Col. Kelsey and higher headquarters. The Army, expecting little, if any, success from Black soldiers, was beginning to recognize the group's strength and valor, though it would never be officially recorded or reported.

THE GLOBAL GAME

Come late July 1944, Gen. Eisenhower and staff concluded that breakout from the expanded beachhead was essential to continuing the fight. The Allies had been waterlogged there since D-Day. Maneuvering into the French region of Brittany was essential in proving American momentum was growing. With this, Operation Cobra was born, and the 333rd Field Artillery Battalion would play a significant role.[43]

Operation Cobra involved a massive collection of Allied Forces, spearheaded by Lt. Gen. Omar Bradley's First Army and composed of the British Second Army and First Canadian Army—a force of almost a half-million soldiers. Their primary objective in Brittany: to capture the Nazi naval bases in the city of Brest. The port city was harboring most of Germany's western submarine fleet, which for months had been destroying US and Allied merchant marine ships ferrying supplies from the American East Coast by way of the Atlantic Ocean to England. With Brest in friendly hands, supplies could ship directly to France without having to trans-ship fromEngland.

By now, Patton's all-Black trucking battalions were ferrying ammunition, fuel, and other supplies to his Third Army combat units, the 761st Tank Battalion a recipient. The day-and-night convoys were given the moniker "Red Ball Express" (adopted from a successful, twenty-five-year-old US civilian moving company established in 1919).[44] With explicit orders from Patton, these trucks had priority road space and were armed with large white flags adorned with a painted red ball to signify the important mission of more than six thousand trucks. At its peak, the Red Ball transported at least twelve thousand tons of supplies every twenty-four hours.[45] They ran for three months, until port facilities opened at Antwerp, and the Allies captured French rail lines and established portable gasoline pipelines.

Note: After WWII, White veterans, with little or no wartime trucking experience, received priority employment with transportation companies over African American veterans, who were the original Red Ball drivers. Sadly, this occurred throughout the US within many industries.

CAPTURING LAND AND SKY

The Germans always knew a successful Allied landing at Calais or Normandy was a possibility, and they had planned to fight the battle from defensive positions in occupied France. To blunt a land invasion from the West, they needed to erect a physical barrier to supplement the ground and air forces they had built up; this became the basis for the Siegfried Line, or Atlantic Wall. The Siegfried Line followed the contours of the Maginot Line built by France along the border of Western Germany to prevent an invasion by the German army, like what had happened in WWI. Unfortunately, France's barricade proved an ineffective deterrent, as the German army successfully maneuvered around it.

Brest (the US Army's main initiative in Operation Cobra) was part of the Siegfried Line, along with hundreds of cities, towns, villages, and hamlets, all part of the massive, man-made barrier.[46] The open terrain and hill areas separating towns were home to supplementary obstacles designed to block, or at least impede Allied offensive operations, especially tanks. The terrain was cluttered with tank barriers—or dragon teeth. These spiked cement blocks of varying heights were bound to buildings and other structures by barbed wire, in hopes of entangling tank treads and causing Allied immobility; once snagged, the enemy would shoot at ensnared tanks from concealed positions.

Before the US Army could ever recognize the 333rd for the eventual capitulation of Brest, they would have to survive the next two months of Operation Cobra. The unit encountered the enemy at every turn with German artillery tucked behind hillsides and inside unsuspecting barns and buildings; our troops were never meant to make it out alive. On July 28, 1944, nearly three years after Pearl Harbor, our 333rd and 969th Field Artillery Battalions, in supporting the 90th Infantry and following a fierce fight, dislodged German infantry from the Brest suburb of Saint-Sauveur-Lendelin. Hitler's army was backed by fighter aircraft disposing ammunition upon our artillerymen. The all-Black unit, blocking the bombardment to the best of its ability and focused on the safety of its fellows, steadied, aimed, and returned fire, downing several Nazi aircraft.[47]

> These men, who back at home were considered secondary citizens (if not half-human), were finally regarded as skilled artillerymen on the ground and now, a quickly rising antiaircraft battalion.

Moving, once again, as in a long-standing match of international chess, the American soldiers inched their way toward St. Aubin-d'ubigné, an old Roman city on the French peninsula of Brittany, lined with sky-high spires atop hilly land. Although they ran into more strafing from the Luftwaffe, there were no Allied casualties this time around. In a follow-up maneuver, the 333rd was attached to lend support to the 8th Infantry moving to secure Brittany's capital city of Rennes. The old city had a tumultuous past stretching back decades, much of its picturesque architecture having been destroyed by a devastating fire. After the rebuild, the city was destroyed a second time—this time, by Hitler's army amidst seizing it from Free French Forces three years earlier. What remained would again be destroyed, this time by US forces and Royal Air Force (RAF) aircraft in an effort to dislodge the remaining Nazi forces.[48]

CHECK

Nearing fall, 1944, which on the French coast is comparable to a Southern California autumn day (but with eighty percent humidity), the group was closer than ever to its main target, the city of Brest, in a mission that surely would obscure the country's sunny, coastal charm.

Note: Before its capture by Germany, Brest, for hundreds of years, had been a key, commercial port city whose commerce was vital as an economic engine for trade. Now, however, civilian trade was almost nonexistent since the Germans had occupied and fortified it as a defensive bastion.

The Americans traveled west toward Dinard and St. Malo, where with 333rd assistance, the infantry division would liberate both towns, which like other Brittany towns, were intermediate objectives for Brest. They combined with their 969th field-artillery sister in Lesneven, only fifteen miles north of Brest, to lend artillery support to another US Division order to attack and assist in the capture of Brest. Major General Middleton, who was still serving as Patton's Third Corps subordinate commander, would face challenges displacing the entrenched German Army in Brest, even with assistance from the 333rd Field Artillery Battalion.

The city's citadel, or Château de Brest, was a military fortress and the center of gravity in Brest. Hitler had carefully chosen one of his most admired generals as its commander, Gen. Herman Ramcke, chief officer of Hitler's palace guard unit, the Führer Begleit Brigade. Ramcke was a decorated veteran of the battle in Crete who had demonstrated an intense loyalty to Hitler and the Third Reich. He was even awarded the Knight's Cross of the Iron Cross, Nazi Germany's highest military honor, presented by the führer himself.[49] Over time, General Ramcke had completely fortified Brest's citadel, touting its impregnable nature and elaborate defensive measures. Ideally, the fortress would thwart Allied incursions by sinking ships upon arrival in its harbor. Within the citadel, slabs of cement were erected with ample firing points to block pillboxes disguised as houses. Numerous antitank ditches and minefields stretched across any and all land approaches, connected by barbed wire (same song and dance as the Siegfried Line) to help entangle treads and wheels on tanks and other war vehicles.[50]

The below-ground command and control center for Ramcke's fortress was a reinforced, cemented internal bunker—a city within a city—that housed an internal power plant, storage and maintenance areas, ammunition dumps, a hospital, and several troop housing quarters, all of which were interconnected by an elaborate tunneling system. And all of this added confidence to the enemy's expectation of fighting off a prolonged Allied siege.

CHECKMATE

A major attack by the American VIII Corps began on August 25, 1944, when three infantry divisions, including the 333rd Field Artillery Battalion, supported by airstrikes, tanks, and engineered explosives, fired highly explosive shells directly at the Brest citadel. It was enough man and firepower to destroy the, supposedly, immovable fortress and end the almost month-long siege. Though Ramcke's confidence in his Nazi Army hadn't wavered midbattle, boasting that *"a German soldier never surrenders,"*[51] Hitler's favorite pawn eventually surrendered four hundred surviving soldiers out of more than thirty thousand; the others were badly wounded, combat ineffective, or killed. The US 8th Corps suffered ten thousand wounded out of their initial group of one hundred thousand men; there was no comparison.

Upon capturing Brest, the Allies discovered the city's railroad system and the harbor's locks, breakwaters, and quays had been destroyed by the Germans. Gen. Middleton surmised it would take months to repair water navigation for future use by US forces.[52] In the meantime, the African American battalion of brothers, rejoicing over their incredible, and doubted, win against Nazi Germany and liberation of its captives, returned to Lesneven to establish shelter, clean and service their weapons, and make necessary repairs to war equipment. Here, the 333rd finally garnered overdue R&R (rest and recuperation) and enjoyed its first-ever United Services Organization (USO) Show.

These shows were the US government's effort to bring a piece of

Hollywood and Broadway to military bases and battle zones for the entertainment and morale of WWII soldiers. Shows were headlined by popular singers, dancers, movie stars, and comedians of the era, usually hosted by famous comedian Bob Hope, known for closing his shows with the song "Thanks for the Memories." For Whites, USO troupes included well-known celebrities, like Betty Grable and her "million-dollar legs,"[53] comedian Eddie Canter, musician Jerry Colona, and German-born American actress and singer Marlene Dietrich. Cast members were even supported by a full orchestra with favorites Harry James[54] and Benny Goodman. Under the USO policy that no soldier face discrimination based on race or creed, Black units enjoyed entertainment provided (strictly) by Negro performers, such as dancer Lena Horne, actress Dorothy Dandridge, singer Eartha Kitt, The Mills Brothers, and vibraphonist Lionel Hampton's orchestra.

And, for the first time, rumors whirred about the possibility of Christmas at home in the US with their loved ones. The men's excitement skyrocketed even further after they finally started receiving long-overdue mail from the States for the first time since crossing the English Channel (mail was delayed due to an extensive backlog in London caused by inefficient sorting and delivery, which was only rectified with the arrival of the 6888th Central Postal Directory Battalion in January 1945, the only American Army unit of all-Black women soldiers in the Theater). In another wave of postwar celebration, battalion Commander Lt. Col. Kelsey, whose confidence in his men seemed ever-wavering, finally presented his 333rd men with accolades for their superior battlefield performance.

CHAPTER FOUR

Before the Bulge

In AN UNPLANNED formation on September 30, 1944, Lt. Col. Kelsey assembled his men to share a special mention from a lengthy story in *Yank*, a weekly WWII magazine published by the US military.[55] On this day, leadership arranged for White units in the area to join the Black 333rd—a rare sighting of normally segregated soldiers standing together. Lt. Col. Kelsey, competing with the frigid cold, congratulated his African American battalion, citing from the popular military magazine: "... You boys arrived in France, fired four rounds in ninety seconds, and knocked out a church steeple more than nine miles. That's the kind of shooting the battalion has done ever since. It was the first Negro combat outfit to face the enemy in France.

> I've heard doughboys of five divisions watch men of the 333rd battalion rumble past in four-ton prime movers and say, 'Thank God those guys are behind us.'"[56]

The 333rd was jubilant, and just as notable, White soldiers standing alongside them shared their joy. Congratulations were given all around, as even White officers paid their respects to Kelsey and his brave battalion—another rare sighting in the segregated military.

BOUND FOR BELGIUM

Just four days earlier, on September 26, 1944, the unit began a 160-mile road march, pushing through France en route to Belgium again and bivouacking for the night in the city of St. Aubin-d'Aubigné.

Note: US soldiers maneuvered in and out of Belgium, crossing back and forth—imagine the men traveling between two cities in, say, California, like Los Angeles and Long Beach. There was constant movement.

The strategic objective in Belgium for Allies and Germans was to control its deep-water port city, Antwerp. It showed potential as a hub for logistics, which could determine the war's outcome. Logistics, or "beans and bullets," were just as important to an army as its weapons and vehicles because it ensured provisions would quickly and safely make their way to our soldiers. Antwerp, if in Allied hands, would allow US ships to offload directly to stevedore units, reducing delivery time to units by several days. Upon arrival, the all-Black unit was greeted by throngs of welcoming French citizens thanking the men for liberating their hometowns just days earlier.[57]

Come dawn in Saint Aubin, the weary unit booted up for another 150-mile trek to their next destination: Chartres. Like other French cities, Chartres (southwest of Paris) was a Gothic town with a troublesome past, having been burned to the ground and built again. During the war, the US 26th Infantry, upon reclaiming the city, had made diligent efforts to preserve Chartres's historic, sky-high cathedral and its towering spires and flying buttresses. For hundreds of years, power over Chartres had shifted from the French to the Normans to the English and then to the Germans—but, thanks to the US Army, the French had, finally, reclaimed their city.[58] The troops were elated to reach Paris, home of the then fifty-five-year-old Eiffel Tower, as they rolled through the city en route to Saint Quintin. The battalion knew both cities had been liberated by the US; Saint Quintin, with support from the all-Black 761st Tank Battalion, and Paris, by Free French of the Interior's (FFI) Second French Armored Division, supported by our troops.

By October 1, 1944, nearly one year before the end of WWII, the 333rd Field Artillery Battalion was crossing the frontier to reenter

Belgium, bivouacking in Houffalize, a city several miles northeast of Bastogne. The weather was bigger than the small town situated in the Ardennes Forest, with rain and snow seemingly swallowing its fields and roads, leaving only knee-deep mud. The rain let up after a couple of days and made way for the team's convoy toward St. Vith, a town located at a vital road junction within the forest; it was just twelve miles from the German front—the Siegfried Line. At that moment, St. Vith was the ideal location to garner a few days rest, but weeks later, it would become the center of attack by the German Fifth Army during the now famous Battle of the Bulge.

Roll in, replenish, repeat—the 333rd pushed through until it reached Belgium at the crossroads of France and Luxembourg.[59] This location was strategically essential to the US military because for decades, especially in the years right before the war, it had served as a major logistical hub for western Europe, with extensive road and rail networks. With a deep-water port at Antwerp, whichever military controlled the extensive transshipment center would have a major advantage in replenishing its troops. Belgium, which was neutral at first and later engaged after the German invasion, was also a country in contrast and provided a direct avenue of attack through the Southern Ardennes Forest, which the Germans occupied during the Battle of the Bulge to interdict American and Allied Forces.

Following weeks of intense warfare, while defending depleting forces (a significant loss of men and equipment), King Leopold III of Belgium surrendered his military, allowing Germany to occupy the country, though he would preserve his king title throughout the war. Once thwarted into battle, the Belgians (many, at the time, speaking French, German, and English) were divided by their loyalties; some advocated for the US Allies and, others, the new German occupation. None wanted to be part of the losing team. After its capture, Belgian soldiers and boys were conscripted into the German Army, and as in France, it became a government in exile with the king resigning at the end of the war.

Still attached to VIII Corps and continually on the move, the American artillerymen surged a few miles east of their rest stop, toward the Schönberg area, in a mission to provide direct support fire to the 2nd Infantry, which was forward of the 333rd and much closer to the Siegfried Line. In the same breath, the unit bravely counterfired during planned attacks by the Germans, who had previously pinpointed land and sea targets and were now launching V-1 rockets overhead, stunning civilian areas in the rear and wounding and killing the people of Schönberg.[60]

GHOST FRONT

November was a quiet month for the 333rd, a rare, crucial opportunity for rest and recuperation, given what December 1944 had in store for the American men. The idle month gave the VIII Corps a chance to recognize Lt. Col. Kelsey with the Bronze Star Medal for his meritorious service[61] and the all-Black battalion's shooting accuracy. The soldiers had nothing tangible to show for their success, a sad reality in the WWII segregated military.

On December 6 and for the next few nights, the 106th Infantry began a relief in place in total darkness, man for man, gun for gun,[62] of the 2nd Infantry Division east of St. Vith, in an area known as the Losheim Gap. Substitute 106th soldiers arrived to occupy friendly fox holes, artillery cannons, and defensive positions held by their 2nd Infantry counterparts. The 333rd Field Artillery Battalion stayed stationary to support the newly arrived infantry and its 422nd, 423rd, and 424th Regiments. The 106th Infantry Division, the greenest of units, had recently arrived in the Theater with no combat experience among its commanding general, officers, and soldiers.[63] Originally, the unit had proficiently trained for combat in the US, but two-thirds of its soldiers were sent ahead to Europe to replace critical losses in infantry divisions. Because of this, the 106th required backfill by new recruits who'd only undergone basic training in the US based on the assumption that the war was winding down and soldiers would be home for Christmas.

With current information and hopes of a smooth transition into the war zone, the 106th was assigned to the Schnee Eifel sector, referred to as the *Ghost Front*,[64] a term used to identify areas with little to no enemy activity,[65] which was exactly what the men were expecting. At the time, the front was a dreary, isolated, snow-covered land of low mountains shrouded by silent, dripping fir forests believed to be inaccessible by Nazi Panzer and Tiger tanks.[66] Adding to the treachery of deep snow and freezing temperatures—inhospitable conditions that further complicated defense measures by infantrymen and artillerymen of General Middleton's VIII Corps—the Army allocated only a single division to help secure the twenty-two mile front of the Belgium border.[67] As a division-sized unit would traditionally deploy to defend a front of five miles, this would become the most difficult location Middleton's overextended Corps line would defend along the border. The Ghost Front was impossibly wide, with a seemingly impenetrable depth of eight miles, and too abundant for a single division to defend.[68] The Germans had occupied and improved the area before being routed by the US months earlier, so it wasn't much different than the garrisons the men were used to.

The soldiers settled into houses, log cabins, and winterized tents to avoid an additional war against the winter elements. Cold-weather gear and uniforms provided by logistical service units started arriving, the battalion anxiously awaiting the extra warmth. Though the silent, almost sleepy territory showed no signs of potentially encountering the enemy, Patton expressed serious concern that the VII Corps hadn't fittingly deployed the 106th—which had never experienced the enemy, was still completing basic training, and sat stationary in a vital avenue of approach of a possible German attack. The new American presence was solid, still with nine battalions of infantry, two cavalry squadrons, five organic field artillery battalions, and eight additional field artillery units attached from VIII Corps (including the all-Black 333rd Field Artillery), all of these men representing sixteen thousand of the eighty thousand US soldiers stationed in the Ardennes Forest;[69] this was a mere fraction of the two hundred fifty thousand to three hundred thousand men in German General Sep Dietrich's Sixth Panzer Army, which, unknown to the Allies, would flood their sector in just a few days.[70]

Hitler's operational plan was to attack through the Ardennes Forest, pass through the Losheim Gap, cross the Meuse River, and move toward Antwerp to secure the city's port. In German hands, this would inhibit the flow of logistics by the Allies, thus possibly ending all Allied attacks and enabling the Germans to sue for peace. If successful, the Nazis would surround the heavily wooded Schnee Eifel landscape, cutting off the 106th Division, and, as an interim objective, capture the all-important road junction and communications center at St. Vith. The African American 333rd Field Artillery Battalion would play the major supporting role of defender in the battle for the forest. In less than a fortnight, the 106th Division would be decimated, and out of the sixteen thousand men who entered the forest, only four thousand would return—their brothers killed, wounded, or captured; all victims of the greatest US defeat in Europe in the Second World War.[71]

CHAPTER FIVE

---★---

Battle of the Bulge

ONE WEEK before Christmas, on December 16, 1944, as the African American 333rd soldiers mentally prepared for another holiday in the trenches, the enemy fired its first shots at Allied troops at three o'clock in the morning from within the pitch-dark Ardennes Forest. Unsuspected by the US, General der Panzertruppe Erich Brandenberger's German Seventh Army, one of four Nazi groups secretly spread throughout the forest, had built up divisions across the Our and Sauer Rivers[72] and was waiting to pull the trigger. Enemy fire rained upon the 106th Division and 333rd Battalion areas. Not only was the Nazi army watching and carefully noting American key positions—they had quietly penetrated with reconnaissance patrols through gaps in our defensive lines. With this intelligence and awareness of the land (after all, they had been in the same positions only months earlier), German cannoneers were hitting their American targets spot on. Before the initial attack, German soldiers were issued a directive from the highest-ranking Generalfeldmarschall (Field Marshal) Karl Rudolf Gerd von Rundstedt.

"Soldiers of the West Front! Your great honor has arrived. Large attacking armies have started against the Anglo-Americans. I do not have to tell you anything more on that. You feel it yourself. WE GAMBLE EVERYTHING! You carry with you the holy obligation to give everything to achieve things beyond human possibilities for our Fatherland and our Fuhrer!"[73]

Before daylight could alert the Allies, Germans troops pushed through our defensive lines and across the front, along the apex of the borders of Luxembourg, Belgium, and France. Enemy manpower was vast and fierce with 250,000 to 300,000 soldiers; their firepower was just as impressive, boasting 2,600 artillery pieces, 382 tanks, and 335 self-propelled guns.[74] The surprise attack allotted American soldiers zero reaction time. Many were immediately killed, leading VIII Corps Headquarters to allow the 106th Division and 333rd Field Artillery Battalion, with the exception of one 333rd battery and half of another to withdraw—they were outmanned and outgunned and losing more by the second.

The US Army ordered Battery Charlie (indicative of the old Able Baker phonetic military alphabet) and a section of a service battery to stay behind and cover the fleeing 106th and their 333rd brothers. The other batteries evacuated wounded soldiers, using whatever nearby vehicles were available in desperate efforts to escape alive, but only after following orders to destroy all equipment and materials such as maps, generators, radios, switchboards, telephones, or anything that could be used by the enemy. They fought fire with fire well into nightfall, expending the last of the ammunition. At that time, the only Allies left on the Ghost Front were Capt. McLeod and twenty Black soldiers.[75] With a final order from Kelsey to McLeod, trucks were sent to rescue what remained of the 333rd, but, by the time the first truck arrived, advancing German soldiers had already directly attacked and wounded or killed several of his men.

Note: Two days after the attack began, a priest ventured out of his cellar to find more than two hundred bodies, American and German, scattered in the vicinity of his church.[76] Faithfully, he offered last rites to each of them, friend, and foe alike.

Still greatly outnumbered and engulfed by tens of thousands of German soldiers, the Americans resorted to everything they had learned back home in basic training about fighting hand to hand; but the ambush was still too powerful. Many of the remaining Allies were shot, stabbed, or butchered. With no ammunition or weapons, and desperate to save the lives of his remaining men, Capt. McLeod surrendered.[77]

CALAMITY AND CAPTIVITY

Surviving soldiers of the decimated 333rd, with the loss of their brothers still fresh, merged with the 969th Battalion—the only other African American field artillery unit in the Third Army. All three regiments under the 106th Infantry (supported by the 333rd) experienced significant loss, many slain during the first day of battle alone, as ammunition and supplies quickly dwindled. The division's reserve was committed.

Note: In combat operations, generally two-thirds of forces are "committed" to the action, keeping one-third in reserve to influence the action. At the proper time, on either side, the reserve is committed to reinforcing the breaking-through of Allied Forces at enemy lines or is committed to thwarting the breaking of friendly lines by enemy forces.

Reinforcements from VIII Corps were en route, including the 7th Armored Division, which was also under heavy fire and losing men and equipment left and right as they battled blankets of rain and muddy snow on their way to assist.

Three days into the Battle of the Bulge, two 106th Infantry Regiments (422nd and 423rd) stood on a hill near Schoenberg in a crescent-shaped defense stance, losing another fight against the Germans. The situation was dire for the Americans, with no fire support from the 333rd or any of the other artillery groups, all of which were simultaneously putting out serious fires of their own. The two regiments were nearly out of small-arms ammunition, and torrential weather meant the option for resupply via skies was out of the question. They were disconnected from division headquarters and other surviving units—the rest of the world—and nobody on the outside knew the enemy had captured US Sherman tanks and was firing down American soldiers with their own ammunition.

Two more days of futile efforts left the 422nd and 423rd weary, thirsty, and stretching withering rations as the Germans continued to collect American casualties. Faced with their own mortality, and determined to save what remained of their men, unit commanders surrendered against the disheartening odds of survival. As of now, St. Vith and surrounding areas, including Schoenberg, were in German hands. The final unit under the 106th was instructed to withdraw to the safety of the arriving 82nd Airborne and 7th Armored Divisions, both of which would take part in the recapture of St. Vith in the weeks to come. The current landscape showed scores of American soldiers killed, wounded, or, if "lucky" enough, captured alive, like many 333rd soldiers and thousands more—the captivity rate surpassing half of what once was an unstoppable, fourteen-thousand-man infantry division. Imprisoned Americans were immediately transported to enemy POW (prisoner of war) holding areas after capture to await processing at the German rear.

Completely surrounded and depleted of food and ammunition, three hundred White-American soldiers dropped their weapons and raised their hands in surrender to Nazi soldiers on December 17, 1944. The men were collected in a field and headed to a prison camp, as far as they knew. But then, on order, German infantry soldiers of the 1st SS Panzer Regiment fired on them with automatic weapons, instantly killing scores of them. Others managed to avoid death by running through deep snow into the forest. Either the soldiers themselves or their leader had no knowledge of the Geneva Convention—or purposely chose to ignore it.

Once Allied prisoners arrived at camp, the Germans segregated the officers from their enlisted men. Since the 333rd Field Artillery Battalion had an all-White officer corps, they were housed with White officers of the 106th Infantry Division. The enlisted soldiers of the 333rd and the 106th were housed together in the same facilities. Ironically, and finally, African Americans were receiving equal treatment in housing, messing, medical attention, and all other facets of daily life. For two years, the soldiers had trained in a segregated military and fought in a segregated war, separate from Whites—and integration had finally come in captivity as POWs, the Nazis never distinguishing White from Black because they were all enemies of the Fatherland.

> It took enemy captivity in a foreign country, in a World War, for African Americans to receive treatment equal to their light-skinned counterparts.

This is not to say that the equal treatment of American soldiers, despite race, was at all humane. Though Germany had signed and agreed to the terms of the 1929 Geneva Convention, which outlines basic, humane treatment of prisoners of war, under such extreme circumstances, the Nazis had shown no interest in upholding their end of the international obligation. Nazi prisoners of war were held in famously unsanitary conditions, malnourished, and forced into intense labor.

With much of the 333rd in captivity, along with their commanding officer, Capt. McLeod, the Germans spared no rod in punishing their Western enemies. Some POWs were even executed by a gunshot to the head without a moment's notice. Even making it to camp was treacherous for the soldiers, who after capture, were forced to walk for days toward Duchenstadt,[78] one of the thousands of camps throughout the Third Reich; some of their wounded did not survive the treacherous trip on foot and succumbed to their war injuries along the way. On the other hand, not all who were captured were forced into POW camps, as more than one hundred American men were murdered directly after capture at Malmedy, Belgium.[79] In another battle eleven men from the 333rd escaped to Wereth, though unsuccessfully, after surrendering to enemy forces during a fight at Schonberg.[80]

CHAPTER SIX

The Wereth Eleven

As THE GERMAN Army exhausted their ammunition upon Schönberg early in the Battle of the Bulge, on December 16, 1994, the American 333rd Field Artillery Battalion was outnumbered and overrun. In an effort to preserve as many lives as possible, the US soldiers, forced to surrender to the Nazis, were captured and sent to prison camps for the remainder of the war. One group of eleven Negro soldiers managed to escape the bloody scene, outrunning the enemy to avoid capture.

The men spent hours on the run, heading in separate directions and hiding among the dense trees of the Ardennes Forest, where, in one spot the eleven came together again—hungry, physically exhausted, and fighting freezing temperatures. For a day and a half they had trudged together, taking cover each time a vehicle passed, never confident of whether the trucks were transporting allies or foes. Their feet and hands were half-frozen as they finally came upon a sign in the snow: *Wereth*—a small hamlet in the Eupen-Malmedy region of Belgium. The soldiers counted nine houses along a narrow street with what appeared to be a cow pasture at one end. Afraid of what—or who—they might encounter, the fleeing men from the 333rd were hesitant to approach civilization and waited to take disguise in the night. Come darkness, the men approached the first house and waved a white flag of surrender, informing any occupants that they were Americans.[81]

The door opened to reveal a family, Mathias and Maria Langer and six of their children. The Langers were a Catholic family who respected the Allied Forces and feared the Germans, their two oldest boys had been sent away to avoid getting drafted into the German Army.[82] The family welcomed the Black soldiers openly, as they had with many victims of the war, and ushered them out of the weather; by now, the men were frozen and could hardly stand. The family wrapped them in blankets, sat them at the kitchen table, and served hot coffee, water, and freshly baked bread, and the soldiers scarfed it down, their first warm meal in days.[83] In an act of compassion and thanks, one soldier traded the Langers a small, half-eaten box of Chiclets chewing gum,[84] the last of his military-issued K-rations.

Because Wereth lies near the border of Germany, and at one time was part of the country, some of its residents were still partial to the Fatherland—so partial, that one neighbor outed Mathias and Maria Langer by alerting the German military about the US soldiers hidden in their home. When Nazi forces arrived at their door, the family scrambled to move the eleven into the basement, where the Langers were already stowing two countrymen on the run but, fearing this would endanger the family's safety, the soldiers surrendered.

> The Langer eight mourned the American Eleven and the inevitable punishment the Germans would impose, as they watched the captors and captives disappear into the pasture.

Now, captured despite their best efforts, the GIs were led with hands above their heads outside into the snow, where they sat for hours as Nazi soldiers terrorized each one, chasing the men in an enemy Volkswagen Schwimmwagen truck, intentionally running over them, breaking bones, and slaying one outright. The other barely surviving men were bayoneted, shot, killed, and dismembered. All of this savagery was in direct violation of the rules of the Geneva Convention, which clearly prohibited the mistreatment of prisoners of war, let alone assassination and murder.[85] The neighbors reported having heard gunshots in the night. To ensure the Americans were dead, even after having bashed in their jaws with the butts of rifles and cutting off fingers, the Nazis shot each soldier in the head; the eleven bodies were dumped out of sight in the snow-ridden cow pasture.[86] The torture, maiming, and murder of the 333rd soldiers—and their remains—wouldn't be discovered for another two months.

Christmas 1944 came and went, and shortly after, a Luftwaffe airplane hovered over Wereth and dropped an explosive near the Langer home, striking and seriously hurting four of their children; Mathias and Maria couldn't help but feel this was long-awaited retribution by the Germans for providing aid and comfort to the Allies. The children were treated and discharged from a hospital just minutes away, and the family who had helped so many, was reluctant to return home in fear of further vengeance. Luckily, their family was spared; but sadly, they would begin the new year on another dreadful note.[87]

AFTER THE SNOW CLEARED

American forces cleared most of the Germans from the area surrounding Wereth by the end of January 1945. Some were captured but most abandoned their battle positions and fled, leaving behind heavy weapons and equipment in the melting snow. The Langer family, and many others, undoubtedly, had not attended Sunday Mass for weeks because the weather was fierce, and the firefight too close to home. But, as Mother Nature allowed and enemy troops fled, replaced by our 99th Infantry Division, it was finally safe to step outside. The oldest child, Hermann Langer, was first to leave the house. As he approached the cow pasture, he spotted a farm tool protruding from the snow—at least, he wished it was only a tool. Hermann quickly realized it was a human hand and ran to get his father.[88] Mathias Langer approached the US Army command post to report his son's discovery. They ushered the Americans toward the pasture, where they found a heap of African American soldiers buried beneath the disappearing snow.

The Army dispatched a graves-registration unit to Wereth, where they snapped photos for the developing investigation. Preliminary findings presented clear evidence that the 333rd soldiers endured excruciating torture before being massacred. Fellow brothers in arms recovered and removed the men's bodies to a hospital unit for identification and autopsy examination, where medical staff discovered gunshot wounds, faces and heads bashed in, and dismembered and missing fingers. There were broken jaws, numerous stab wounds—including bayonets to eyes—and evidence that some had been run over by enemy vehicles.[89] Identification was found on some of the bodies, but rings, watches, and necklaces had been removed and stolen by German soldiers. A few other personal effects were discovered on or near the men's bodies; a Bible, photographs, an old pocket watch, and some coins.[90] When it came to finding those responsible for the massacre, there was no clear evidence as to which German unit was responsible, though the Waffen-SS, First SS Panzer Reconnaissance Battalion, commanded by Major Gustav Knittel, had been in the area at the time. The Langer family knew which neighbor had given them up to the Germans (a woman married to a Nazi soldier) but never publicized an identity.[91]

In 1947, two years after the bodies were discovered, the superficial investigation was officially closed—and not a single newspaper shared the story of the Black 333rd soldiers and what they had endured during the war for their country. The investigative report was classified "secret," sealed, closed, and completely forgotten.[92] A 1949 Senate Armed Services Committee carefully documented, in official records, twelve, specific incidents of American soldiers and Belgian civilian massacres by Nazi troops, publishing them in a final 1949 Congressional Report on War Crimes. The committee listed, in detail, the name of every massacred victim—civilian and military—and where each crime took place. African American GIs, massacred on December 17, 1944, in Wereth, Belgium, were omitted from the report.[93]

Is it possible that Americans, including members of the Black press, voiced their belief that our media failed to report the atrocity to avoid offending German American citizens, completely lacking concern for African American citizens—or the truth?

Despite its (shallow) investigation and documentation, and next to twelve other massacres of American troops and Belgian civilians during the Battle of the Bulge, the Wereth massacre was the only war crime labeled *CLASSIFIED* by the US Army.[94]

BECAUSE OF A BELGIAN BOY

For decades, the tragedy had seemed to escape everyone except one person—Hermann Langer, the twelve-year-old Belgian boy who ventured out that one winter day. Hermann left Wereth in 1961 but never forgot the African American soldiers his family had welcomed into their home. Instead, to remember the fallen, he erected a stone cross at the site of the massacre fifty years later, on September 11, 1994, to honor the "Wereth Eleven." For the rest of his life, Langer would suffer from nightmares of finding the mutilated bodies[95] of those American heroes, but he had also never forgotten their kindness:

> "I will be very surprised if one day an American came here to see this cross. Who knows—if one comes, maybe he will give me a Chicklet, like the GI s did in 1944."[96]

And he was surprised. In 1998, a group held the first, official ceremony at that same pasture in Wereth, coming together to honor the valor of the eleven, once-unknown, African American soldiers. In 2001, Belgians, and the now officially recognized US Wereth Memorial

Committee, started raising funds for a permanent memorial. The money raised was used to purchase pastureland surrounding the original shrine at the massacre site, where the committee established a monument and plaque, dedicating the site on May 23, 2004, to the 333rd Black Battalion[97] and all segregated US units that fought in Europe during World War II. The memorial is believed to be the only one of its kind in Europe.[98]

At the annual remembrance service on May 1, 2007, US Army General Dennis Via, commanding general, US Army Europe and 7th Army, delivered a speech[99] and the Army Color Guard presented the colors of the United States and Belgium. Each guest, American and Belgian, was presented a small box of Wrigley's Chiclets chewing gum to symbolically commemorate the heartfelt exchange of compassion by the 333rd soldiers. In 2013, the US Congress introduced a Congressional Resolution, calling upon the Senate Armed Services Committee to amend the 1949 subcommittee report to include a proper recognition of the massacre of the eleven Black soldiers on December 17, 1944.[100] The resolution read:

> Our country shall be forever grateful to every member of the Greatest Generation who contributed to the defeat of Nazism in Europe and laid down their lives so that future generations could enjoy the blessings of freedom. Every now and then, it takes history a while to accurately reflect the monumental moments that have helped chart the course. The valiant efforts and unequal sacrifice of the Wereth Eleven soldiers deserved to be commemorated in our country's history. These are men whose heroic story has been lost to time, but whose names must be honored, and whose account we must share today and in the future.[101]

The African American soldiers from the 333rd Field Artillery Battalion, forever known as the Wereth Eleven, were identified as:[102]

Private Curtis Adams, age twenty-four, South Carolina

Corporal Mager Bradley, age twenty-seven, Mississippi

Private First Class George Davis, age twenty-six, Alabama

Staff Sergeant Thomas Forte, age twenty-nine, Mississippi

Technical Corporal Robert Green, age twenty-two, Georgia
Private First Class James Leatherwood, age twenty-four, Mississippi

Private Nathaniel Moss, age twenty-three, Texas

Private First Class George Moten, age twenty-two, Alabama

Technical Sergeant William Pritchett, age twenty-two, Alabama

Technical Sergeant James Stewart, age thirty-seven, West Virginia

Private First Class Due Turner, age twenty-two, Arkansas

Initially, these war heroes were buried with military honors at the American Henri-Chappelle military cemetery in Liege, Belgium, but following the war, by family request, some of the men were returned to the US and reinterred at military or hometown cemeteries. All eleven men received full military honors. The fully funded memorial site is still attracting military personnel, history buffs, tourists, and civilians paying homage to the American GIs, who were once lost beneath the snow, found by a Belgian boy, and memorialized forever.

CHAPTER SEVEN

At War's End

MONTHS BEFORE the declaration of the end of WWII, survivors of the 333rd Field Artillery Battalion were absorbed into their sister unit, the 969th, and, together, they delivered devastating fire support to the 101st Airborne Division in the siege of Southern Belgium's Bastogne from December 20–27. By battle's end, the American death toll had climbed, but the Allies finally repulsed the German incursion, killing, or maiming many of its men. Bastogne was encircled by the enemy one day and liberated by an array of American infantry that week, many from Lt. Gen. Patton's Third Army, including multiple African American units.

The heroic 969th (including remnants of the unrelenting 333rd) was awarded the Presidential Distinguished Unit Citation for its actions supporting the Bastogne encirclement, the highest honor bestowed by the president of the United States upon an army unit during World War II.[103] The battalion also received the Belgian Croix de Guerre (War Cross) with Palm for their heroic actions defending Bastogne.[104] During the Battle of the Bulge, the 333rd Battalion sustained more casualties than any other VIII Corps Field Artillery Battalion within General Patton's Third Army. Of the 500 officers and enlisted men serving, at least 220—nearly half—were killed, wounded, or captured by Nazi forces. The Battalion was officially dissolved in late 1945, after earning a reputation as one of the best field artillery units in the European Theater of Operations. By the time bodies of the Wereth Eleven were discovered in February 1945, the Battle of the Bulge had ended; the cost of victory proved heavy with substantial

American losses, though, despite its extensive fighting force and weaponry, the enemy had lost even more.

On May 8, 1945, World War II ended after the Germans surrendered to Allied Forces.

After the war, the US Army investigated half a million Belgians for collaboration with Germany and, of these, almost fifty-six thousand were prosecuted. The majority received prison sentences and thousands were executed.[105]

SLOW JUSTICE

After commanding the massacre of the White US soldiers at Malmedy, the path of justice for German SS Lieutenant Colonel Peiper was long but sure. In 1946, he and other German leaders were arrested, charged with war crimes, tried, and convicted.

He and others received death sentences but commuted to life sentences two years later following their confessions. In 1956, he was released from prison when it was revealed that his confession had been coerced by threats and physical violence to his family.[106] His arrest had come about following extensive investigation and follow-up by the US Military.

Now free from prison, he was hired to manage American sales for Porsche, Inc. Later, he worked for the Volkswagen Corporation in the same position while also serving as an interpreter and becoming active in German veteran organizations.[107]

By now he had changed his identity, believing he could hide in plain sight. Unbeknownst to him, he had been tracked by former Free French Resistance Fighters who are believed to have orchestrated the firebombing of his home in Traves Haute-Saome, France in 1976. He was burned to death. "His judgment cometh and that right soon."[108] It didn't come soon, but it did come.

Although extensive investigation and follow-up had resulted in

Lieutenant Colonel Peiper's arrest, there was no follow-up by US authorities in the massacre and dismemberment of the eleven Black soldiers at Wereth, Belgium. Why would the war department waste the time? It seems clear that an extensive investigation and follow-up was not conducted due to racism, plain and simple. After all, the victims were just Black soldiers. Their lives were worth less than their White counterparts. This easily followed the trend of treating them as second-class soldiers even while at war, and often not caring what did, or did not, happen to them.

Much of this was evidenced by the Army's policy of not presenting Black soldiers an award higher than the coveted Silver Star medal, no matter the valor,[109] their wounds not being treated by White Army nurses. The war was almost over and there appeared to be a rush to return to "normal."

FINAL VICTORS

It's appalling that it took sixty years for the US government and Belgian civilians to provide proper recognition for the sacrifices made by these African American soldiers during the Second World War. Members of the 333rd Field Artillery Battalion always knew their patriotic service would be treacherous or fatal. And for many, like the Wereth Eleven, it was both.

When a person enlists, or is drafted, into the military, there is the silent, inherent understanding that he or she could end up going to war. When soldiers enter a war zone, there's an inherent expectation they could be wounded, lose their life (or, if fortunate, captured and their life spared), fighting for a noble cause—it's all part of the agreement. Still, today, under the Geneva Convention, if a soldier survives battle but is captured by the enemy, he or she can expect to leave captivity and safely return home; such soldier has no reason to believe they might be hunted down, murdered, dismembered, and left in a field in the name of winning a war. It should never happen now, and it was never supposed to have happened then.

In the end, the men of the 333rd Field Artillery Battalion were the victorious contenders. Perhaps some of their German executioners who had masqueraded as noble soldiers were killed running from a later fight, their bodies riddled by fire from the 969th Field Artillery, Black brothers of the 333rd. Some of the murderers could have even escaped, eventually throwing away their weapons as cowards, having lost face and lost the war. The Wereth Eleven were buried with full military pageantry and honors, their names now preserved on scrolls and monuments for the world to see in all posterity.

African American artillery troops on march in Belgium. Photo courtesy of National Archives and Records Administration.

Men of the 333rd emplace 155-mm howitzers in a Normandy field, June 28, 1944. Photo courtesy of National Archives and Records Administration.

Body of American soldier borne on stretcher near Malmedy, Belgium, where the Germans committed many atrocities. Photo courtesy of National Archives and Records Administration.

Surviving members of the 333rd Battalion, TSgt William E. Thomas and PFC Joseph Jackson (part of 969th Field Artillery Battalion at the time) prepare Easter eggs for Hitler, 1945. Photo courtesy of National Archives and Records Administration..

6888 soldier sorting mail. Source: Photo courtesy of US Signal Corps.

PART FOUR

We Deliver
6888th Central Postal
Directory Battalion

Captain Adams drilling her company at the first WAAC training center in Fort Des Moines, Iowa, 1943. Photo courtesy of National Archives and Records Administration.

Whatever made you 'blankety-blank' women think you could be soldiers?[1]

—6888th Recruit Gertrude LaVigne
Quoting an unknown drill sergeant

INTRODUCTION

In the mid-1990s I attended a memorial service for the mother of one of my childhood friends; she was also *my* mother's close friend, the two of them part of the same women's religious organizations and having had sons who grew up in the same neighborhood, at the same school. When I stepped into the chapel to celebrate her life and mourn the community's loss, I was astonished to learn she was even more than a mother, friend, and churchgoer. It wasn't her good works in our community that surprised me, and we all knew how patriotic she was, always displaying a flag for special observances. What was most mesmerizing was a single passage toward the end of the program:

> "As a young woman, she was a World War II soldier in the Women's Army Corps (WAC) and served overseas in a post office Unit."

As a boy who was fascinated with the military and had been in her home many times, I would have noted any photos or certificates hanging, but there were none. No one, as far back as I can remember, ever mentioned her military service—neither her, her son, nor my mother. She was a member of the "Greatest Generation,"[2] as television news anchor and writer Tom Brokaw deemed it. She joined the war, performed her mission, came home, raised a family, and carried on with civilian life, just as the other hundreds of thousands of women in WWII. Because of her, and people from her generation (and my own military career), I became enthralled with the history, and bravery, of the WWII "Post Office Unit."

★ ★ ★

During the Vietnam War (1963–1975), combat scenes of the battle aired on local and national television, after having been filmed in Vietnam a day, or two earlier, inviting the controversial war into the living rooms of millions of Americans. Family members of soldiers and marines were stuck to their screens back at home, realizing their spouses, fathers, brothers, or children had talked about those very places—the war zone—in recent letters home.

The almost real-time reporting was chalked up to advanced technology in the form of wire services, radio and TV, and major newspapers and magazines. The rapidly released news over current events could now inundate the Department of Defense with floods of telephone calls and inquiries from concerned family and friends acknowledging their loved one's involvement in the war and asking whether they had been reported missing, wounded, or dead. The US government took extraordinary measures to ensure that information regarding ongoing or future operations, no matter how small, were never leaked to the press. But to err is human, and many servicemembers were not aware they may have unintentionally violated military policy by divulging closely held information regarding confidential military overseas unit locations or pending tactical operations. The information may not necessarily have been top secret, but, perhaps, operationally sensitive as to something further down the chain, like FOUO (for official use only) or as basic as the "need to know."

The humanity of enterprise is that military personnel in the intelligence business can unknowingly be the culprit—especially a low-ranking, eighteen-year-old messenger stationed at headquarters who, on a prideful mission to impress his peers, wants to be the first to give the scoop—the lowdown—of the operation to fellow servicemen. In some instances, media and news correspondents positioned themselves at or near the line of departure of a planned military operation in an effort to capture on film the units' arrival by air insertion or ground convoy. Such footage quickly made its way back to the US on our five-o'clock news. With the advent of cassette and 8-track tape recorders, soldiers could record and send voice messages from Vietnam to their loved ones, the greetings arriving home just days after posting their packages at the local APO (Army Post Office) facility on base in Southeast Asia. Such convenient technology inevitably led to a decline in letter writing, now that receivers back home could *hear and feel* the thoughts and emotions of the men they loved; the written word in the form of letters home would never be quite the same again.

The new generation of communicating between the battlefield and home—outwardly connecting American soldiers in places like Iraq and Afghanistan in times like the 1990s and 2000s—was generated by the rise of cellular phones (and today, smartphones and satellite phones), which conveniently allow soldiers the ability to speak to family and friends even during an actual combat firefight, much like a scene from a campy sci-fi movie.

Note: The real danger of real-time communication was, and is, discouraged by the Defense Department with active measures in place to thwart exchanges under the pretext of violation of operational security (OPSEC).

Today's technological advances in communication would be alien (and frightening) to a 1940s soldier who solely relied on long-hand letters delivered by a WWII postal system. For the millions of soldiers transitioning from country to country and town to town, through bloody battlefields in all kinds of severe weather, receiving these highly valued, personal letters was their only connection to home, and they could take weeks to arrive.

THE RIGHT ROBERT SMITH

Unlike modern warfare, World War II was a mobile war in which military units, Allied and enemy alike, were on the never-ending move. The constant maneuvering of forces across several countries in Southern, Eastern, and Northern Europe, executing each one's unique operation, wreaked havoc on the US military mail-delivery system, causing extensive backlogs of overseas mail. Most incoming mail to Europe from the US at the time was processed in England, which became the epicenter of the stagnation. The on-the-go nature of operations made it extremely difficult for postal personnel to know where to send or forward letters and packages; even when a unit *was* located, it was already on the move, again—always here today and gone tomorrow.

During wartime (and in peace), no matter the decade or circumstance, it's impossible to overstate the importance of mail for the morale of soldiers. For most, incoming mail is almost as important as food, pay call, and ammunition, and the shortage of any of those would affect the outcome of any combat operation. The critical nature of mail efforts was addressed in the 1942 annual report by the then postmaster general, which stated,

> "The Post Office, War, and Navy Departments realize fully that frequency and rapid communication with parents, associates, and other loved ones strengthen fortitude, enlivens patriotism, makes loneliness endurable, and inspires to even greater devotion the men and women who are carrying on our fight far from home and from friends."[3]

YOU'VE GOT MAIL (SOMEWHERE)

During the war against Hitler, and for months after, the US military was significantly challenged with delivering the *correct* mail to the *correct* soldier. It was a challenge for a number of reasons. With more than seven million American personnel in the European Theater alone, many shared common names. For example, there were more than 7,500 variations of the name Robert Smith[4] within the Army, Navy, Marine Corps, Air Corps, and Seabees (including tens of thousands of other staff and congressmen) with first names like Rob, Robbie, Robby, Bob, Bobbie, Bobby, Bert, Sonny, Bubba, and Junior, and last names Smith, Smyth, Smithy, or Schmidt—all written on envelopes headed overseas. Thousands of outgoing letters and packages were often incompletely addressed to "Company A" (with more than five hundred Company A's in existence) or "Headquarters Company F" with no unit identification.

By autumn 1944, warehouses and airplane hangars in Birmingham, England, were crammed with millions of pieces of mail addressed to American servicemen and women, Red Cross, and government employees. Sluggish delivery was affecting morale, one general predicting it would take the latter part of six months to one year to clear out, even if the mail had stopped flowing in that very second. In a single month, with workers manning three shifts around the clock, processing sixty-five thousand pieces of mail per shift, seven days per week, the total amounted to almost five million processed pieces.[5] It was clear to postal workers that thousands of service members, and others, were receiving letters from home much later than intended and, in some cases, had never received a single letter or package from parents, spouses, friends, neighbors, or the church members who frequently held letter-writing campaigns for our military.

Throughout WWII, the European Theater also suffered a shortage of qualified postal officers, which naturally contributed to the ever-growing backlog. To help the cause, the postal division continuously sought to secure additional officers by requisition from the reinforcement system.

CHAPTER ONE

---★---

Women to the Rescue

UNEASY—THOUGH BRAVE—in their realities of giving up husbands, sons, fathers, and brothers to World War II efforts, American women would go on to play equally important roles, at home and in uniform, during the war against Nazi Germany. The United States was committed to full-on war after the December 1941 attack on Hawaii's Pearl Harbor, using every last asset to our advantage, including women.

General Eisenhower felt that he could not win the war without the aid of the women in uniform:

> "The contribution of the women of America, whether on the farm or in the factory or in uniform, to D-Day was a sine qua non of the invasion effort."[6]

Sensing the nation would require all hands on deck, nearly three hundred fifty thousand women would ultimately enlist and serve in uniform, at home, and abroad, volunteering within organizations like the Women's Army Auxiliary Corps (WAAC, later called WAC—Women's Army Corps), Navy Women's Reserve (WAVES: Women Accepted for Voluntary Emergency Services), Marine Corps Women's Reserve, Coast Guard Women's Reserve (SPARS: Semper Paratus—Always Ready), Women Airforce Service Pilots (WASPS), and Army and Navy reserve corps.

Note: Unlike Allied powers, the Axis forces (Germany, Italy, Japan) hesitated to appoint women to WWII efforts; Hitler, especially, considered Americans immoral for putting our women to work, as German wives and mothers were expected to tend to the home and produce more children for the Third Reich.

The WAAC (specifically, because of its uniqueness) originated with female recruits and enlistees from across the country, mainly in the South and mostly from Texas. This is where its first director, Oveta Culp Hobby, wife of 1915–1917 Texas Governor William P. Hobby,[7] was tasked with the widespread search. After Hobby had petitioned White women from her home state, she expanded her outreach toward the West Coast and opened the opportunity to African Americans.

WASHING MACHINES TO WAR HEROES

Black women were only accepted into the WAAC because of pressure placed on the War Department by African American political organizations demanding racial equality. Black activists closely monitored the War Department's plans for developing a women's corps. When it was revealed that a Texan (Hobby) was appointed director of the WAAC, they protested on grounds that Hobby, because of her Southern background, would discriminate against Negro women. Under pressure, and only after Director Hobby allocated forty of the first officer trainee slots to African American women, did the opposition to her new position taper off.

The original goal for the WAAC was to serve alongside male soldiers in the US, in logistical, administrative, and technical positions, which would free more men to serve in combat units overseas. It was the Army's policy at the time, however, that Black men were relegated to only support units and would never see actual combat. During the early months of the WAAC, because of overt racism, Black women received the same treatment, in that their positions within the Army were domestic, like cleaning White WAAC barracks and as charwomen and laundresses[8]—civilian duties deemed unfit for their light-skinned counterparts, who were automatically appointed the more sought-after jobs.

It wasn't long until First Lady Eleanor Roosevelt and her activist friend, Mary McLeod-Bethune, would take a stand and push for permanent change and eventually win back the rights of African American women to fill the positions for which they had originally volunteered or were recruited. Early on, McLeod-Bethune was a champion for the African American women in the WAAC. She praised their accomplishments and provided emotional, political, and economic support as the women swam against the tides of institutional racism. She was not only active in social causes—she was well known in Black communities throughout the country for having founded (and served as president of) the Bethune-Cookman College. She went on to become the formative president of the National Council of Negro Women,[9] a large "organization of organizations" still influential for African American women, and their families and communities, to this day.

The Women's Army Auxiliary Corps activated in March 1942[10] and, shortly after, converted to the Women's Army Corps (WAC).[11] It had become an official branch of the Army, and after just a couple months,[12] the women of the WAC were officially eligible for the same pay and benefits as men within the same rank. Director Hobby was given a direct commission to the US Army rank of lieutenant colonel but retained her title of director.[13] She was eventually promoted to colonel in July 1943.[14]

McLeod-Bethune closely monitored what she called, "My WACs," especially when it came to racial slander and injustice,[15] as ignorance and bigotry ran just as rampant toward the new WAC as the old. As if spirit was never part of the change, the WAC maintained restrictive quotas on the number of African American women joining the ranks versus the continued open-door policy afforded to White women. Black females were capped at 10.6 percent[16] (theoretically, the percentage of Blacks in the nation), but their numbers never exceeded 9.5 percent during the war. The Army Nurse Corps fared even worse—African American nurses equaled *less than 1 percent* of the US Army Nurse Corps in World War II.[17]

There were numerous cases of proven, deliberate discrimination toward Black women within the newly established WAC. For example, in June 1944, four members protested their assignment to perform "dirty duties" in an alleged spirit of blatant racism. A court-martial board convened including the nine White officers who had charged the WACs with insubordination and laziness. The women's defense was simple: the officers' order to carry out menial tasks was unfair and unjust. Even then, all four members were convicted and sentenced to one year at hard labor followed by dishonorable discharge.[18] It wasn't until a year later, after learning about the discharged women, that three congressmen requested an investigation, which was supported by multiple letters of protest to the War Department written by the Black press and organizations.[19] After an official inquiry and thorough review of the case facts, coupled with new witness statements, the court overturned the women's verdicts, citing blatant racism as a factor. The four Black WACs were restored to duty.[20]

The court-martial sentences were voided on the grounds that the court had improperly convened. An investigation revealed that the accuser, a general officer, summoned the board *and* served as the board chairman. This meant the court proceedings were not only inappropriate but illegal.

This was just a microcosm of the discrimination faced by female, African American soldiers throughout the war. In another unit, which was combined with a White women's hospital unit at a Southern installation, Black women possessing training and education were also assigned menial jobs like washing walls and carrying bedpans at a hospital for White soldiers.[21] One of these soldiers had even earned a doctorate in theology, was an ordained minister, and joined the military to serve as a chaplain—only to end up scrubbing the floors for people[22] who saw her as less than a White woman.

The intervention of national Black leaders would be the only reason these commonplace issues were ever addressed and, *some*, rectified. After several White WAC units were dispatched overseas to serve in the European Theater, African American organizations pressed the War Department to extend the opportunity to Black WAC units. Finally, in early December 1944, the War Department reluctantly conceded and assigned an overseas opportunity to what would later be known as the 6888th Central Postal Directory Battalion. With war ablaze and military postal issues on the rise (and unknown to the women at the time), the future all-Black battalion would set out to make the difference they fought so hard to make.

HERSTORY IN THE MAKING

The US military began accepting volunteers for its new postal battalion from existing African American WAC units in air and service forces. Despite the slow-moving success, 824 enlisted women and thirty-one officers would make up the all-Negro "Six-Triple-Eight." The new, fully female battalion boasted a headquarters company for administrative and service support and line Companies A, B, C, and D, all of which were commanded by a captain or first lieutenant. The unit would eventually bear the responsibility of receiving, processing, and arranging for mail delivery to the field within the European Theater, under the authority of the highly qualified Black major (later lieutenant colonel) Charity Adams.

Higher education was highly stressed in Adams's home, especially as her parents were both college graduates with advanced degrees, her mother a former schoolteacher and her Latin- and Greek-speaking father an ordained minister in the African Methodist Episcopal

Church. Adams followed closely in their footsteps, especially her mother's, as she graduated college and taught mathematics for four years at a public school in her hometown in Columbia, South Carolina. She had only completed half of her master-level studies when the War Department invited her to join the WAAC, and later, the WAC. Adams graduated from officer candidate school as part of the first African American WAC unit and had served as a captain for more than two years when she was granted the opportunity to command a company at the Fort Des Moines Provisional Army Officer Training School (OTS) in Iowa, the first of its kind for WAC recruits.

She had extensive experience traveling the United States on previous assignments, leaving her mark in nearly every region, including in Washington, DC. She maintained superior officer efficiency reports and developed a sparkling reputation as a leader and, upon selection, was promoted to the field-grade rank of major. Adams became one of the only two female Negro WAC majors in the Army at the time, her counterpart stationed at the nation's Pentagon. Considering racial and social climates at the time in segregated America and with the roaring of Hitler's War, it's easy to understand why the United States's first Negro, female battalion commander found life-changing inspiration in activists Eleanor Roosevelt and Mary McLeod-Bethune. Adams cherished an existing personal connection with both advocates, having been interviewed by Roosevelt and McLeod-Bethune, along with other influential African American women, before her appointment as commander of the 6888th.

With that, and with millions of women in factory positions back in the US and serving in the Red Cross, America's military was thrust into a new, progressive direction with the addition of Black women into World War II. The Army continued to recruit and fill command positions in the 6888th Postal Unit, assigning the remainder from units throughout the country, each of them graduates of Fort Des Moines with previous command and leadership experience. Once fully organized, the battalion began training to relocate for an undisclosed mission to another location, Fort Oglethorpe, Georgia—a totally segregated facility, complete with separate drinking fountains to remind Negroes that, despite their voluntary efforts in a global war fueled by hate, militarism, and economic depression, their rights to equality weren't as inherent as those of their White sisters and brothers. And once the 6888th arrived at Oglethorpe, the women were assigned training regimes similar to men in the Army, minus any weapons, because—like Negro men—women were never intended to deploy overseas, period. To (hardly) compensate for weapons, the women were trained in jiu-jitsu, a close-combat martial art,[23] the Army believing (or simply not caring) that if they were forced to engage in literal hand-to-hand combat, *maybe* the women could subdue the enemy with nonlethal force.

Either way, traditional weapons training was never provided to the 6888th. Training at Fort Oglethorpe taught the postal unit how to respond if captured, how to board a ship via cargo net, and how to climb ropes. They learned to distinguish between friendly and enemy ships, aircraft, and weapons of all grades, crawled beneath fire on infiltration courses, practiced gas drills, and were instructed on how to occupy roadside ditches when attacked by enemy aircraft.

> Even with intense training under their belts, the soldiers had zero clue as to what would be their mission—aside from a simple mention from leadership about crossing international waters with the possibility of German U-boat attacks. Now, the women had an idea that they must be headed for war-torn Europe.

In early January 1945, the women traveled by train to their demarcation point, Camp Shanks, New York, where many Black brothers in arms had also waited for war. Come February 3, after hanging tight for three extra days until U-boat activity halted in the North Atlantic, the first wave sailed for Britain in a convoy of several ships, with blessings in tow from Colonel (and WAC Director) Hobby, who had flown from Washington DC to see them off. The second wave would follow in fifty-five days on a vessel, the SS *Île de France*, a former fancy French cruise ship turned military transporter, which hauled the hundreds of troops—all men, except for the women of the 6888th—plus, military equipment, bombs, and ammunition overseas. For segregation purposes, female soldiers were assigned to two-person billets on the upper deck, while men, all White, took the lower, each level with its own mess facility. During the eleven-day crossing, the soldiers survived several enemy-boat scares but ultimately arrived safely at Prestwick, just outside of Glasgow, Scotland, on February 11.

The green group of soldiers, Black and White, female and male, were instantly launched to war when a German V-1 rocket exploded near the unloading dock, forcing the newcomers to seek cover—the women with no weapons and limited combat training, which the Army still had no intentions of fixing, even after the enemy explosion on day one.

CHAPTER TWO

—⭐—

The House Women Built

THE NEWLY FORMED, and undoubtedly eager, Six-Triple-Eight made it overseas to Europe in two waves and three contingents, beginning January 1945, with Maj. Adams and Executive Officer Capt. Noel Campbell, the first to bid loved ones farewell and head for Europe, the eye of the war storm.

The two women shared the Douglas C-54 Skymaster cargo plane (practically nonexistent today but occupied the skies throughout WWII) with thirteen male officers, engaging with thick, Southern accents, other male, civilian war correspondents, and one other woman, an unidentified civilian. Because it was customary for civilian VIPs, like Hollywood celebrities, to travel to war zones to perform for troops, it wasn't rare for soldiers to share the skies with entertainment big wigs. On this flight, reportedly, Adams and Campbell spotted a woman who could have been Judy Garland, Bette Davis, Lauren Bacall, or one of the many celebrities who entertained American troops overseas in WWII—with a heaping luggage pile, hat boxes, and floor-length gowns in bags, all carried onboard by enlisted men[24] who were surely delighted to assist the star.

Unaware of military security classifications, the African American women assumed they would share a plane with scores of other soldiers headed overseas and were shocked to discover they were granted Priority II clearance, with Priority I reserved for the president and top military officials; the soldiers had bumped some congressman on an inspection tour or junket, a lavish trip paid for with American tax dollars. As directed, their sealed orders were opened one hour into the flight and they discovered they were en route to London via Glasgow, Scotland. The pilot took the southern route, landing in Bermuda for their first stop and overnight stay before reaching the Azores Islands to refuel. Another touchdown and two more to go, Maj. Adams and Capt. Campbell later descended into Prestwick, just outside Glasgow, Scotland, before they were finally routed to London aboard a small, propeller-driven DC-3 plane.

Once the Black women landed on United Kingdom soil, they were, officially, the first female African American officers on the war-torn continent, other than our military nurses.

White officers and enlistees were alarmed by their presence, so much so that Adams and Campbell were rarely saluted by fellow officers junior to them, and enlisted soldiers, who probably had never seen African American Army women in their lives. But the new arrivals had a mammoth task ahead, so they pushed forward to coordinate duties and responsibilities in London, despite the UK's warm welcome they had received. Quickly, it was off to Paris to report to Lt. Gen. John H. Lee, commanding general within the communications zone (COMMZ) in the European Theater of Operations.

Note: This was the rear area of operations where all wartime support functions and logistics were planned, coordinated, and executed. With Paris liberated after the D-Day landings, General Lee had relocated Comm-Z headquarters from England to across the English Channel and into Europe.

Once the plane touched down in Paris, The City of Love, Light, and Romance, the soldiers were warmly welcomed by their host, WAC headquarters director Maj. Mary Weems of the COMMZ team.

At a reception in their honor, hosted by Gen. Lee in his military quarters at Hotel George Cinq, the American women were introduced to COMMZ senior officers and staff. (Later, Adams and Campbell had the honor of meeting Benjamin O. Davis Sr., the first-ever African

American to rise to the rank of brigadier general—a progressive step for Black minorities in the WWII era.) That night, in the same breath, Lee commanded Adams and her 6888th Battalion to "Pass in Review" (a traditional military inspection), just two days after her unit's arrival in England. There is no doubt Adams anticipated a speedy entry into the war, but never did she imagine her first mission would be a Pass in Review in the presence of Gen. Lee. She accompanied Gen. Davis as he conducted an inspection of the troops upon their arrival aboard the *Ile de France*. Surely intimidated, Adams would solely march her troops before the general. She knew her soldiers were walking off their "sea legs" after having arrived just two days before from Glasgow. But orders were orders.

Note: Earlier-arriving units, Black and White, may have been welcomed by an Army band, but a Pass in Review was reserved for specific occasions. The age-old military tradition was typically carried out for large units welcoming a new commander, or for when a new unit was added to the command, like the first all-Black WAC unit arriving in the Theater. The new troops marched before their commander, as he observed them for the first time to evaluate their readiness, including factors like fitness.

PRECISION TESTED AND APPROVED

Adams's and Campbell-Mitchell's advance-party mission (arriving first to pave the way for the first wave 6888th soldiers) required ensuring all administrative and logistical requirements were finalized before bringing in the troops, including lodging, meals, transportation, and work facilities. Later, leaving Campbell-Mitchell behind to finish arrangements, Maj. Adams returned to Glasgow, Scotland, accompanying Gen. Davis to meet the early-arriving soldiers.

With high morale and fierce spirits in tow, the first wave of history-making WACs landed in Glasgow to greet the woman who would boldly lead them into WWII, Major Adams, who anxiously awaited the arrival of her all-Black battalion.

The next day, Adams, with the first of the WACs alongside her, departed Glasgow for the four-hundred-mile train ride to London (a five-hour trip), where the women were greeted by a thirty-piece Army band; a White band, at that—*it really was a strange, new world for these African Americans.* Bagpipes fading into the background, the soldiers trooped toward their temporary home at King Edward's School in London's suburb of Birmingham, hauling hefty, Army-provided duffel bags. This was the first Negro WAC unit within the European Theater, and its members were the first Negro women some residents of Birmingham had ever seen.

Two days after their London landing, the women underwent their Pass in Review, as requested by Lee, who had flown from France to London to meet his new 6888th battalion. The soldiers paraded the streets of Birmingham dressed in their Army Service Uniforms (ASUs): a fitted, buttoned jacket paired with a midlength, below-the-knee skirt, spotless cream-colored gloves, and military berets, called "Hobby Hats," named for Lieutenant Colonel Oveta Hobby, the WAC Director.[25] Onlookers in the area couldn't ignore the sound of dress heels hitting the pavement in unison, as the women marched in silence, except for the audible Army cadence deciding their every step. The all-woman, African American battalion strode toward their general, who stood off to the right with staff behind him. Going with tradition, it's safe to assume that Maj. Adams loudly commanded, "Eyes *right*," simultaneously rendering a right-hand salute to the general and signaling soldiers to sharply execute a quarter turn with just their heads, continuing to march. Once the battalion was completely past the general, Adams would command, "Ready, *front*," at which time the soldiers sharply returned their heads one-quarter turn to the front.

After completing their two-block Pass in Review, the early arrivers of the 6888th marched back to their quarters. The women received surprise accolades from the unexpected crowd of onlookers and, more importantly, Gen. Lee, who commented on the unit's impressive precision. Their review was a tremendous success.[26] The next day the new arrivals gathered in the assembly hall to soak in welcome speeches from General Davis, Major Adams, and military officers from the area with whom the 6888th would coordinate in the future. In her opening comments, Major Adams, their leader and fellow Black woman, remarked to her soldiers:

> "We are the best WAC unit ever sent into a foreign theater . . . the eyes of the public [will] be upon us, waiting for one slip in our good conduct or performance."[27]

And Adams was right—these women were history in the making, even though their role in WWII was still a mystery. Until that day.

The Army designated the battalion, in its infancy, as provisional (temporary and organized for a certain time and place) and attached to the First Base Post Office APO 640 for duty under Maj. Patricia Jernigan. On March 8, 1945, they received official designation as the 6888th Central Postal Directory, becoming the largest self-sustaining battalion in Birmingham at the time. Maj. Adams waited weeks for the senior headquarters to officially appoint her as battalion commander. With no response, Adams proceeded to publish her own orders (unsurprisingly) and forwarded a copy to higher headquarters, where Gen. Lee finally authenticated and approved her position as commander. Official orders were important because they authorized Adams to acquire and disburse pay, promote and demote soldiers, award decorations, and administer nonjudicial punishments, such authority granted to a battalion commander.

FROM SHAMBLES TO SHINGLES

All of the welcome bands and positive reviews in the world could not atone for the housing mess the 6888th would march into as the unit approached King Edward's school in Birmingham. The former swanky, first-class boys' school turned WAC military housing, was founded by King Edward VI in 1552 as part of the King's Foundation of the Schools.[28] The building had suffered extensive damage from the war, so much that the women described it as depressing and in shambles with holes in the roof, minimal heat, and insufficient hot water; the soldiers, at first having to communally bathe in cold water with no privacy. Each room suffered ventilation problems, and every hall was dark and narrow. The nearly four-hundred-year-old school was now a monument of the ravages of war—a half-hearted welcome to the African American soldiers and a "depressing" home away from home, according to some; four thousand miles away from everything they knew.[29]

But over time and with loads of (wo)manpower, the 6888th transformed the centuries-old boys' school into the first home of the first, all-Black, all-female American Army unit to live in barracks overseas in WWII. The soldiers restored the roof and worked manual carpentry, electrical, and plumbing jobs, each one using skills learned back at home in the US. The women brought back to life the boarding school's essential offices, classrooms, dormitories, gymnasium with basketball court, and kitchen facilities, and it finally felt like a home away from home. The unit would become self-contained, meaning the women operated their own mess hall, motor pool, and supply room.

The unit recruited clerks and payroll staff in its own members, each offering their expertise and experience to organize and fill positions, including a weaponless military police element for security and patrol of the barracks. Even their chapel was staffed with an organist, chaplain, and choir—all recruited from within. The in-house beauty parlor was staffed by former beauticians turned WWII soldiers, which drew in patrons from the area, once word spread of the women's operation, proving again that Europeans supported Black soldiers more than our own military and much of the US. When men arrived in war, they were given the essentials; when women—Black women—joined the war, they were left to their own devices.

Note: While overseas, the battalion even had to recruit three of its members, all former civilian morticians, to embalm the remains of two of their own soldiers who died in a jeep accident. There were no provisions for funerals, so the unit raised money to purchase a casket from a civilian vendor and buried their own with military honors.

The next wave of self-sufficient soldiers arrived in Scotland fifty-five days later, aboard the HMS *Queen Mary* (now permanently stationed in Long Beach, California) and was simply met by the battalion commander, the fanfare of the bagpipe band and dignitaries apparently reserved for their landing in London, where they would unite with the earlier arriving 6888th members. However, the last of the battalion received an underwhelming welcome from London, almost as if the African American Army women were already old news, or perhaps, no news at all.

CHAPTER THREE

England: Mission Commenced

WITH ALL FEET firmly on European soil, and with all hardworking hands on deck, the soldiers were organized by line companies and ready to contribute eight-hour shifts for twenty-four-seven operations. The 6888th Postal Battalion was open for business and enthusiastic to begin its mission in the Second World War: to receive, sort, process, and forward mail.

Maj. Adams's infant unit replaced a White postal battalion that had been redeployed to the United States because it was unable to successfully carry out its mission. The magnitude of the mail problem was overwhelming, mainly because the original team had failed to establish a coherent system for mail input and output. Of course, the Army *could* have created overlap between the two postal units to encourage continuity and communication within their mutual operation, but it never happened. The 6888th swooped into the unknown days after the White unit deployed home. Generally, in military operations the *gaining unit* sends liaison personnel to affect direct coordination with the *losing unit*, which would receive a briefing on the given, current situation, allowing the incoming unit to observe operations firsthand and gain some situational awareness. Had the US military provided the 6888th proper onboarding, the women's entry into Europe would have had a running start. Instead, they were forced to develop a completely new sorting system—from nothing. And the gap between the old unit leaving and the new battalion arriving, no matter how insignificant, exacerbated the already atrocious mail situation, stagnating the issue even further.

First order of business? To evaluate the issue of undeliverable mail caused by the on-the-go nature of Army units. With no system in place to buttress the *billions* of letters and boxes that would, by 1945, enter and leave the Army postal operation,[30] and with shortages in civilian and military workforces, mail had been accumulating for months (up to two years) before the 6888th arrived. In Birmingham, warehouses and airplane hangars were stacked from floor to ceiling with mail bags, some of which contained cakes and cookies baked for soldiers but eventually became food for nearby rats and mice. The women could not even be sure how many of these men were still alive and well enough to enjoy any sweets sent by their sweethearts. So, it became one of their first projects to help establish a system that would clear any backlog by determining which soldiers had been wounded and hospitalized, transferred, or discharged—or worse, killed in action.

Part of the fix was to assign each woman a role. From there, the crucial job clerk role was born. These officials were assigned boxes full of cards containing the numbers of the seven million military and serving civilians stationed in Europe, and when a unit moved, the postal directory was notified, and new locater cards were made for every soldier in a given unit, regardless of service branch (and with popular last names, like "Smith," they required multiple boxes dealing with a single surname). Often, mail was forwarded to soldiers whose units had already moved *before* the directory received new unit locator cards, resulting in returned mail, which was held by the postal unit until it received an updated locator card. Patton's Third Army, including various corps, divisions, and battalions, presented a greater challenge than most other units with the constant, speedy movement of his troops.

Only the new postal unit, with zero slack cut by the Army, could make the Third Army's mail miracle a reality with its new, proprietary system—and the women did. Patton's men began receiving mail *on par* with the Army's slower-moving units. The new locator process was one of many ways the 6888th Postal Battalion contributed to WWII, ensuring American soldiers continued receiving mail, which undoubtedly resulted in higher morale among our forces. The military expected the women would take at least six months to a year to clear the longstanding postal backlog. The all-Black female unit, working in a White man's world, boasted an unexpected work ethic and unfailing determination to accomplish and exceed its mission. The battalion worked around the clock seven days a week and cleared the entire backlog within three months; the 6888th had proved successful in half the allotted time and remained driven by their new motto:

No mail, low morale.[31]

The women of the only Black Army unit within Europe were assigned full responsibility and authority over their mail mission *without* male or White female control. Their leaders filled positions that African American females could never occupy before, becoming pioneers in the making. They led by example, were educated, trained, and competent—everything Blacks were not, according to conditions back in segregated America at the time.

To get word back to the States and to help solidify the Negro women's presence and efforts in WWII, an in-house public-relations officer took charge of interviewing battalion members and sending photos and newspaper stories focused on unit activity and ongoings back to America (all information, first cleared by Army Intelligence). A weekly battalion bulletin, *Special Delivery*, communicated current events to civilians with articles written by 6888th women. Public relations also headed fundraisers for charitable organizations, like the United Negro College Fund, one drive netting five thousand dollars to benefit African Americans attending what would later be termed *historical Black colleges*.

DISARMING HARMONY

With their around-the-clock operation, necessitating little to no disruption, an official set of established procedures would help eliminate, or at least avoid, any authorized, routine, or mundane non-mission-essential tasks. Major Adams knew that on any given day and without notice, a general (within their chain of command) could walk into the building and request an in-rank inspection. With that, she installed a military-standard protocol, directing one-third of her soldiers who had worked overnight shifts to sleep during the day, while the second shift staffed the mail. The major's quick thinking would ensure zero stops in the unit's twenty-four-seven operation.

During the battalion's first official inspection at the postal center, and with Adams's military-standard protocol in play, Gen. Lee unexpectedly walked into a half-empty inspection, demanding to know why so few soldiers were in formation. After his subordinate referenced military protocol, Lee abruptly suggested that every soldier be present for inspections, even though this wasn't the case for any other day-and-night Army operation (as soldiers were expected to switch off, unless in emergency situations like an enemy attack). Firmly, and with respect for Lee's higher rank, Adams reminded him that *his* higher headquarters demanded zero disruption to mail processing, given the extensive wartime backlog. The general scoffed: "Send a White lieutenant down to show her how to run the unit!"

Major Adams's response, in hindsight offhanded and off the cuff: "Over my dead body, sir."[32]

Their hasty exchange led to the general's departure, inspection outstanding, but not before Lee assured his subordinate that she would hear from him again. Adams's regret was instant. Just days later, court-martial charges were filed against her. Now *fully* lamenting the outburst toward her superior, the major was frightened of criminal charges that could banish from her command position on the grounds of disrespecting a senior officer and failing to obey orders.

But after wisely reviewing military regulations, Adams discovered that Lee had disobeyed a directive from Gen. Eisenhower's SHAPE Headquarters (Supreme Headquarters Allied Powers Europe), which prohibited unit commanders from using language that stressed racial segregation and could lead our allies to suspect disharmony among American troops. Authorized by her position (and considering Lee's inappropriate actions), Adams drew up court-martial charges against the general. Eventually, all legal action, against the major *and* general, was dropped.[33]

Note: Surprisingly, Adams and Lee would later serve under the same headquarters command—harmoniously.

With all potential charges negated and Maj. Adams's operational protocol secured in place, the 6888th resumed its uninterrupted mission to ensure war-weary soldiers received their letters and packages from home. But, while in *unsegregated* England, the battalion would continue to experience similar, egregious small-mindedness from Army leaders. For example, leaders would allow off-duty African American soldiers to participate in sports to help maintain their physical strength, mental health, and battle morale. Recreation specialists organized the Negro women into teams at their barracks for intramural play. Eventually, Blacks were allowed to compete against other WAC teams—*all White, naturally*—but because of fundamental racism on the US Army's part, the 6888th required permission to participate in head-to-head volleyball, softball, table tennis, and basketball tournaments against White women.

Even the American Red Cross was guilty of persecution of African American Army women, simultaneously touting its patriotic mission to spread morale among US troops with concerts, socials, and dances. Red Cross hotels and dance clubs were wide open for Whites (and even cordial to Black men), but the African American WACs were turned away at the door—no room for Negro women here.[34] In the same breath, Red Cross personnel located what they considered a "suitable" space, without informing Maj. Adams, and opened an unofficial African American women's Red Cross Club, furnishing the building with subpar equipment, in hopes the Negro women would quietly accept the bargain. But the 6888th refused to use the space, their leader and advocate Maj. Adams declaring that

> Negro women were not about to allow the Red Cross to practice segregation in their unit. The 6888th Central Postal Directory Battalion had already experienced enough racism from the US Army.[35]

UNDERDOGS ON TOP

The soldiers' time in progressive England was drawing to a close and unveiled a more positive, accepting side of humanity, compared to what African Americans were experiencing back home in segregated America (a place where women had finally won the right to vote just twenty years earlier—except for Black women in the South, of course). The female soldiers were treated with acceptance and respect in the UK, the British having witnessed our women take on and conquer key roles within a major mission, starting from the bottom with few resources. British citizens even refused to serve White American service members who disrespected Black WACs in their presence. Our overseas allies saw past the stereotype that Blacks were inherently subservient to Whites, as represented in film, print, and other forms of major media.

With their mail mission accomplished in England, and still residing in Birmingham, the 6888th received word that US President Franklin D. Roosevelt had died on April 12, 1945; a shocking revelation for everyone, including our mourning friends in the United Kingdom. Six-Triple-Eight commanding officer Maj. Adams received orders less than a month earlier to report to Paris in mid-May, but with the president's passing, her orders were revoked, and she would attend five of the thirty-plus memorial services in Roosevelt's honor;

the 6888th Central Postal Directory Battalion was represented by one member at each of the other services. Adams's orders were reissued on May 5, confirming her arrival in Paris on May 7, 1945. The first female, African American battalion commander touched down in France the day the Germans signed their formal act of military surrender—French citizens were celebrating in the streets, embracing and kissing each other and anyone in uniform, including Maj. Adams. Today, the world acknowledges Victory in Europe Day (VE Day) every year on May 8.

CHAPTER FOUR

---★---

Mission Accomplished: Moving Forward

AFTER VICTORIOUSLY clearing the mail backlog in Birmingham, England, on June 9, 1945, the 6888th transferred to Rouen, France, first by train to Southampton, then by boat across the English Channel, debarking at Le Havre en route, via another train, to Rouen.

Word spread of the women's pending arrival, and the unit was warmly welcomed with a surprise party, where they met the graces of many Black male soldiers who had traveled in military and civilian vehicles, including horse-drawn wagons,[36] to meet the now notable postal battalion; many had not seen an African American woman in three years. Awestruck, the men surrounded their counterparts with anticipation and curiosity and with questions about what schools they had attended and what people they knew, all while carrying the women's duffle bags and offering tours of their new, temporary home—it may have been the first time in their military careers that someone had offered to carry their bags.

The party was a rare, bright moment for the African American brothers and sisters in arms that left everyone with a renewed sense of family and purpose. The soldiers were elated to mingle with folks from back home and, hopefully, learn more about each other's war experiences and what was happening in Negro communities, since Army publications released zero news on African Americans in the US at the time; even in sports, most news sources would not print a story about Blacks, including Negro National Baseball League scores.

Note: The unexpected party was, perhaps, where the men

learned about the women's success in the European WAC Basketball Championship. After initial rejection from higher-ups because of inherent racism on the US Army's part, the women had finally been granted permission to go head-to-head in volleyball, softball, table tennis, and basketball tournaments against White women. The 6888th had put their mental and physical strength to the test, powered forward, and won the European WAC basketball championship.

HIGH MAIL AND LOW MORALE

Rouen's large, two-story, historic (even in WWII) Kaserne Tallandier, now part of a modern retail center, was the former military headquarters of nineteenth century French military leader Napoleon[37]—and, in postwar 1945, it served as the 6888th postal headquarters in France. Not without imperfections left by time and periods of war, the building was in running shape when the women arrived thanks to German prisoners of war (POWs) who had prepared it, allowing the unit to hit the ground running. The soldiers were also assigned living quarters in a nearby four-story building, equipped with proper ventilation and security walls, basic comforts denied early in the unit's formation.

The recent declaration of peace, after six bloody, agonizing years of international war, had sealed the end of an era for the entire world, but it was just the beginning, again, for the postal unit. Its mission to sort, process, and forward mail was as daunting as ever (if not more) with a similar situation as in England—run-ins with rodents in ceiling-high stacks of two- to three-year-old mail; this time, the unit ran into issues of open packages, torn and rummaged through by underprivileged prisoners and civilians. Theft became a major issue in Rouen when the US Army recruited German POWS and local civilians to work the years-old mail backlog. They had gone years without simple necessities, and the workers must have felt they hit a gold mine in backlogged American mail. Though the unit faced the same overwhelming challenge of locating and delivering to ever-moving units in the field, the war was over, and what was once floods of incoming mail were beginning to subside. Now, the women could focus on delivering long-overdue love letters never received by many homesick soldiers. The 6888th employed their England-born, tried-and-true mail system to help solve postal problems in Rouen.

Along with theft, morale issues heightened as French civilians were uncomfortable working side by side with the enemy, voicing, "Germans were prisoners, and French were free!"[38] Leaders made every effort to keep the two separated and assigned the 6888th to supervise the respective groups.

> For the first time in American history, Blacks supervised Whites.

The European Theater was closing the curtain on WWII, and soldiers from units all over were redeployed to the United States—1.4 million men and women would return home by September 1945 and in 1946, this number would double.[39] This upswing affected the 6888th as much as any unit still left in the field. They still had work to do in Rouen, France, but with fewer soldiers, summer 1945 would prove a mammoth challenge physically, mentally, and emotionally.

Come October, the remaining members of the battalion motor-marched from Rouen to Paris in a thirty-five-vehicle convoy that was expected to take three hours but, instead turned into a ten-hour trek due to heavy fog and accidents along the way. Upon arrival late at night, there was no warm welcome for the weary soldiers; this would be their final duty station in Europe before reuniting with family and friends in America.

Living conditions in Paris for the 6888th soldiers still overseas had vastly improved since Birmingham and Rouen, the military now reserving rooms at the Bohy Lafayette Hotel and booking officers at the first-class Hôtel États (*to the victors belong the spoils!*), both a thirty-minute drive to their postal directory center. The greatest issue faced by the remaining women was a worker shortage, as incoming mail was again rapidly increasing with Christmas 1945 around the corner, and more than one-third of the unit already returned to the States, including Maj. Adams and executive officer Capt. Noel Campbell. With fewer feet on the ground, and according to the Army's senior leaders, there was no longer a need for a major and captain, so, the Army assigned a first lieutenant over the remaining postal battalion.

It seemed more and more that the Army simply wanted these Black WACs out of Europe as soon as possible, to prohibit any socializing with French society, as the women had done in Europe when it was a team of eight hundred. Still in the war zone, and with mail flooding in, assigning a lieutenant would greatly challenge that commander's ability to effectively lead a unit that was *still* one of the largest in the area.

CHAPTER FIVE

Home, Unsweet Home

By JANUARY 1946, the 6888th Central Postal Directory Battalion's presence in Europe was further dwindling, and by March 1946, almost a year after the war's end, each of the 855 battalion members had returned home to the United States, the soldiers' arrival uncelebrated, once again.

The American 6888th had triumphed over its one-of-a-kind mission with unending support from its fearless female leaders and the team's ability to cooperate, maintain morale, and practice pride and patriotism, despite hailing from the racially segregated US. They had an unwavering goal behind every mission accomplished—to prove to every White senior leader in the military (and to Whites and men, in general) that Black women could perform any task handed to them—and they did.

The Army officially deactivated the postal unit in May 1946 at Fort Dix, New Jersey. There wouldn't be a welcome-home parade; no grand speeches from leadership or public appreciation from Americans, and no official recognition of their history-making wartime accomplishments. The women never received the Distinguished Unit Citation, as anticipated, but instead, a simple, verbal confirmation of a job well done.[40] It was a moment that wasn't recorded in the unit's history until decades after WWII when the US Army eventually recognized the 6888th for its success. In a slight nod (which may have felt more like a slight), battalion commander Maj. Adams was promoted to lieutenant colonel upon her return to the United States. Her band of women would never deny that Adams deserved the honors she received, though it could never repay those who had worked twenty-four-seven to help deliver hope and morale to American soldiers out in the field.

THE CHANCE AT A FUTURE

In eras of war *and* peace, there is a laundry list of reasons men and women volunteer their time and skills to the United States military. In World War II, however, race, gender, and class—innate fates of the eighteen-to-nineteen-year-old women—played a key role in their decisions to enlist. For more than one million African Americans in segregated America during WWII, unlike their White brothers and sisters in arms, enlisting was one of the few opportunities to receive a paycheck and future educational opportunities at the time. Though some 6888th soldiers had college experience before entering the service, several having earned degrees, many took advantage of the opportunity to obtain higher education on the federal government's dime (although the soldiers more than deserved the investment). So, postwar, some women went on to enroll in colleges and universities throughout the country but, for the most part, the now veterans settled near the hometowns they had left to serve their country overseas.

Even after arriving home from their courageous war efforts, all public and private colleges and universities in the South *still* barred Negroes from attending, but historical Black colleges swooped in with an effort to accept African American women en masse. Other institutions included Ohio State University, where Adams had attended graduate school before she was invited to lead the 6888th, Salmon P. Chase College, University of Cincinnati, Georgia State University, Compton College, Columbia University, State University of New York at Albany, and the University of Colorado—among *many* others. Several of the women went on to graduate from law school[41] while others became teachers, nurses, and administrators for Black businesses.

In a still segregated America, postwar employment opportunities for Negro women were not as plentiful as the veterans had expected (or maybe were even promised), and the same, surprisingly, stood for White females, even with access to the Veterans Administration (VA). It was business as usual for women of all colors; despite their experience and eagerness, they were the last people considered. Men were handed combat roles while women were assumed domestic; services had quotas on Black women (only ten percent to match the percentage of Black women in the US) with zero quotas on White women. White men were encouraged to join, en masse, while Black men battled strict quotas prewar and during the first months of WWII. Segregation, sexism, and bigotry ruled the system before, during, and after Hitler's War. It was a dark period of our nation's history.

Note: Though never officially assigned as a combat unit in WWII because of gender and race, history indicates the 6888th was in fact met by enemy fire when a German bomb exploded near a dock at Prestwick, Scotland. This makes the battalion the first all-woman African American unit to see combat.

The US military would not support, on a grand scale, the complete integration of women into the armed forces until 1948, when President Harry S. Truman signed the Women's Armed Services Integration Act into motion. Then, one month later, he passed the Integration of the Armed Forces Act, which *desegregated* the military, promising (in theory) uniformity and enforcing racial and gender equality across its branches.[42]

Nearly fifty years following WWII and Truman's integration acts, Dr. Brenda Moore, PhD, a leading military sociologist, conducted a 1991–1993 survey to gain insight on the women from the 6888th Central Postal Directory Battalion regarding their wartime service and postmilitary life.[43] The women reported joining the WAC, and WAAC prior, for a wealth of reasons. Some had wanted to improve their status in order to climb the social ladder (an unfortunate reality for minorities, including all women, in America); many looked forward to greater employment opportunities, and most required access to adequate healthcare and greater employment opportunities, plus, as promised, the postwar GI Bill was reserved for all US veterans. But, almost expectedly, the women (Black and White) realized their military benefits would not satisfy employment and health demands, a dishonor that would carry on another fifty years, through multiple wars, before the VA implemented specialized programs and services for women.

HONORS, FINALLY

In 1996, just six years before Adams-Earley (married, at the time, to the late Stanley A. Earley, former WWII translator and US medical doctor) passed away in Dayton, Ohio, the Smithsonian Institution's National Postal Museum in Washington, DC, hosted a program in honor of her for her commendable time as commander of the 6888th Central Postal Directory Battalion. On October 19, 1997, she received additional honors at the dedication of the Women in Military Service for America Memorial at Arlington National Cemetery. In 2005, Charity Adams-Earley Girls Academy opened in Dayton, Ohio, as part of the Dayton School System. It's still up and running today.

The 6888th has been highlighted at exhibits and educational programs since the late 1990s at the US Army Women's Museum at Fort Lee, Virginia. Their history-making actions are also maintained in records held by the National Archives for Black Women's History, in Washington, DC, and the Library of Congress, which contains the Charity Adams-Earley papers, an archive of correspondence, notes, records, press clippings, speeches, and other details surrounding her experience as the first Black commissioned officer in the Women's Army Corps during World War II.

On February 25, 2009—sixty-four years after the Second World War—at the Women in Military Service for America Memorial at Arlington Cemetery, surviving members of the 6888th gathered for an honors ceremony by US Army Freedom Team Salute, an official US Army commendation program to honor the women's heroic, history-making actions in WWII. Three of the unit's surviving members, Alyce Dixon, Mary Ragland, and Gladys Schuster, each in their nineties,[44] received official certificates and letters of appreciation signed by the secretary of the Army and the chief of staff of the Army.[45] The celebration, though better late than never, was the first time the battalion had been thanked by the military face-to-face for their wartime services; surely, these women held the memory close for the rest of their days on earth.

The unit's supreme caliber of dedication, and its triumph over its special mission, rocketed the 6888th women into the Big Top, and away from the sideshow, alongside their Black brothers from the 320th Barrage Balloon Battalion, 761st Tank Battalion, and the 333rd Field Artillery Battalion. Though never fully and deservingly recognized for the many brave acts committed in the 1940s (and beyond), each of these veterans was an integral part of Gen. Patton's heroic army in the war against Hitler.

AFTERGLOW

Lt. Col. Charity Adams-Earley published her autobiography in 1989, titled, *One Woman's Army: A Black Woman Remembers the WAC*. Her purpose for publishing was to help trailblaze Black former military women who served throughout World War II and had been virtually ignored and forgotten, even decades later. Shortly after, in June 1994, Dr. Brenda L. Moore, a sociology professor at the State

University of New York at Buffalo, published a study for the US Army Research Institute for Behavioral and Social Sciences, entitled: *African American Women Who Served Overseas During World War II: Toward a Life-Course Analysis*. Two years following, Moore published a book, *To Serve My Country, To Serve My Race: The Story of the Only African American WAC Unit Stationed Overseas During World War II*. Dr. Moore's research study and book provided substantial, critical information about the Black women of World War II; a great honor for Moore and everyone involved.

In 2022, the US Congress paid a final and groundbreaking honor to Lt. Col. Adams-Earley when it approved the US Naming Commission's recommendation to rename Virginia's Fort Lee, named for Confederate Gen. Robert E. Lee, as Fort Gregg-Adams. The official name change occurred in 2023 when it was authorized by the secretary of defense. Now, the East Coast Army base is a testament to trailblazing Black officers like Adams-Earley in World War II and Lt. Gen. Arthur J. Gregg in the Korean and Vietnam wars.

The 6888th Central Postal Battalion participates in a victory parade, May 1945, in Rouen, France. Photo courtesy of the National Archives and Records Administration.

Maj. Charity Adams inspects her troops in Birmingham, England, 1945. Photo courtesy of the National Archives and Records Administration.

Mail stacked to the ceiling in Birmingham. Photo courtesy of National Archives and Records Administration.

Brig. Gen. Benjamin O. Davis Sr. somewhere in France, August 8, 1944." Pvt. Ruth L. James on guard duty at an open house for the 6888th in Rouen, France, May 1945. Photo courtesy of the National Archives and Records Administration.

Pvt. Ruth L. James on guard duty at an open house for the 6888th in Rouen, France, May 1945. Photo courtesy of the National Archives and Records Administration

POSTFACE

America entered World War II on December 8, 1941, two years after warfighting had broken out in Europe as the Germans invaded adjacent countries in Western Europe and declared war on the United States, following our declaration of war on Japan.

The war would eventually spread African American units across multiple countries to fight in the European Theater—the 320th Barrage Balloon Battalion, 761st Tank Battalion, and 333rd Field Artillery Battalion, all supported by the women's 6888th Central Postal Directory Battalion. These minority men and women entered the Second World War as mere sideshows, as dictated by America's military leaders and segregated society, but each one ended their service as the main attraction, bolstering General Patton's Third Army. Unlike the Vietnam War, which divided our country into hawks and doves, World War II brought together the American nation. Just hours after the bombing of Pearl Harbor, the general population coalesced to support our military, even as the president declared war on the aggressors. And, like the steady swell of a wave at the beach, patriotic fever quietly rose within the US. The military draft, which had been instituted months earlier, dramatically increased, and industry repurposed its products and people to manufacture war machines and military uniforms.

In three-and-a-half years, starting with the Japanese bombing of Pearl Harbor in December 1941, and ending with the surrender of Germany and Japan in 1945, America had produced the following: 10 battleships, 29 aircraft carriers, 33 sloops, 52 cruisers, 338 corvettes, 396 destroyers, 1,014 frigates and destroyer escorts, 23,900 transport aircraft, 58,085 training aircraft, 96,872 bombers, 99,456 fighter aircraft, 105,055 mortars, 108,410 tanks, 2,382,311 trucks and other vehicles, 257,390 artillery pieces, and 2,679,840 machine guns.[46]

The Greatest Generation—the same generation to develop the atomic bomb and ultimately conquer Japan and Germany while neutralizing Italy—put 16.1 million men and women in uniform and recruited them into the armed services, including more than one million African Americans.[47] Our forces invaded Africa, Sicily, and Italy, won the battle in the Atlantic, and successfully executed D-Day on French soil. Alongside Allies, the seldomly sung Black protagonists liberated Western Europe with lesser training, fewer resources, and nearly zero faith from their leaders or Americans back home.

EPILOGUE

With World War II on the horizon, the United States military and civilian leaders intended to perpetuate the disparate treatment of Black people, true to the prewar culture, and maneuver it into the military for the coming war.

From the beginning, with a running start, America planned to build a strong fighting force composed of White soldiers serviced by Black soldiers (or Negroes or Colored people, the common vernacular of Whites *and* Blacks, at that time). Black soldiers were assigned to rear echelon billets on the battlefield, the only roles the 1925 Study deemed these men capable of performing, while White counterparts were trusted with the heavy lifting of combat. White military leaders believed weapons should never be in the hands of Colored soldiers for fear they would attack and kill White soldiers, friends or foes. The US Army stuck to its plan during the early war years, at least in Europe, but come D-Day, followed by the Battle of the Bulge, it all changed.

Though Black combat units were activated beginning in late 1941 and well into 1942, the master plan was to retain the men in a training status until the war's end. Was it not for heavy losses of American White soldiers on the beaches of Normandy, followed by the Bulge, the 761st Tank Battalion and the 333rd Field Artillery Battalion would never have been baptized by fire on French soil. Even the 320th Barrage Balloon Battalion, the only Negroes unit to suffer casualties on Omaha Beach along with their White brethren, was not scheduled to deploy. Why would they, as twenty identical White battalions were warming up and in the queue? The 320th got the call because, theoretically, according to the Army, their presence on the beaches would never register as a combat force but merely a "technical" presence. With respect to the 6888th Central

Postal Directory Battalion, their overseas deployment happened only because their White predecessors had failed their given mission.

Throughout World War II, these heroic Black units, supporters of Patton's Third Army and so much more, seldom received the accolades warranted for battle action or logistical and administrative efficiency. Positive public pronouncements about Blacks were rare, even after all the battalions had accomplished. Their valorous battles and skirmishes saw minimal military or civilian press coverage, and there was a cap placed on awards and decorations at the highest levels. Revelations known today, proved there could not have been just one "most heroic" or "decorated" American soldier in the European Theater during World War II, as more than one million Black soldiers had awards capped at the Silver Star Medal because of blatant ignorance and racism, as reported by the US Army seventy years later. However, all soldiers in the war, whether White or Black, man or woman, from all Theaters, had earned recognition as members of The Greatest Generation.

The disparate treatment of Black units continued at war's end and beyond. Case in point—war crimes committed by German soldiers against White and Black American soldiers, such as the mass killings during the Battle of the Bulge, had differing conclusions. The incident involving our murdered White soldiers was investigated until the end, resulting in the identification, arrest, military trial, conviction of war crimes, sentencing, and punishment, all of which were widely reported by the media of the day. In comparison, when it came to the slaughter of Black US soldiers, the entire race saw injustice in the Army's handling of things. The superficial investigation was short-lived, and the Army never identified even potential perpetrators. The case was closed and filed away; the results marked *Top Secret*, with no media reports until many years later.

GEN. GEORGE S. PATTON JR.

George Patton was an enigma. He generally followed to form the age-old civilian managerial and military command protocols of praising subordinates in public and harshly critiquing them in private. The most colorful of World War II generals and strategic planners, Patton seldom shared public praise regarding the abilities of Colored units in his Third Army. And when he did speak publicly, Patton was quick to save face, offering positive feedback on his troops. But his daily journals and diaries, as well as letters to his wife, all published following his tragic death in December 1945, showed us the real Gen. Patton. Few, if any, of his privately written thoughts about Blacks were positive, as most of his entries contained expletives demeaning his Black soldiers' work, character, and abilities. To this day, soldiers of all hues admire Patton, as he clearly understood that the priority of the military is to win every war.

AFTERWARD

Though German military leader Maj. Gustav Knittel was held responsible for the White American massacre at Malmedy and sentenced to death in 1946, his sentence was reduced to life in prison in 1948. Knittel was released in 1956, only to become gainfully employed. His first job out of prison was managing American sales for Porsche Motor works in Germany, and, later, holding the same position at Volkswagen. In 1976, unknown assailants firebombed his home, which resulted in his death.

The eleven murdered Black soldiers of the 333rd Field Artillery Battalion whose bodies were uncovered at Wereth received awards and decorations prior to their internment, in Europe and the United States, all with full military honors. Their names and home states were engraved on a monument dedicated in their honor at the site of their demise. Sixty years after the war, the 761st Tank Battalion, believed to have been the most successful armor unit in Patton's Third Army, and in the European Theater, as a whole, was finally recognized with the Distinguished Unit Citation. A monument and street were named in the unit's honor in Fort Hood and Killeen, Texas. Staff Sgt. Reuben Rivers, nominated but denied the Medal of Honor, received the award posthumously, following a review of his actions seventy years later.

Corporal Waverly Woodson, 320th Barrage Balloon Battalion, had distinguished himself with valor at Normandy on D-Day and was recommended for the Congressional Medal of Honor but denied due to "lack of documentation." His cause was recently taken up by members of Congress who petitioned for a more thorough review, which is currently pending as of this book. It was not so for William Dabney. As a surviving member of the same unit, he was the recipient of the French Legion of Honor in 2009, at a special ceremony in Paris. The award was presented by US President Barack Obama.

Upon returning home from their postal mission in Europe, after the war, the 6888th Central Postal Directory Battalion was not immediately recognized with a unit award, only comments of "job well done." Over the years, as information became more available regarding their superb performance in England and France, the unit and its surviving members were recognized at a number of ceremonies, culminating with a special engagement in their honor by the US Army Freedom Team Salute, an official US Army commendation program. Lt. Col. Charity Adams-Earley, promoted upon returning from the war zone, having been the first Black female officer in the US Army, became the first woman of color to achieve her new rank. In 2018 the 6888th Central Postal Directory Battalion was nominated to receive the Congressional Gold Medal. In early 2022, US President Joe Biden signed an Executive Order authorizing the award. As of this book, the presentation date is still pending.

The Congressional Gold Medal seeks to honor those, individually or as a group, "who have performed an achievement that has an impact on American History and culture that is likely to be recognized as a major achievement in the recipient's field long after achievement."

When asked to comment on the long overdue award, Stanley Earley III, son of 6888th commander Lt. Col. Charity Adams-Earley said,

> "It's wonderful, and it's time. It should have happened fifty, sixty years ago. But there is now the opportunity for recognition that these folks did all these things that were so important."

THE FUTURE

Neither the authors of the 1925 Army Study, nor captains of American units in World War II Europe, could have foreseen the US climate seventy-five years later. What would be their reaction to know the American people would elect a Black president and a Black female vice president, appoint an African American four-star general as chairperson of the joint chiefs of staff, and, over time, see more than three hundred Black US Army soldiers as general officers? This includes me, a retired commanding general of a tank-heavy mechanized infantry division, who served side by side with two of my eight veteran brothers, one serving a combat tour of duty in Vietnam, and the other retiring as a command sergeant major, the highest enlisted rank in the Army, who commanded Black as well as White soldiers. Unlike Black soldiers of World War II, he held the rank of private only once. The United States and segregated America, at the time, would have eaten their words in utter disbelief.

We are Black, and we all went in—and came out—fighting.

ACKNOWLEDGMENTS

I want to thank and acknowledge the following World War II veterans for unknowingly inspiring me and playing a pivotal role in my childhood and later in my military career. Thank you for seeing my potential.

- Brigadier General Thomas O. Lawson, US Army
- Lieutenant Colonel Theodore "Ted" Lumpkin, Jr., (Original) Tuskegee Airman
- Major Franchon Blake, US Women's Army Corps
- Major Aaron Herrington, (Original)Tuskegee Airman
- Captain Edna Woodward, Fort Huachuca, Arizona, US Women's Army Corps
- Petty Officer Second Class James Harris, US Navy (my uncle)
- 2nd Lieutenant Vernon Butcher, Sr., USMC, Montfort Point Marine
- Sergeant Morris Barton Gilmore, USMC, Bataan Death March Survivor
- PFC Clarence Gravett, Sr., 99th Fighter Squadron, Tuskegee Air Unit (my father)
- Corpsman Second Class Donald McClure, US Navy (my father-in-law)
- Mine Man Third Class Willie Garrison, US Navy (my stepfather)
- PFC Normal Beasley, 6888th Central Postal Directory Battalion, US Women's Army Corps
- PFC Robert L. Harris, General Patton's Third Army and US Army Constabulary, Post-War Germany (my uncle)
- PFC L.D. Jackson, General Patton's Third Army, Red Ball Express
- Trooper Harold Cole, Buffalo Soldier, National President, 9th and 10th US (Horse) Calvary Association
- Trooper Fred Douglas Jones, Buffalo Soldier, 28th US (Horse) Cavalry Regiment, 4th Cavalry Brigade, 2nd Cavalry Division

SPECIAL THANKS:

To Liana Whitehead for her assistance with editing
To my brother, Command Sergeant Major Melvin E. Gravett,
US Army, (Retired) for his assistance with this book.

To Judge Todd Irby, California Superior Court,
for providing vital material.

INTRODUCTION FOOTNOTES

Introduction: The Mighty Malicious Pen

1. Excerpts from the *Memorandum for the Chief of Staff regarding Employment of Negro Manpower in War.* 1925. President's Official Files, 4245-G: Office of Production Management Commission on Fair Employment Practices. War Department. 1943; Archives of the Franklin D. Roosevelt Library. ("The Study"). pp.1-33

2. ibid, pp. 1-33

3. Potter, Lou with Miles, William and Rosenblum, Nina. *Liberators Fighting on Two Fronts in World War II*. Harcourt Brace Jovanovich. New York. 1992. p. 61

4. Smith, Graham. *When Jim Crow met John Bull: Black American Soldiers in World War II*. p. 26

5. Axelrod, Alex. *World War Two: What Really Happened*. Fall River Press. New York. 2008. pp. 12-16

6. ibid, pp. 92, 93

7. Hervieux, Linda, Forgotten: The Untold Story of D-Day's Black Heroes, at Home and at War, Collins Publishers, New York, New York 2015. p. 24

8. ibid, p. 26

9. Lanning, Michael Lee. The African American *Soldier: From Crispus Attucks to Colin Powel*, New York, Citadel Press, 2004. p. *135*

10. Hervieux, p. 23

11. The Study, pp.1-33

12. The Study, pp.1-33

13. Hervieux, p. 29

14. ibid, p. 63

15. ibid, p. 30

16. ibid, p. 30

17. Interview with author's mother

18. Hervieux, p. 62

19. Interview with author's father

20. Interview with author's father

21. Potter, p. 58

Introduction: The Mighty Malicious Pen
Books

Axelrod, Alex, World War Two: What Really Happened, Fall River Press, New York, 2008.

Hervieux, Linda, Forgotten: The Untold Story of D-Day's Black Heroes, at Home and at War, Collins Publishers, New York, New York 2015.

Lanning, Michael Lee. The African American Soldier: From Chrispus Attucks to Colin Powel, New York, Citadel Press, 2004.

Potter, Lou with Miles, William and Rosenblum, Nina, Liberators Fighting on Two Fronts in World War II Harcourt Brace Jovanovich, Publishers, New York, 1992.

Smith, Graham, When Jim Crow met John Bull: Black American Soldiers in World War II Britain (London: I.B. Tauris), 1987.

Interviews
Gravett, Alice M. Author's Mother. Various times, and dates.

Gravett, Clarence, World War II Veteran, Author's Father. Various times, and dates
Memorandum

Memorandum for the Chief of Staff regarding Employment of Negro Man-Power in War, November 10,1925, President's Official; Files 4245-G: Office of Production Management Commission on Fair Employment Practices: War Department, 1943; Archives of the Franklin D. Roosevelt Library. (The Study)

Part One Footnotes: 320th Barrage Balloon Battalion
Epigraph
1. Greenspan, Jesse. History Channel: *A Black Medic Saved Hundreds on D-Day. Was He Deprived of a Medal of Honor?* June 4, 2019. https://www.history.com/news/d-day-hero-medal-of-honor-waverly-woodson. 2021.

High Flight Poem
2. Gillespie, John. *Pilot John Gillespie Magee: High Flight.* September 1941. https://www.nationalmuseum. af.mil/Visit/Museum-Exhibits/Fact-Sheets/Display /Article/196844/pilot-officer-john-gillespie-magee-high-flight/. 2021.

Introduction
3. Legout, Colonel Gerard. *D-Day and the Battle for Normandy.* Philipe Pique. Zorilla Productions. Imperial War Museum. US Archives. 1998. p. 4

4. Kershaw, Alex. *The First Wave: D-Day Warriors who Led the Way to Victory in World War Two.* Dutton Caliber. New York. 2019. p. 8

5. History on the Net: Encyclopedia.com: *D-Day Statistics,* Updated Version, July 17, 2020. https://www.historyonthenet.com/d-day-statistics.

Chapter One: Sky's the Limit
6. Shock, James R., *The US Army Barrage Balloon Program*, Bennington VT: Merriam Press, 2006, p. 74

7. Hervieux, p. 73

8. ibid, p. 76

9. ibid, p. 74

10. ibid, p. 84

11. ibid, p. 86

12. ibid, p. 85–87

13. ibid, p. 87

Chapter Two: Hiring Away the Help
14. McFarlin, Shannon. *As If They Were Ours: The Story of Camp Tyson, America's Only Barrage Balloon Training Facility.* Merriam Press. World War Two History. Bennington, Vermont. 2016. p. 50

15. ibid, p. 40

16. United States War Department. *Barrage Balloon Operational of Material and Employment of Personnel*. Coast Artillery Field Manual FM 4–17. June 1, 1942.

17. Shock, p. 50

18. ibid, p. 50

Chapter Three: Nothing Less Than Victory

19. Axelrod, p. 309

20. Hervieux, p. 225

21. ibid, p. 223

22. ibid, p. 224

23. ibid, p. 235

24. ibid, p. 232

25. ibid, p. 241

26. ibid, p. 242

27. McFarlin, p. 134

28. Brown, Jessica Wambach. *"Last Stop USA."* World War II Magazine. Vienna, Virginia. August 2020. p. 57

29. Shock, p. 77

30. Hervieux, pp. 262–263

Chapter Four: The Beginning of the End

31. Hervieux, p. 251

Part One Bibliography

Books

Adams-Earley, Charity, *One Woman's Army, A Black Officer Remember The WAC*. Texas A&M University Press. College Station. First Edition. 1989.

Axelrod, Alex. *World War Two: What Really Happened*. Fall River Press. New York. 2008.

Buckley, Gail. *American Patriots: The Story of Blacks in the Military from the Revolution to Desert Storm*. New York: Random House. 2001.

Crouch, Tom D. *The Eagle Aloft: Two Centuries of Balloons in America*. Washington, DC: Smithsonian Institution Press. 1983.

Darman, Peter, *Deception Tactics of World War II: Cunning Camouflage, and the Art of Misdirection/* Metro Books. New York. 2017.

Edgerton, Robert B. *Hidden Heroism: Black Soldiers in America's Wars*. Boulder, Colorado. Westview Press. 2001.

Eisenhower, Dwight D. *Crusade in Europe*. Garden City, NY. Doubleday. 1948.

Harrison, Gordon A. *The European Theater of Operations-Cross Channel Attack*. New York. BBD Special Editions. 1993.

Hervieux, Linda. *Forgotten: The Untold Story of D-Day's Black Heroes, at Home and at War*. Collins Publishers. New York, New York. 2015.

Hyslop, Stephen G. *Eyewitness to World War II, Unforgettable Stories from History's Greatest Conflict*. National Geographic Partners. Washington, DC. 2018.

Kershaw, Alex. *The First Wave: D-Day Warriors Who Led the Way to Victory in World War Two*. Dutton Caliber. New York, 2019.

Lanning, Michael Lee. *The African American Soldier: From Crispus Attucks to Colin Powel*, New York. Citadel Press. 2004.

Lee, Ulysses. *The Employment of Negro Troops. United States Army in World War II*. Honolulu, Hawaii. University Press of the Pacific. 1994.

Lee, Ulysses. The Employment of Negro Troops. Office of the Chief of Military History. United States Army. Washington, DC. 1966.

Legout, Colonel Gerard. *D-Day and the Battle for Normandy*. Philipe Pique. Zorilla Productions. Imperial War Museum. US Archives. 1998.

Lewis, John E. *Voices From D-Day: Eyewitness Accounts from The Battle for Normandy*. MJF Books. New York. 2014.

McFarlin, Shannon. *As If They Were Ours: The Story of Camp Tyson, America's Only Barrage Balloon Training Facility*. Merriam Press. World War Two History. Bennington, Vermont. 2016.

McRae, Bennie, Jr. *Lest We Forget, African American History: The All Black 320th Anti-Aircraft Barrage Balloon Battalion, VLA, They Landed on D-Day*. Bill Dawson's Letter to the History Net. Waynesburg, PA.

Moore, Christopher Paul. *Fighting for America: Black Soldiers: The Unsung Heroes of World War I*. New York. Ballantine. 2006.

New York Times. *Complete World War II 1939–1945: All the Courage from the Battlefields to the Home Front*. Articles by New York Times Staff. 2013.

Paone, Thomas. *75th Anniversary of World War Two Protecting the Beaches with Balloons: D-Day and the 320th Barrage Balloon Battalion*. Aeronautic Department. June 4, 2019.

Potter, Lou with Miles, William and Rosenblum, Nina. *Liberators Fighting on Two Fronts in World War II*. Harcourt Brace Jovanovich. New York. 1992.

Shock, James R. *The US Army Barrage Balloon Program*. Bennington, Vermont. Merriam Press. 2006.

Shock, James R. *US Army Airships, 1908–1942*. Atlantis Productions. Edgewater, Florida. 2002.

Smith, Graham. *When Jim Crow met John Bull: Black American Soldiers in World War II*. Britain (London: I.B. Tauris). 1987.

US Army War College. *The Army War College Studies Black Soldiers*. HERB: Resources for Teachers (The Study).

US Army War College. *Barrage Balloon Operational of Material and Employment of Personnel*. Coast Artillery Field Manual FM 4–17, 1 June 1942.

Bulletins
OPC Bulletin, Bouchard, Chad, The Monthly Newsletter of The Overseas Press Club of America, New York, New York, November 2015, Linda Hervieux, Author of *"Forgotten"* Addresses Capacity Crowd.

Internet
Center for Media and Learning. *The Army War College Studies Black Soldiers*. Social History for Every Classroom. https://shec.ashp.cuny.edu/items/show/808. 2021.

Gillespie, John. *Pilot John Gillespie Magee: High Flight*. September 1941. https://www.nationalmuseum.af.mil/Visit/Museum-Exhibits/Fact-Sheets/Display/Article/196844/pilot-officer-john-gillespie-magee-high-flight/ 2021.

Greenspan, Jesse. History Channel: *A Black Medic Saved Hundreds on D-Day. Was He Deprived of a Medal of Honor?* June 4, 2019. https://www.history.com/news/d-day-hero-medal-of-honor-waverly-woodson. 2021.

History on the Net: Encyclopedia.com: *D-Day Statistics*, Undated Version, July 17, 2020. https://www.historyonthenet.com/d-day-statistics. 2021.

Wikipedia. *320th Barrage Balloon Battalion.* https://en.wikipedia.org/wiki/320th_Bar rage_Balloon_ Battalion. 2021.

Magazines

Brown, Jessica Wambach. *"Last Stop US"* World War II Magazine. The National World War II Museum, Inc. Vienna, VA. August 2020.

Hervieux, Linda. *"He Served With D-Day's Only African American Combat. His Widow Is Still Fighting for His Medal of Honor."* Time Magazine. June 4, 2019.

Memorandum

US War Department. Cover Letter for *Memorandum for The Chief of Staff: Employment of Negro Manpower in War.* November 10, 1925. President's Official. Files 4245-G. Office of Production Management Commission on Fair Employment Practices. War Department. 1943. Archives of the Franklin D. Roosevelt Library. ("The Study"). pp.1–33.

US War Department. *Memorandum for the Chief of Staff regarding Employment of Negro Man-Power in War.* November 10,1925. President's Official Files 4245-G. Office of Production Management Commission on Fair Employment Practices. War Department. 1943. Archives of the Franklin D. Roosevelt Library. ("The Study"). pp.1–33.

Newsletter

Hervieux, Linda. *Daily Beast Newsletters.* November 9, 2018.

Sherman, Ben. Fort Sill Newsletter. May 1, 2014.

Part Two Footnotes

Epigraph

1. Potter, p. 115

Chapter 1: Bitterly Opposed South

2. The Study, pp.1–33

3. Potter, p. 20

4. ibid, p. 119

Chapter 2: Come Out Fighting

5. DiNicolo, Gina. *The Black Panthers at War: The 761st Tank Battalion and General Patton's Drive on Germany.* St. John's Press. 2016. Originally Titled: *The Black Panthers: A Story of Race, War, and Courage.* 2014. p. 63.

6. Lee, Ulysses. *The Employment of Black Troops,* Office of Military History, United States Army. Washington, DC. 1966. p. 661

7. DiNicolo, p. 42

8. Williams, David. *Hit Hard.* Bantam Books. New York, Toronto, London, Sydney. 1983. p. 34

9. Kelly. *Red Legs of the Bulge,* p. 55

10. Sasser, Charles W. *Patton's Panthers: African-American 761st Tank Battalion in World War II.* Pocket Books. New York, London, Toronto, Sidney. 2004. p. 16

11. DiNicolo, p. 126

12. Potter, p. 128

13. Gates, Henry Louis Jr. *The Black Church: This Is Our Story This Is Our Song.* Penguin Press. New York. 2021. p. 23

14. Abdul-Jabbar, Kareem and Walton, Anthony. *Brothers in Arms.* Broadway Books. New York. 2004. p.35

15. Potter, p. 119

16. Lee, p. 338

Chapter 3: Lock and Load

17. Lewis, Jon E. *Voices From D-Day.* MJG Books. New York. 1994. pp. 178–180

18. Davidsmeyer, Jo. *Normandy Hedgerow Battles in World War Two.* 1995–2011. https://www.jodvavidsmeyer.com/combatmilitary/hedgerow.html. 2021.

19. DiNocolo, p. 141

20. Kershaw, p.143

21. Abdul-Jabbar, p. 77

22. The Study, pp.1–33, Lee, p. 69

23. Sasser, p. 54

24. Abdul-Jabbar, p. 67
25. Lee, pp. 623–624

26. Abdul-Jabbar, p. 86

27. ibid, p. 79

28. Wilson, Joe Jr. *The 761st Black Panther Tank Battalion in World War II.* McFarland & Company, Inc. Jefferson. North Carolina & London. 2006. p. 49

29. Lee, p. 661

30. Sasser, p. 63

31. Abdul-Jabbar, p.78
    Sasser, p. 58

Chapter 4: Prelude to Battle

32. DiNocolo, p. 228

33. Patton, General George S. *The War as I Knew It.* Annotated by Colonel Paul D. Harkins. Houghton Mifflin Company. Boston, Massachusetts. The River Press. Cambridge, MA. 1947. pp. 242–243

34. Sasser, p. 263

35. DiNocolo, p. 146

36. Abdul-Jabbar, pp. 81 and 89

37. Axelrod, p. 320

38. Potter, p. 162

39. Abdul-Jabbar, p. 89

40. DiNocolo, p. 142

41. Abdul-Jabbar, p. 87

42. ibid, p. 87

43. Patton/Harkin, p. 160

44. Lee, p. 661

45. Williams, p. 142

46. Abdul-Jabbar, p. 92

47. Wilson, p. 65

Chapter 5: From Victory to Victory

48. Sasser, p. 229

49. ibid, p. 183

50. Wilson, p. 55

51. Wikipedia. *Third Geneva Convention.* https://en.wikipedia.org/wiki/Third_Geneva_Convention. 2021.

52. Abdul-Jabbar, pp. 121–122

53. Patton/Harkin, p. 170

54. Wilson, pp. 86, 256–257

55. Military Hall of Honor. https://militaryhallofhonor.com/. Military Hall of Honor, LLC. 2021.

56. Wilson, p. 62

57. Lee, p. 665

58. Wilson, p. 79

59. DiNocolo, p.179

60. Wilson, p. 113

Chapter 6: Battle after Battle

61. Von, Clausewitz, Carl. *On War.* Indexed Edition. Edited and translated by Howard, Michael and Brodie, Bernard. Princeton University Press. Princeton, New Jersey. 1976. pp. 361

62. Nye, Roger H. *The Patton Mind: The Professional Development of An Extraordinary Leader.* Avery Publishing Group Inc. 1993. p.71

63. Wilson, p. 118

64. Potter, p. 182

65. Wilson, p. 119

66. Patton/Harkin, p.185

67. ibid, p. 185

68. Potter, p.189

69. National Archives Foundation. *Surrender? "Nuts!" Gen. Anthony McAuliffe's 1944 Christmas Message to His Troops. 1944.* https://www.archivesfoundation.org/documents/surrender-nuts-gen-anthony-mcauliffes-1944-christmas-message-troops/. 2021.

70. Sasser, p. 243–244

71. Potter, p. 195

Chapter 7: Calling All Negros

72. Lee, p. 688

73. ibid, p. 688

74. ibid, p. 689

75. ibid, p. 693, 689

76. Potter, pp. 198–200

Chapter 8: Steel Coffins

77. Foote, Shelby. *The Civil War: A Narrative*. Random House. New York. 1958–1974. p. 58

78. The Study, pp.1–33

79. Wilson, p.144

80. Sasser, pp.197–200

81. ibid, pp. 197–200

82. ibid, pp.197–200

83. ibid, p.186

84. ibid, pp. 260, 264–265

85. DiNocolo, p. 230

86. Wilson, p.159

87. ibid, p.161

88. Sasser, p.280

89. ibid, p. 280

90. Wilson, p. 168

Chapter 9: Damn Good Soldiers

91. Potter, p. 182

92. Abdul-Jabbar, p. 260

93. Sasser, p. 287

94. Wilson, p. 163

95. Abdul-Jabbar, pp. 81–82

96. Moore, Brenda L. *To Serve My Country to Serve My Race*. New York University Press. New York and London. 1996. p.6

97. Sasser, p. 333

98. Potter, p. 232

99. US Holocaust Memorial Museum

100. Martin. *The Patton Papers*. 1940–1945. Da Capo Press. New York. 1974. pp. 787–789. Wilson. p. 224.

101. Potter, p. vi

102. Potter, p. 217

103. ibid, p. 217

104. ibid, p. 217

105. Abdul-Jabbar, p. 246

106. ibid, p. 247

107. DiNocolo, p. 260

108. Wilson, p. 200

109. ibid, pp. 203–204

110. DiNocolo, pp. 255–256

111. Wilson, p. 204
　　Potter p. 260

112. Potter, p. 260

113. ibid, p. 260

Chapter 10: Home, Unsweet Home

114. ibid, p.259

115. The Study, pp.1–33

116. Wilson, p. 199

117. Sasser, p. 344

118. DiNicolo, p. 260

119. Abdul-Jabbar, p. 261

120. Potter, p. 279

121. Military History Fandom. *761st Tank Battalion.* https://militaryhistory.fandom.com/wiki/76 1st_Tank_Battalion_United_States. 2021.

122. Abdul-Jabbar, p. 268

Part Two Bibliography
Books

Abdul-Jabbar, Kareem and Walton, Anthony. *Brothers in Arms.* Broadway Books. New York. 2004.

Anderson, Trezzvant. *Come Out Fighting: The Epic Tale of the 761st Tank Battalion.* 1942–1945. University of Chicago Press. January 1, 1945.

Army Field Manual. pp. 3–20, 12. Abrams Main Battle Tank. US Army Publishing Directorate. Fort Belvoir, Virginia. 22060-5447. 2009.

Axelrod, Alan. *World War I: What Really Happened.* Fall River Press. New York. 2008.

Atkinson, Rick. *The Guns at Last Light, The War in Western Europe.* 1944–1945. Volume Three of the Liberation Trilogy. Henry Holt and Company. New York, New York. 2013.

Foote, Shelby. *The Civil War: A Narrative.* Random House. New York. 1958–1974.

Bowers, William T., Hammond, William, MacCarrigle, George, L., *Black soldiers White Army The 24th Infantry Regiment in Korea.* United States Army Center for Military History. Washington DC. 1996.

Blumenson, Martin. *The Patton Papers* 1940–1945. DA CAPO Press. New York. 1996.

Boatner III, Mark Mayo. *The Biographical Dictionary of World War II.* Presidio Press, Navato, CA. 1996.

Bradley, Omar N, and Blair, Clay. *A General's Life*, New York. Simon and Schuster. New York. 1983.

Carter, Allene and Allen, Robert L. *Honoring Sergeant Carter, Redeeming a Black World War II Hero's Legacy*. Harper-Collins Publishers. 2003.

Child, Robert. *Immoral Valor: The Black Medal of Honor Winners of World War II*. Osprey Publishing. New York, New York. 2022.

Congressional Medal of Honor Foundation. *Medal of Honor, Portraits of Valor Beyond the Call of Duty*. Third Edition, Artisan. Workman Publishing Company. New York, New York. 2011.

Darman, Peter. *Deception Tactics of World War II*. Metro Books. New York. 2017.

Davies, Norman. *Europe, A History*. Oxford University Press. Oxford, New York. 1966.

DiNicolo, Gina. *The Black Panthers at War: The 761st Tank Battalion and General Patton's Drive on Germany*. St. John's Press. 2016. Originally Titled: *The Black Panthers: A Story of Race, War, and Courage*. 2014.

Eisenhower, Dwight D. *Crusade in Europe*. Isha Press International. Bronx, New York. 2011.

FM 3-20.12. *Abrams Maintenance Battle Tank*. US Army Publishing Directorate. Fort Belvoir, Virginia. 22060-5447. Nov. 3, 2009.

Gates, Henry Louis Jr. *The Black Church: This Is Our Story This Is Our Song*. Penguin Press. New York. 2021.

Gabel, Christopher R. *The US Army GHQ Maneuvers Of 1941*. Center of Military History United States Army. Washington, DC. 1991.

George, Denise and Child, Robert, *The Lost Eleven; The Forgotten Story of Black American Soldiers Brutally Massacred in World War II*, Caliber, New York, 2017.

Gravett, Peter J. *From East Garrison to the Ranch House and Beyond*. P&B Publishing. Rancho Palos Verdes, California. 2018.

Hervieux, Linda. *Forgotten: The Untold Story of D-Day's Black Hero's at Home and at War*, Harper-Collins Publishers. New York. 2015.

Hogg, Ian V. *The Biography of General George S. Patton*. Gallery Books, Smith Publishers, Inc. New York City, New York. January 1, 1984.

Hyslop, Stephen G. *Eyewitness to World War II: Unforgotten Stories from History's Greatest Conflict*. National Geographic. Washington, DC. 2018.

Jefferson, Robert F. *Brothers in Valor, Battlefield Stories of the Eighty-Nine African Americans Awarded the Medal of Honor*. LP Publishers, Guilford, Connecticut. 2019.

Kahn, Charles H. *The Art and Thought of Heraclitus, An Additions of the Fragments with Translations and Commentary*. Cambridge University Press. December 1979.

Kahn, Louis I. Duke University. Museum of Art (1989). *"The Art Museum of Louis I. Kahn."* Duke University Press. Durham, North Carolina. 1989.

Kershaw, Alex. *The Longest Winter: The Battle of the Bulge and the Epic Story of World War II's Most Decorated Platoon*. MJF Books. New York. 2004.

Lanning, Lt. Col. (Ret), Michael Lee. *The American Soldier from Crispus Attucks to Colin Powell*, A Birch Lane Press Book. Carol Publishing Group, 1997.

Lee, Ulysses. *The Employment of Black Troops*, Office of Military History, United States Army. Washington, DC. 1966.

Lewis, Jon E. *Voices From D-Day*, MJG Books, New York, 1994.

McFarlin, Shannon. *"As if They Were Ours: The Story of Camp Tyson, America's Only Barrage Balloon Training Facility,"* Merriam Press, Bennington, VT, 2016

Morelock, J.D. *Generals of the Ardennes, American Leadership in The Battle of The Bulge*, National Defense University Press, 1994.

Moore, Brenda L. *To Serve My Country to Serve My Race*. New York University Press. New York and London. 1996.

Morris, Robert V. *Black Faces of War: A Legacy of Honor from Revolution to Today*, Zenith Press. Minneapolis, Minnesota. *2011*.

Mosley, Leonard. *Marshall: Hero of Our Times*. Hearst Books. New York. 1982.

New York Times. *Complete World War II*. 1939–1945. Black Dog and Leventhal Publishers. New York. 2013.

Nye, Roger H. *The Patton Mind: The Professional Development of an Extraordinary Leader*. Avery Publishing Group Inc.1993.

Patton, General George S. *The War as I Knew it*. Annotated by Colonel Paul D. Harkins. Houghton Mifflin Company. Boston, Massachusetts. The River Press. Cambridge, MA. 1947.

Potter, Lou; Miles, William; Rosenblum, Nina. *Liberators, Fighting on Two Fronts in World War II*. Harcourt, Brace Jovanovich. Publishers. New York, San Diego, London. 1992.

Roush Jr., John H. Jr. *World War II Reminiscences: A Collection of Vivid Memories of Combat During World War II, by California Veterans for the Most Part*. Second Edition. 1996. Revised and Expanded, Third Printing. 2002. Sponsored by the Reserve Officers Association of the United States, California Department.

Sasser, Charles W. *Patton's Panthers: African- American 761st Tank Battalion in World War II*. Pocket Books. New York, London, Toronto, Sidney. 2004.

Shock, James R. *The US Army Barrage Balloon Program*. Merriam Press. Benning, VT. 2012.

Sloan, Sam. *Dwight D. Eisenhower: Crusade in Europe*. Ishi Press. New York, Tokyo, 2011.

Smith, Jessie Carney. *Black Firsts: 4,000 Ground-Breaking and Pioneering Historical Events*. Third Edition. Canton, Michigan. 2003.

Stewart, Jeffery C. *1001 Things Everyone Should Know About African American History*, Broadway Books. New York. 2006.

The Study US Army War College. *The Army Studies Black soldiers. 1925 HERB: Resources for Teachers*.

Von, Clausewitz, Carl. *On War*. Indexed Edition. Edited and translated by Howard, Michael and Brodie, Bernard. Princeton University Press. Princeton, New Jersey. 1976.

Williams, David. *Hit Hard*. Bantam Books. New York, Toronto, London, Sydney. 1983.

Wilson, Joe Jr. *The 761st Black Panther Tank Battalion in World War II*, McFarland & Company, Inc. Publishers. Jefferson, North Carolina, and London, 2006.

Yeide, Harry. *"Fighting Patton, George S. Patton, Jr. Through the Eyes of His Enemies."* Zenith Press. Minneapolis, Minnesota. 2011.

Newspapers

Herald/Review Media. *"A Special Supplement. D-Day 75th Anniversary."* Gate House Media. 2019.
James, George. *"Ben Bender Letter."* New York Times. October 7, 1991.
Stars and Stripes. November 27, 1944.

Internet

National Archives Foundation. *Surrender? "Nuts!"* Gen. Anthony McAuliffe's 1944 Christmas Message to His Troops. https://www.archivesfoundation.org/documents/ surrender-nuts-gen-anthony-mcauliffes-1944-christmas-message-troops/. 2021.

American Rifleman. *Remembering the Men and the Guns of the Battle of the Bulge.* https://www.americanrifleman.org/content/remembering-the-men-and-guns-of-the-battle-of-the-bulge/. 2021.

Holocaust Encyclopedia. *Afro Germans during the Holocaust.* https://encyclopedia.ushmm.org/content/en/article/afro-germans-during-the-holocaust. 2021.

Geneva Convention. Chapter 7: Medical and Religious Personnel and Objects (rules 25–30). Henckaerts, Jean-Marie. International Committee of the Red Cross. Publisher: Cambridge University Press. pp 79–104, DOI: https://doi.org/10.1017/CBO978051 18044700.011. 2021.

Wikipedia. *Heraclitus.* https://en.wikipedia.org/wiki/Heraclitus. 2021.

Davidsmeyer, Jo. *Normandy Hedgerow Battles in World War Two.* 1995–2011. https://www.jodvavidsmeyer.com/combatmilitary/hedgerow.html. 2021.

Military History. *761st Tank Battalion.* https://military-history.fandom.com/wiki/761st_Tank_Battalion_(United_States). 2021.

Military Hall of Honor. https://militaryhallofhonor.com/. 2021.
Wikipedia. Medical Neutrality. https://en.wikipedia.org/wiki/Medical-neutrality. 2021.

Magazines

Barrett, Claire. "*Interview: Guy Stern, War of Words.*" Military History. History Net Publisher. Arlington, Virginia. Sept. 2020. p. 14

Blum, Howard. "*Destination Iran.*" World War II History. August 2020. p. 30.

Brown, Jessica. "*Last Stop USA.*" World War Two History. August 2020.

Miskimon, Christopher. "*Third Armored Division: Sherman Tank Ace.*" World War II History. Aug./Sept. 2020. p. 8.

Marszalek, John and Sherman, William Tecumseh. In a speech to the graduating glass of the Michigan Military Academy (June 19, 1879). "*Sherman: A Soldier's Passion for Order.*" The Free Press. 1993. p. 331.

Stiffer, Jeff. "*We Are Commanders Now.*" The American Legion. September 2020. p. 18.

Part Three Footnotes
Epigraph
1. Wilson, p.10

Introduction

2. Wikipedia. *Third Geneva Convention.*
PBS. *Japan, POWs, and the Geneva Conventions.* Bataan Rescue. 2007. https://www.pb s.org/wgbh/americanexperience/features/bataan-japan-pows-and-geneva-conventions/. 2021.
3. Newspapers.com. *Survivor's story of Americans being killed by German forces during the Malmedy Massacre in 1944.* https://www.newspapers.com/clip/25426 877/survivors-story-of-americans-being/. 2021.

Chapter One: Black Blood

4. Schuyler, George. Smithsonian American Art Museum Newsletter. Washington, DC. November 2021. p. 3

5. Randolph, A. Phillip. Smithsonian American Art Museum Newsletter. Washington, DC. November 2021. p. 1.

6. Taylor, James T. Letter to The New York Times: "*Negros Seek Equality, War to Them Is National and Not Racial Matter*". New York Times Complete World War II 1939- 1945, Coverage from the Battlefield

to the Home Front. Black Dog and Leventhal. New York, New York. 2013. p. 253.

7. Brown, Edgar G. *"Negros Pledge Loyalty"* Telegram to President Roosevelt. New York Times Complete World War II 1939–1945 Coverage from Battle front to Home Front. Black Dog and Leventhal. New York, New York. 2013. p. 222.

8. Lee, p. 88
   Hervieux, p. 26

9. Hervieux, p. 26

10. Wilson, p. 96

11. Lee, pp. 133–134

12. Moore, p. 69

13. The Study, pp.1–33

14. George, Denise and Child, Robert, *The Lost Eleven, The Forgotten Story of Black American Soldiers Brutally Massacred in World War II,* Calibre, Published by Berkley, Penguin Random House, New York, New York, 2017. p.85

15. Lee pp. 24–27

16. ibid. p.5

17. George, p. 81–82

18. ibid p. 81

19. ibid p. 82–83

20. Kelly. *Red Legs of the Bulge,* p. 55

Chapter Two: Becoming the Weapon

21. George, p. 75

22. Wikipedia. *333rd Field Artillery Regiment.* https://en.wikipedia.org/wiki/333rd_Field Artilery Regiment. 2021.

23. Kelly. *Red Legs of the Bulge,* p. 39

24. George, p. 108

25. ibid p. 108

26. ibid p. 88

27. ibid p. 90

28. ibid p.90

29. ibid pp. 90

30. Laughlin, Kurt. *US Army Pneumatic Tires of World War II.* http://www.usarmymodels.co m/ARTICLES/Tires/tires.html. 2021.

31. George, pp. 130–132

32. Hervieux, pp.171–172

33. Potter, p. 76

34. George, p. 147

35. Sasser, p. 53

Chapter Three: Bullets, Balloons, and Bombs Away

36. Legout, p.4

37. Bradley, pp. 552–553

38. George, p. 163

39. George, p. 166

40. ibid p.168
41. ibid p. 168
42. ibid p. 169

43. George, p. 180

44. American Red Ball. *Our Rich History.* www.redball.com/long-distance-moving-company/our-rich-history/. 2021.

45. Wikipedia. *Red Ball Express.* https://en-wikipedia.org/wiki/red_ball_express. 2021

46. George, p. 190, 191, 226, 227

47. ibid, p. 180

48. ibid, p. 181

49. ibid, p. 197

50. ibid, p. 190

51. ibid, p. 197

52. ibid, p. 188, 197

53. McGee, Tom. *Betty Gable: The Girl with The Million Dollar Legs.* Madison Books. New York, New York. 1997

54. Brander, Eric. *USO Shows in Prose: Entertainment during World War II.* United Service Organization. October 2015. https://www.uso.org/stories/61-uso-shows-in-prose-entertainment-during-world-war-ii. 2021.

Chapter Four: Before the Bulge

55. George, p. 219

56. ibid, p. 219

57. George, p. 253

58. ibid, pp. 214–215

59. George, 222, 253

60. George, p. 236

61. ibid, p. 238

62. Dupuy, Colonel R. Ernest. *St. Vith: Lion in the Way, the 106th Infantry Division in World War II.* Arcadia Press. Charleston, North Carolina. 2018. p. 16 Tolhurst, Michael. *Battle Ground Europe: Battle of the Bulge, St. Vith, US 106th Infantry Division.* Combined Publishing. Pennsylvania. 1999 p. 39

63. Kelly. *Red Legs of the Bulge,* p. 19

64. Whiting, Charles. *Death of a Division: The True Story of the 16,000 Green Troops of the US 106th Infantry Division Destroyed in The Battle of The Bulge.* Stein and Day Publishing, New York, New York. 1984. p. 11

65. George, p. 226

66. Whiting, p. 11

67. George, p. 237

Tolhurst p.42

68. Dupuy, p. 18

69. Whiting p. xv, 6, 7

70. George, p. 248
Tolhurst p. 59

71. Whiting, p. xvi

Chapter Five: Battle of the Bulge

72. Vannoy, Allyn. *"The Cold Shoulder."* World War II Quarterly Journal of The Second World War. McLean, Virginia. Winter 2021. p. 40.

73. Tolhurst, p. 59

74. George, p. 248

75. ibid, p. 267

76. Tolhurst, p. 66

77. George, p. 273

78. Tolhurst, pp. 124 and 128

79. George, p. 281–282

80. George, p. 281
Kelly, *Red Legs of the Bulge*, p. 116

Chapter Six: The Wereth Eleven

81. George, pp. 285–287

82. ibid, p. 288

83. ibid, p. 287

84. ibid, p. 289

85. George, 275

86. Kelly. *Red Legs of the Bulge*, p. 116
George, p. 289

87. George, p. 301

88. ibid, p. 302

89. Kelly. *Red Legs of the Bulge*, p. 116

90. George, p. 303

91. Discovering Belgium. *Remembering the Wereth Massacre*. 2021. https/www.discovering belgium.com/wereth-massacre. 2021.
Kelly. *Red Legs of the Bulge*, p. 116

92. George, p. 304

93. ibid, p. 304

94. ibid, p. 304

95. ibid p. 304

96. ibid p. 317

97. Kelly. *Red Legs of the Bulge*, p. 117

98. George p. 308

99. ibid, p. 308

100. ibid, p. 309

101. Historynet. *The Wereth 11: A Little-Known Massacre during the Battle of the Bulge.* https://www.historynet.com/the-wereth-11-a-little-known-massacre-during-the-battle-of-the-bulge.htm. 2021.

102. Kelly, C.J. *Forgotten Massacre.* July 19, 2022. https://owlcation.com/humanities /Forgotten-Massacre. 2022.

Chapter Seven: At War's End

103. National World War II Museum. *Sacrifice: The 333rd Field Artillery at the Battle of the Bulge.* August 21, 2020. https://www.nationalww2museum.org/war/articles/african-american-333rd-field-artillery-battle-of-bulge. 2021.

104. ibid

105. Wikipedia. *Belgium in World War II.* https://en.wikipedia.org/wiki/Belgium_in_World _War_II. 2021.

Epilogue

106. George, p. 326

107. ibid, p. 326

108. Movie: *Shawshank Redemption*

109. Wilson, p. 256

Part Three Bibliography

Books

Abdul-Jabbar, Kareem and Walton, Anthony. *Brothers in Arms.* Broadway Books. New York. 2004.

Allen, Colonel Robert S. *Lucky Forward: The History of Patton's Third US Army.* The Vanguard Press. New York, New York. 1947.

Anderson, Trezzvant W. *Come Out Fighting: The Epic Tale of the 761st Tank Battalion.* 1942–45. Advocate Press. New Haven, Connecticut. 1979.

Atkinson, Rick. *The Guns at Last Light, The War in Western Europe.* 1944–1945. Henry Hold and Company, LLC. New York, New York. 2013.

Blumenson, Martin. *Eisenhower.* Ballentine Books, Inc. New York. 1972.

Blumenson, Martin. *Mark Clark: The Last of the World War Two Commanders.* Congdon and Weed. New York, New York. 1984.

Blumenson, Martin. The Patton Papers. 1940–1945. DA CAPO Press. New York. 1974.

Boatner III, Mark Mayo. *The Biographical Dictionary of World War II.* Presidio Press, Navato, CA. *1996.*

Bradley, Omar N. and Blair, Clay. *A General's Life.* Simon and Schuster. New York, New York. 1983.

Brown, Edgar G. *Negros Pledge Loyalty.* Telegram to Teddy Roosevelt. New York Times Complete World War II 1939–1945 Coverage from Battle front to Home Front. Black Dog and Leventhal. New York, New York. 2013

Dupuy, Colonel R. Ernest. *St. Vith: Lion in the Way, the 106th Infantry Division in World War II.* Arcadia

Press. Charleston, North Carolina. 2018.

Edgerton, Robert B. *Hidden Heroism: Black soldiers in America's Wars.* Westview Press. Boulder, Colorado. 2001.

Eisenhower, John S.S. *The Bitter Woods: The Battle of the Bulge.* G.P. Putnam's Sons. New York, New York. 1969.

Fargo, Ladislas. *Patton: Ordeal and Triumph.* Ivan Oblensky Publishers. New York, New York. 1964.

George, Denise and Child, Robert. *The Lost Eleven: The Forgotten Story of Black American Soldiers Brutally Massacred in World War II.* Berkley, Penguin, Random House. New York, New York. 2017.

Gerlach, Jim (PA-6th District) and US Representative Chaka, Fattah (PA-2nd District), Congressional Resolution 68. US Representative. Washington, DC. 2013.

Hervieux, Linda. *Forgotten: The Untold Story of D-Day's Black Heroes, At Home and At War.* Harper-Collins. New York, New York. 2015.

Hirschon, Stanley P. *General Patton: A Soldier's Life.* Harper-Collins. New York, New York. 2002.

Hyslop, Stephan G. *Eyewitness to World War Two.* National Geographic Partners. Washington, DC. 2018.

Isserman, Maurice. *The Winter Army: The World War II Odyssey of the 10th Mountain Division, America's Elite Alpine Warriors.* Houghton Mifflin Harcourt. New York, New York and Boston, Massachusetts. 2019.

Kelly, C.J. *Red Legs of the Bulge: Artillerymen of the Battle of the Bulge.* Merriam Press. World War II History. Bennington, Vermont. 2014.

Kershaw, Alex. *The Longest Winter: The Battle of the Bulge and the Epic Story of World War II's Most Decorated Platoon.* MJF Books. New York, New York. 2004.

Lanning, Lt. Col. (Ret.) Michael Lee. *The American-Soldier, From Crispus Attucks to Colin Powell.* A Birch Lane Press Book. Carol Publishing Group. Secaucus, New Jersey. 1997.

Lee, Ulysses. *The Employment of Negro Troops in World War Two.* Office of the Chief of Military History. United States Army. 1966.

Lee, Ulysses. *The Employment of Negro Troops.* Office of the Chief of Military History, United States Army. 1994.

Legout, Colonel Gerard. *D-Day and the Battle of Normandy.* Imperial War Museum. US Archives Philippe Pique. Zorilla Productions. Rainier, Washington, DC. 1999.

McGee, Tom, Betty Gable: "The Girl with The Million Dollar Legs," Madison Books, New York, New York, 1997.

Meriam, Robert E. *Dark December.* Ziff-Davis. Chicago/New York. 1947.

Moore, Brenda. *To Serve My Country, To Serve My Race.* New York University Press. New York. 1996.

Morelock, J.D. *Generals of the Ardennes, American Leadership in the Battle of the Bulge.* National Defense University Press. US Government Printing Office. Washington, DC. 1994.

Motley, Mary Penick. *The Invisible Soldier: The Experience of the Black soldier, World War Two.* Wayne State University Press. Detroit, Michigan. 1987.

Nye, Roger H. *The Patton Mind "The Professional Development of an Extraordinary Leader."* Avery Publishing Group. Garden City Park, New York. 1993.

Nobecourt, Jaques. *Hitler's Last Gamble.* Schocken Books. New York. 1967.

Orlando, Robert. *The Tragedy of Patton: A Soldiers Date with Destiny, Could WWII's Greatest General Have Stopped the Cold War?* Humunix Books. West Palm Beach, Florida. 2021.

Price, Frank J. *Troy H. Middleton, A Biography.* LSU Press. Baton Rouge, Louisiana. 1974.

Randolph, A. Phillip. *Smithsonian American Art Museum Newsletter.* Washington, DC. November 2021.

Schuyler, George. *Smithsonian American Art Museum Newsletter.* Washington, DC. November 2021.

Taylor, James T. *Letter to The New York Times: Negros Seek Equality, War to Them Is National and Not Racial Matter.* New York Times Complete World War II 1939- 1945 Coverage from the Battlefield to the Home Front. Black Dog and Leventhal. New York, New York. 2013.

Toland, George. *Battle: The Story of the Bulge.* Random House. New York. 1959.

Tolhurst, Michael. *Battle Ground Europe: Battle of the Bulge, St. Vith, US 106th Infantry Division.* Combined Publishing. Pennsylvania. 1999.

Whiting, Charles. *Death of a Division: The True Story of the 16,000 Green Troops of the US 106th Infantry Division Destroyed in The Battle of The Bulge.* Stein and Day Publishing, New York, New York. 1984.

Wilford, Melissa K. *US Army Military Institute.* October 19, 2007.

Williams, David J. *Hit Hard.* Bantam Books. New York, New York. 1983.

Wilson, Joe W. Jr. *The 761st Black Panther Tank Battalion in World War II.* McFarland & Company. Jefferson, NC. 1999.

Film

Darabont, Frank, Producer; Marvin, Niki. Director; King, Steven, Screen Writer; *Shawshank Redemption*, Steven Spielberg Production. Hollywood, California. 1994.

Internet

American Experience. *Japan, POWS, and the Geneva Convention.* Bataan Rescue. 2007. https://www.pbs.org/ wgbh/americanexperience/features/bataan-japan-pows-and-geneva-conventions/. 2021.

American Red Ball. *Our Rich History.* www.redball.com/long-distance-moving-company/our-rich-history/. 2021.

Brander, Eric. *USO Shows in Prose: Entertainment during World War II.* United Service Organization. October 2015. https://www.uso.org/stories/61-uso-shows-in-prose-entertainment-during-world-war-ii. 2021.

Discovering Belgium. *Remembering the Wereth Massacre.* 2021. https/www.discovering belgium.com/wereth-massacre. 2021.

Historynet. *The Wereth 11: A Little-Known Massacre during the Battle of the Bulge.* https://www.historynet.com/the-wereth-11-a-little-known-massacre-during-the-battle-of-the-bulge.htm. 2021.

Kelly, C.J. *Forgotten Massacre.* July 19, 2022. https://owlcation.com/humanities /Forgotten-Massacre. 2022.

Laughlin, Kurt. *US Army Pneumatic Tires of World War II.* http://www.usarmymod els.com/ARTICLES/Tires/tires.html. 2021.

Military History Fandom. *Artillery.* https://military-history.fandom.com/wiki/Artillery. 2021.

National World War II Museum. *Sacrifice: The 333rd Field Artillery at the Battle of the Bulge.* August 21, 2020. https://www.nationalww2museum.org/war/articles/african-american-333rd-field-artillery-battle-of-bulge. 2021.

Nye, Logan. *These 17 Photos Show Why Artillery is King of the Battlefield.* January 25, 2021. https://www.wearethemighty.com/mighty-tactical/why-artillery-is-king-of-the-battlefield/. 2021.

Wikipedia. *333rd Field Artillery Regiment* https://en.wikipedia.org/wiki/333rd_Field _Artillery_ Regiment. 2021.

Wikipedia. *Belgium in World War II*. https://en,wikipedia.org/wiki/Belgium_in_World_War_II. 2021.

Wikipedia. *Red Ball Express*. https://en-wikipedia.org/wiki/red_ball_express. 2021

Wikipedia. *Third Geneva Convention*. https://en.wikipedia.org/wiki/Third_Geneva_Convention. 2021.

IMagazines

Armor, Clark Bruce K. "*The Battle for St. Vith: Armor in the Defense and Delay.*" US Armor School. Fort Knox, Kentucky. November/December 1974.

Dennis, William, G. "*Beyond the Breakout: The Battle for Brittany.*" World War II Quarterly Journal of the Second World War. McLean, Virginia. 2020.

Hymel, Kevin, M. "*Peiper's Bloody Blitz Through Belgium.*" World War II Quarterly Journal of the Second World War. McLean, VA. Fall 2019.

Prefer, Nathan, N. "*Forest of Death.*" World War II Quarterly Journal of The Second World War. McLean, VA., Fall 2018.

Schultz, Dennis. "*Coming Home.*" World War II Quarterly Journal of the Second World War. McLean, Virginia. Oct/Nov 2020.

Vannoy, Allyn. "*House to House in the German Heartland.*" World War II Quarterly Journal of the Second World War. McLean, VA., Fall 2020.

Vannoy, Allyn. "*The Cold Shoulder.*" World War II Quarterly Journal of The Second World War. McLean, Virgina. Winter 2021.

Webb, Mason, B. "*Destroying Dresden, Was Operation Thunder Clap: The 1945 Air Raid on The German City- A Military Necessity or An Allied War Crime? The Question Is Still Debated.*" World War II Quarterly Journal of The Second World War. McLean, Virginia. Spring 2019.

Newspaper

Michaels, Jim. *The Wereth 11: A Little Known Massacre During the Battle of The Bulge*. USA Today. November 8, 2013.

Part Four Footnotes

Epigraph

1. Moore, p.1

Author's Notes

2. Brokaw, Tom. *The Greatest Generation* (book cover/title). Random House Trade Paperbacks. New York, New York. 1998.

Introduction

3. National WWII Museum, New Orleans. *Mail Call: V-mail*. December 7, 2019. https://www.nationalww2museum.org/war/articles/mail-call-v-mail. 2021.

4. Adams-Earley, Charity. *One Woman's Army: A Black Officer Remembers the WAC*. Texas A&M University. College Station, Texas. 1989.

5. ibid, p. 151

Chapter One: Women to the Rescue

6. Essay Writer. *The Role of American Women during World War II*. Literature Essay Samples. November 3, 2020. https://literatureessaysamples.com/the-role-of-american-awomen-during-world-war-ii/. 2020.

7. Moore, p. 2

Lee, p. 421, 422

8. Moore, p. 20
9. Brokaw, p. 187
10. Lee, p. 421

11. Adams-Earley, p. 94

12. ibid, p.94

13. Moore, p. 35

14. Adams-Earley p. 39

15. Brokaw, p.187

16. Moore p. 29

17. National Women's history Museum. *African American Nurses in World War II*. July 8, 2019. htps://www.womenshistory.org/articles/African-american-nurses-world-war-ii. 2021.

18. Moore, p. 78

19. ibid, p. 78

20. ibid, p.78

21. ibid, p.69

22. ibid, p. 69

23. Airman 1st Class Gredyon Furstenau. *WWII Veteran Romay Davis Awarded Congressional Medal*. Aerotech News. August 5, 2022. https://aerotecnews.com/blog/20 20/02/29/6888th-central-postal-directory-battalion/. 2022.

Chapter Two: The House Women Built

24. Adams-Earley, p. 130

25. ibid, p. 26

26. ibid, p. 142

27. US Department of Defense. *Sorting Mail, Blazing a Trail: African American Women in World War II*. February 13, 2017. https://www.defense.gov/Explore /News/Article/Article/1081817/sorting-the-mail-blazing-a-trail-african-american-women-in-the-world-war-II/. 2021.

28. Wikipedia. *King Edwards School, Birmingham*. https://en.wikipedia.org/wiki/K ing_Edward%27s_School_Birmingham. 2021.

29. Moore, p. 112

Chapter Three: England: Mission Commenced

30. National World War II Museum. *Mail Call*.

31. Adams-Earley, p. 151

32. ibid, p.160

33. ibid, p.161

34. ibid, p. 161

35. ibid, p.163

Chapter Four: Mission Accomplished: Moving Forward

36. Moore, p. 116

37. ibid, p.116

38. Adams-Earley, p. 181

39. National World War II Museum, New Orleans. *Home Alive by '45: Operation Magic Carpet.* October 2, 2020. https://www.nationalww2.org/war/articles/operation-magic-carpet-1945. 2021.

Chapter Five: Home, Unsweet Home

40. Moore, p. 143

41. ibid, pp. 160–165

42. Feng, Patrick. *Executive Order 9981: Integration of the Armed Forces.* Army History. https://armyhistory.org/executive-order-9981-integration-of-the-armed-forces/. 2021.

43. Moore, p. 211

44. Fargey, Kathleen AAMH-FPO/14. *6888th Central Postal Directory Battalion (Women's Army Corps).* US Army Center for Military History. February 2014. https://histor y.army.mil/html/topics/afamFargey. 2021.

45. ibid, p.6

A Rear View of World War Two

46. Wikipedia. *Military Production during World War II.* July 2014. http:/Wikipedia.org/wi ki/Military_production_during_World_War_II/. 2021.

47. Brokaw, p. 163

Epilogue

1.-Wikipedia. *Congressional Gold Medal.* https://en.wikipedia.org/wiki/Congressio nal_Gold_Medal. 2021.

Part Four Bibliography
Books

Adams-Earley, Charity. *One Woman's Army: A Black Officer Remembers the WAC.* Texas A&M University. College Station, Texas. 1989.

Apple, Rhonda. *Celebrating Black Women*, Pentagram, Washington DC., 10 February 2012.

Bowers, William T., Hammond, William M., MacGarrigle, George L., *Black soldier White Army*, United States Army Center of Military History, Washington DC., 1996.

Brokaw, Tom, *The Greatest Generation*, Book Cover and Title, Random House Trade Paperbacks, New York, New York, 1998

Clark, Alexis, *These Black Female Heroes Made Sure US WWII Forces Got Their Mail*, The National Archives, Washington DC., Feb 1, 2019.

Edgerton, Edgar B., *Hidden Heroism: Black soldiers in America's Wars*, Westview Press, Boulder, CO., 2001.

Lanning, Lt. Col. (Ret) Michael Lee, *African American Soldier from Crispus Attacks to Colin Powell*, Carol Publishing Group, Secaucus, New Jersey, 1997.

Lee, Ulysses, *US Army In World War II, The Employment of Negro Troops*, Office of The Chief of Military History, United States Army, 1996.

Moore, Brenda L., *To Serve My Country, To Serve my Race*, New York University, New York, New York,1996.

Morris, Robert V., *Black Faces of War*, Zenith Press, Minneapolis, Mn. 2011.

Motley, Mary Penick, ed. *The Invisible Soldier: The Experience of the Black soldier, World War II*, Wayne State University Press, Detroit, Michigan, 1987.

Mullenbach, Cheryl, Double Victory: *How African American Women Broke Race and Gender Barriers to Help Win World War II*, Chapter 3, "WACs Go Overseas" Chicago Review Press, Chicago, Illinois, 2013 Royster, Jacqueline, Jones, *Profiles of Ohio Women, 1803–2003*, Ohio University Press, Athens, Ohio, 2003.

Stewart, Jeffery C., *1001 Things Everyone Should Know About African American History*, Broadway Book, New York, New York, 1996.

Warrington, Beth A., *"No Mail, Low Morale" The 6888th Central Postal Directory Battalion*, Military Review, The Professional Journal of the US Army, Army University Press, January-February 2019.

Internet

Army University Press. *Military Review*. January-February 2019. https://www.armyupress.army.mil/Journals/Military-Review/English-Edition-Archives/Jan-Feb-2019/Washington-Mail/. 2021.

Essay Writer. *The Role of American Women during World War II*. Literature Essay Samples. November 3, 2020. https://literatureessaysamples.com/the-role-of-american-awomen-during-world-war-ii/. 2020.

Fargey, Kathleen AAMH-FPO/14. *6888th Central Postal Directory Battalion (Women's Army Corps)*. US Army Center for Military History. February 2014. https://history.army.mil/html/topics/afamFargey. 2021.

Feng, Patrick. *Executive Order 9981: Integration of the Armed Forces*. Army History. https://armyhistory.org/executive-order-9981-integration-of-the-armed-forces/. 2021.

Furstenau, Greydon Airman 1st Class. *WWII Veteran Romay Davis Awarded Congressional Medal*. Aerotech News. August 5, 2022. https://aerotecnews.com/blog/2 0 20/02/29/6888th-central-postal-directory battalion/. 2022.

National Park Service. *National Archives for Black Women's History*. Mary McLeod Bethune Council House. https://www.nps.gov/mamc/learn/historyculture/mamc_n abwh.htm

National Women's history Museum. *African American Nurses in World War II*. July 8, 2019. htps://www.womenshistory.org/articles/African-american-nurses-world-war-ii. 2021.

National World War II Museum, New Orleans. *Home Alive by '45: Operation Magic Carpet*. October 2, 2020. https://www.nationalww2.org/war/articles/operation-magic-carpet-1945. 2021.

National WWII Museum, New Orleans. *Mail Call: V-mail*. December 7, 2019. https://www.nationalww2museum.org/war/articles/mail-call-v-mail. 2021.

US Department of Defense. *Sorting Mail, Blazing a Trail: African American Women in World War II*. February 13, 2017. https://www.defense.gov/Explore/News/Article /Article/10818 17/sorting-the-mail-blazing-a-trail-african-american-women-in-the-world-war-II/. 2021.

Walker, Frank C. *Well, Happy and Safe: Wartime Postmaster General Details the Work of Mail Delivery in WWII*. April 2, 2012.

Wikipedia. *Congressional Gold Medal*. https://en.wikipedia.org/wiki/Congressional_Go ld_Medal. 2021.

Wikipedia. *King Edwards School, Birmingham*. https://en.wikipedia.org/wiki/King_Ed ward%27s_School_Birmingham. 2021.

Wikipedia. *Military Production during World War II*. July 2014. http:/Wikipedia.org/wi ki/Military_production_during_World_War_II/. 2021.

Wikipedia. *Pony Express.* https://en.wikipedia.org/wiki/Pony_Express. 2021

Magazines

The American Legion. "*The Six Triple Eight.*" Indianapolis, Indiana. February 2021. pp 30–32

Newspapers

Fisher, Christina Brown. "*The Black Female Battalion That Stood Up to a White Male Army.*" New York Times. June 17, 2020.

Lynn's Stamp News. "*American Armed Forces Airmail During World War II.*" April 7, 2014.

McCarthy, Dennis. "*World War II: All Black Women's Army Corp Rescued. Mail Call.*" Torrance Daily Breeze. Torrance, California. Monday, January 18, 2022.

Thomas-Lester, Avis. "*Neither Rain, Nor Racial Bias.*" The Washington Post. February 26, 2009.

INDEX

3

320th Barrage Balloon Battalion (US Army)
3, 14, 23, 30–32, 39, 40, 43, 44, 46–48, 50, 52–56, 68, 167, 245, 247, 249, 250, 252

333rd Field Artillery Battalion (US Army)
3, 42, 55, 108, 117, 118, 143, 149, 155, 159–62, 164, 167, 168, 170, 171, 173, 174, 177, 179, 181–85, 187, 192, 194, 196–99, 240, 245, 247, 249

6

6888th Central Postal Directory Battalion (US Army)
3, 175, 201, 214, 222, 230, 231, 236, 238, 239, 242, 245, 247, 250, 252

7

761st Tank Battalion (US Army)
3, 55, 60, 61, 65–68, 72–82, 84, 86, 87, 89, 92–95, 97–99, 102, 104–7, 109, 111–13, 117–24, 126–32, 134–46, 160, 164, 170, 177, 240, 245, 247, 250

A

Academy (Charity Adams-Earley Girls Academy)
239
accolade
100, 128, 175, 222, 248
activated
30, 39, 72, 73, 155, 212, 247
activist
72, 159, 211, 212, 215
actress
175
Adams, Clifford Pvt (Medic)
98
Adams, Curtis Pvt (333rd Field Artillery Battalion)
193
Adams-Earley, Charity (Major; Lieutenant Colonel)
202, 214, 215, 218–22, 228–31, 235–37, 239–42, 250, 251
Adamson, Garland "Doc" Capt (761st Tank Battalion Medical Officer)
98, 102
administrative
5, 14, 38, 40, 211, 214, 220, 238, 248
aerial
33, 35, 40, 46, 164, 169
Afghanistan
36, 71, 207
Africa
8, 246
African American, African
2, 3, 5–7, 11, 13–17, 30–32, 37, 38, 40–42, 50, 52, 65, 68, 72, 74, 75, 77, 79, 81, 86–88, 96, 98, 99, 113, 116, 118, 119, 126, 129–32, 137, 141, 144, 150, 153, 155, 156, 158–60, 165, 167, 169, 170, 174, 176, 181, 182, 184–86, 190–92, 194, 196, 198, 211–15, 218, 219, 221, 223, 224, 227, 229–32, 237, 238, 241, 245, 246, 251
aid (medical, stations)
36, 51, 98, 102, 130, 162, 189
Aiea, Hawaii, US
54
air
1, 3, 23, 27, 31, 32, 35, 38, 39, 42, 43, 45, 46, 49, 50, 52, 53, 55, 80, 97, 106, 109, 111–13, 119, 124, 135, 136, 157, 162, 167, 168, 171, 172, 185, 194, 206, 208, 214, 252
aircraft
1, 13, 29–31, 35, 67, 68, 79, 169, 172, 216, 245
airfields
42, 141
airman
1, 3, 13, 45, 157, 252
airplane
11, 30, 35, 36, 43, 46, 168, 169, 189, 209, 226
Alabama, US
193
Albany, New York, US
237
Alexander, Clifford (Secretary of the Army, 1977-81)

142
allies
 19, 21, 29, 31, 34, 35, 42, 45, 46,
 48–50, 52–55, 59, 67, 68, 74, 84, 85,
 89, 106, 108, 109, 112, 119, 124, 126,
 129, 135, 137, 142, 167, 168, 170–74,
 177, 178, 181–85, 187–89, 194, 195,
 207, 210, 229, 230, 246
Amberg, Bavaria
 131
ambush
 125, 183
America, United States of
 1–3, 5–8, 10–17, 23, 30–38, 40–43,
 46, 47, 49, 50, 52, 58, 65, 67, 68,
 70–75, 77, 79, 81, 85–89, 92, 93, 96,
 98, 99, 101, 105, 108–13, 116, 118–20,
 123–27, 129–37, 139, 141, 142,
 144, 147, 150, 153, 155–60, 165–70,
 172–76, 178–96, 198, 199, 206–15,
 218–21, 223, 224, 227, 229–34,
 236–41, 244–49, 251
ammunition
 12, 41, 47, 80, 81, 83, 84, 96, 109, 115,
 126, 129, 134, 141, 168, 170, 172, 174,
 183–85, 187, 208, 217
amphibious
 43, 46, 47
antiaircraft
 23, 31, 32, 35, 50, 52, 162, 167, 172
antitank
 85, 100, 119, 124, 125, 141, 173
Antwerp, Belgium
 170, 177, 178, 181
aquatic
 46
Ardennes (Forest, Operation)
 97, 108, 109, 115, 135, 178, 181, 182,
 187
Arizona, US
 252
Arkansas, US
 1, 193
Arlington National Cemetery, US
 239, 240
armada
 30, 31, 167
armies
 68, 74, 129, 136, 142, 182
armor
 4, 11, 63, 65–67, 73, 76, 80, 82, 85–87,
 92, 93, 95–97, 99, 102, 106, 109, 111,
 115, 120–22, 125–27, 130, 136, 143,
 145, 153, 159, 167, 168, 177, 184, 185,
 190, 216, 232, 237, 250
Army Officer Training School (OTS)
 215
Army, United States
 1–3, 5–7, 10–12, 14–17, 30, 32, 34,
 37–43, 47, 49–52, 55, 65, 67, 68,
 70–82, 84, 85, 87–89, 91–94, 99, 100,
 102, 103, 105–9, 112, 113, 115–21,
 124, 126–29, 133–38, 140–43, 153,
 155–61, 163, 168–72, 175, 177, 180,
 182–84, 189–92, 194–96, 205, 207,
 208, 210–13, 215–17, 219–30, 232,
 233, 235, 236, 239–41, 245, 247–52
arrest
 195, 196, 248
artillery
 3, 12, 14, 32, 35, 40, 42, 50, 52, 55, 71,
 85, 92, 95, 98, 99, 101, 102, 108, 111,
 117, 118, 125, 126, 136, 141, 143, 148,
 149, 153, 155, 159–62, 164, 167–74,
 177, 179–81, 183–85, 187, 192, 194,
 196–99, 240, 245–47, 249
Asia
 1, 2, 207
assault
 31, 43, 44, 46–48, 50, 67, 85, 86, 93,
 101, 102, 104, 111, 119, 123, 131
ASU (Army Service Uniform)
 221
Atlantic
 53, 137, 165, 170, 171, 216, 246
atomic
 54, 246
attack
 12, 29, 30, 33, 42, 47, 68, 75, 91, 98,
 104, 105, 108, 109, 111, 113, 115, 119,
 123, 124, 130, 137, 158, 169, 173, 174,
 178–83, 210, 216, 228, 247
Attucks, Crispus (Boston Massacre, US)
 5
Austria
 68, 129, 134, 136, 138
Auxiliary (Women's US Army Auxiliary
Corps)
 158, 210, 212
aviation
 53
award
 6, 51, 52, 100, 102, 113, 114, 122, 138,
 142, 173, 194, 196, 222, 248–51

INDEX | 279

Axis powers
   12, 111, 157, 210
Azores Islands, Portugal (Europe)
   219

B

balloon
   3, 14, 22, 23, 29–37, 39–41, 43, 44, 46, 48–50, 52–58, 67, 68, 77, 87, 167, 240, 245, 247, 250
barracks
   37, 79, 211, 223, 229
base (military bases)
   16, 17, 39, 170, 175, 207, 222, 241
baseball
   77, 147, 232, 244
basketball
   223, 229, 233
Bataan (Death March, Philippines)
   252
battalion
   3, 4, 11, 14, 23, 30–32, 39, 40, 42–44, 46–48, 50, 52–56, 60, 61, 65–69, 72–82, 84–87, 89, 92–99, 102, 104–9, 111–13, 115, 117–24, 126–32, 134–46, 149, 155, 159–64, 167–77, 179–85, 187, 190, 192, 194, 196, 197, 199, 201, 214, 215, 220–22, 224–32, 234–36, 238–40, 242, 245, 247–50, 252
battery
   40, 43, 53, 54, 183
battle
   5, 9, 29, 32, 34, 45, 48, 52, 66–68, 71, 74, 76, 83, 87, 90, 91, 93, 96–99, 101, 102, 104, 105, 107, 108, 111–14, 119–28, 130, 131, 135–38, 142, 149, 155, 158, 159, 161, 162, 168, 169, 171, 173, 175, 178, 181, 182, 184, 186, 187, 189, 191, 194, 196, 205, 207, 229, 246–48
Bavaria, Germany
   124, 130, 131
beaches (Normandy, France)
   24, 25, 29, 30, 35, 41, 46–51, 53, 55, 58, 67, 68, 84, 85, 89, 167–69, 177, 224, 245, 247
Beasley, Normal PFC (6888th Central Postal Directory Battalion)
   252
Belgium
   68, 106, 109, 113, 121–23, 136, 155, 176–78, 180, 183, 187, 190–96, 198, 199
Berlin, Germany
   129
Bermuda
   219
Bezange-la-Grande, France
   96
Bezange-la-Petite, France
   96
bigotry
   5, 39, 52, 54, 212, 238
BII (basic issue items)
   88
bill (legislative)
   13, 15, 16, 140, 239
billets
   217, 247
bivouac
   79, 177, 178
Black (as in race)
   1–3, 5, 6, 10–17, 25, 32, 34, 37, 38, 42, 47, 51, 52, 65, 67, 68, 71–79, 81, 86–88, 90, 92, 95, 97–100, 102–6, 109, 112, 113, 115, 117–23, 126, 127, 130, 132–34, 139–43, 153, 155–65, 167–69, 175, 176, 183, 186, 188, 190–92, 196, 197, 211–17, 219, 220, 222, 224, 227, 229, 230, 232, 234–41, 246–51
Blake, Franchon Maj. (US Women's Army Corps)
   252
Blies River, Germany
   106
blimps
   35
Blitz (German, London)
   29, 34, 68, 106
boat
   41, 47, 89, 131, 167, 232
Bois-de-Hessling, France
   102
Bollenborn, Germany
   97, 125
bomb
   18, 30, 31, 34, 35, 48–50, 53, 54, 68, 106, 167, 217, 238, 245, 246
Bonaparte, Napoleon
   33
border
   91, 130, 171, 180, 183, 188
Boston, Massachusetts, US

5, 77
    Bougaktroff, France
    97, 100
Bradley, Mager CPL (333rd Field Artillery Battalion)
    193
Bradley, Omar N. (General of the Army)
    5, 31, 167
Bragg, Fort (North Carolina, US)
    39
branch
    52, 153, 212, 226, 238
Brandenberger, Enrich Gen. (German Seventh Army)
    182
Brazil, South America
    13
Brest, France
    170–74
brigade
    33, 52, 66, 87, 111, 173, 252
brigadier
    10, 37, 52, 82, 110, 113, 116, 220, 243, 252
Britain
    11, 12, 31, 33, 49–51, 124, 164–66, 170, 216, 230
Brittany, France
    170, 172, 173
Brokaw, Tom (US news anchor)
    205
Bronze Star
    52, 54, 102, 113, 118, 142, 179
Brown, Edgar G. (Director of the National Negro Council)
    157
Buchenwald, Germany
    131, 133
Buffalo Soldier
    15, 157, 252
Bulge, Battle of the (aka Ardennes Offensive)
    108, 109, 111, 118, 119, 128, 155, 176, 178, 182, 184, 187, 191, 194, 247, 248
Bulwark Camp, Wales
    43
Butcher, Vernon Sr. 2nd Lt. (US Marine Corps)
    252

C

Cajun
    38
Calais, France
    68, 171
California, US
    1, 2, 76, 98, 172, 177, 224
camp (various U.S. and foreign military camps)
    8, 14, 32, 37–43, 53, 54, 57, 73, 76, 77, 79, 81, 82, 84, 92, 96, 131, 132, 141, 161, 162, 164, 185–87, 216
campaigns
    135, 142, 209
Campbell, Noel Capt (US Army 6888th Central Postal Directory Battalion)
    218–20, 235
Canada
    12, 13, 27, 49, 70, 170
cannon
    71, 81, 82, 123, 131, 153, 179
Capitol, United States
    15
captain, US Army
    74, 75, 98, 99, 101, 102, 113, 122, 145, 160, 163, 183, 186, 202, 214, 215, 218, 219, 235, 251
captivity
    108, 131, 185, 186, 196
captured
    30, 34, 53, 81, 95, 108, 126, 127, 130, 131, 141, 170, 172, 173, 178, 181, 184–89, 194, 196, 206, 216
Cardiff, Wales
    42, 43
career
    2, 65, 67, 76, 122, 153, 158, 160, 205, 232, 252
cargo
    6, 216, 218
Carolina, North and South, US
    39, 77, 157, 193, 215
Carter, Jimmy (US President)
    142
castle
    131
casualties
    36, 47, 89, 101, 105, 126, 131, 141, 168, 172, 185, 194, 247
Catholic
    17, 157, 177, 187
Caucasian
    39, 75, 156
cavalry
    15, 36, 73, 76, 157, 158, 180, 252

celebrities
  175, 218
cemetery
  58, 193, 239, 240
ceremony
  52, 143, 191, 240, 250
chaplain
  12, 107, 157, 205, 213, 223
Chapman, Carlton Corp (US Army 761st Tank Battalion)
  60
Chartres, France
  177
Château de Brest (citadel in France)
  173
Checkendon, England
  42
Cherbourg, France
  53
Chicago, Illinois, US
  77
chief
  7, 10, 30, 31, 40, 73, 118, 131, 142, 157, 173, 240, 251
children
  1, 14, 16, 78, 90, 132, 162, 187, 189, 206, 211
Chinese
  2
Christmas
  75, 107, 108, 116, 175, 180, 182, 189, 235
church
  101, 120, 163, 168, 176, 183, 209, 214
Cincinnati, Ohio, US
  237
citadel
  173, 174
citation
  138, 139, 141, 142, 194, 236, 250
civilian
  10, 17, 76, 77, 79, 91, 153, 158, 165, 170, 173, 179, 190, 191, 193, 196, 205, 212, 218, 224, 226, 227, 232–34, 247–49
Claiborne, Camp (Army; Louisiana, US)
  73, 76, 77, 79, 96
Clark, Mark Lt Gen (US Army)
  5, 160
classified
  190, 191
clerk
  136, 223, 226
Cleveland, Ohio, US
  112
climate
  78, 80, 111, 142, 159, 160, 215, 251
Clinton, Bill (US President)
  100
coast
  3, 29, 30, 32, 42, 43, 49, 68, 75, 77, 85, 89, 98, 157, 164, 167, 170, 172, 210, 211, 241
Cobra, Operation (333rd Field Artillery Battalion)
  170, 171
Coburg, Germany
  146
College, Army War (US)
  5–7, 10, 13, 71, 141, 158
college (various US colleges)
  76, 78, 140, 153, 157, 162, 212, 214, 227, 237
Collins, Joseph Gen (US Army)
  5
colonel (US Army)
  4, 39, 74, 75, 80, 89, 93, 97–99, 105, 121–25, 135, 139, 160, 163, 169, 175, 176, 179, 195, 212, 214, 216, 221, 236, 240, 241, 250, 251, 252
Colorado, US
  237
colored (people)
  1–3, 5, 10, 15, 17, 32, 39, 43, 63, 65, 71, 81, 87, 94, 95, 103, 108, 116–18, 122, 126, 128, 141, 156, 158–60, 162, 247, 249
combat
  2, 3, 5, 6, 8, 10–12, 14, 32, 33, 41, 42, 44, 47, 48, 50, 51, 55, 61, 65–68, 71, 74, 78–84, 91–93, 98, 100–102, 105, 106, 108, 115, 117, 119–23, 129, 135, 138, 140–42, 147, 156, 158, 159, 162, 164, 170, 174, 176, 179, 184, 205, 207, 208, 211, 216, 217, 238, 247, 251
comedian
  42, 175
command
  4, 9, 13, 31, 32, 34, 39, 40, 48, 49, 51, 52, 59, 65–67, 74, 76, 80–82, 86, 89, 92, 93, 95, 97–100, 102, 104–10, 112–18, 121–24, 128–31, 134, 135, 137, 138, 151, 153, 157, 160, 161, 167, 173, 175, 179, 185, 186, 189, 190, 192,

195, 214, 215, 219–22, 224, 228–31, 236, 239, 249, 251
commendation
52, 106, 107, 113, 114, 135–37, 240, 250
commercial
32, 33, 173
commissioned officer (CO)
66, 76, 240
committee
7, 190, 192
communists
131
COMMZ
116, 117, 219
company
16, 34, 35, 40, 45, 75, 79, 81, 92, 93, 100–102, 104, 105, 108, 119, 121, 123, 124, 129–31, 170, 202, 209, 214, 215, 225
concentration camp
131, 141
Confederate
17, 33, 34, 241
Congress
6, 13, 15, 51, 57, 62, 142, 190, 192, 209, 213, 218, 239, 241, 250
Connecticut, US
164
convoy
170, 178, 206, 216, 234
corporal (US Army)
52, 117, 193, 250
corps
1, 32–34, 52, 65, 68, 70, 87, 91, 92, 106, 107, 109, 121, 128, 138, 142, 143, 153, 157, 158, 161, 164, 167, 173, 174, 179–81, 183–85, 194, 200, 205, 208, 210–13, 226, 240, 252
Cotentin Peninsula, France
53, 168
counterattack
99, 105, 108, 115
country
6, 10, 11, 13, 15, 16, 32, 50, 53, 66, 69, 70, 73, 77, 84, 85, 94, 109, 117, 121, 126, 131, 141, 143, 154, 156, 157, 159, 178, 186, 188, 190, 192, 207, 211, 212, 215, 237, 241, 245
court martial
74, 76, 99, 213, 228, 229
Crete, Greece
173
crimes
153, 190, 191, 195, 228, 248
Croix de Guerre (French Army honor)
6, 194
Cuba
34
Czechoslovakia
68, 129, 130

D

Dabney, William Garfield Corp (US Army 320th Barrage Balloon Battalion)
52, 250
Dachau concentration camp, Germany
131
Danube River, Europe
131
Davis, Benjamin O. Sr. Gen (US Army)
13, 116, 157, 219, 220, 222, 243
Davis, George PFC (US Army 333rd Field Artillery Battalion)
193
Dawley, Ernest J. Brig Gen (US Army)
82, 83
Dayton, Ohio, US
239
D-Day
24, 25, 29–32, 34, 43, 45–48, 51–55, 67, 68, 85, 89, 124, 167, 168, 170, 210, 219, 246, 247, 250
death
35, 49, 53, 66, 84, 89–91, 98, 101, 105, 112, 120, 125, 126, 128, 130, 133, 135, 163, 168, 185, 189, 194, 195, 206, 228, 249, 252
debarkation
87, 137, 164, 232
decorated
13, 121, 173, 222, 248, 249
defeat
12, 74, 136, 141, 163, 181, 192
defense
34, 49, 52, 71, 85, 141, 157, 180, 184, 206, 207, 213, 241
defensive
29, 46–48, 66, 67, 85, 86, 91, 104–6, 124, 129, 130, 163, 171, 173, 179, 182
democracy
156, 157
demoted
117

department
7, 10, 29, 51, 65, 71, 81, 86, 106, 121, 122, 196, 206–8, 211, 213–15
deploy
2, 6, 30, 32, 40–42, 50, 65, 66, 68, 80, 82, 85–87, 92, 120, 134, 135, 159, 161, 163, 164, 180, 216, 225, 247, 248
Depression, The Great
159, 216
desegregated
71, 238
destroy
29, 30, 45, 49, 50, 76, 80, 89, 91, 99–101, 104, 112, 116, 117, 120, 123, 126, 130, 137, 141, 162, 170, 172, 174, 183, 245
Detroit, Michigan, US
77
Devers, Jacob Gen (US Army)
124
Dietrich, Sep Gen (German Army)
181
Dieuze, France
97, 102, 104, 107
director
15, 16, 157, 159, 211, 212, 216, 219, 221
dirigibles (zeppelins, blimps)
35
disability
70
disabled
66, 80, 85, 145
disarm
11, 123
disaster
35, 85
discrimination
1, 15, 17, 39, 51, 119, 142, 156, 159, 165, 175, 211, 213
disease
103, 141, 162
dispatched
5, 190, 214
distinguished
51, 100, 138, 142, 194, 236, 250
dive-bombers
46
division
3, 4, 9, 42, 65, 67, 68, 85–87, 91–93, 95–97, 99, 102, 106–11, 113, 115, 119, 121, 123–31, 136–38, 142, 159, 161, 168, 173, 174, 176, 177, 179–85, 189, 194, 209, 226, 251, 252
Dixie
17
Dixon, Alyce CPL (US Army 6888th Central Postal Directory Battalion)
240
doctorate
213
domestic
37, 211, 238
doughboys
176
Douglas C-54 Skymaster cargo plane
218
drachen (German war balloon)
34
draft
1, 6, 13, 15, 16, 70, 71, 100, 154, 156, 158, 188, 196, 245
drill
73, 78, 80, 162, 202, 203, 216
Duchenstadt, Germany
186
Dunkirk, France
12, 31
duty
9, 40, 45, 70, 77, 84, 89, 95, 99, 100, 102, 107, 122, 140, 142, 158, 212, 213, 219, 222, 234, 243, 244, 251

E

Earley, Stanley (son of Maj Charity Adams-Earley, 6888th Central Postal Directory Battalion)
251
economic
173, 212, 216
Eddy, Manton S. Maj Gen (US Army)
128, 138
education
7, 14, 16, 78, 140, 153, 162, 213, 214, 227, 237, 239
Egypt
33
Eisenhower, Dwight D. Gen (Supreme Commander Allied Forces)
5, 10, 31, 45, 52, 59, 74, 86, 109, 116, 118, 129, 138, 139, 142, 169, 210, 229
Ely, H.E. Maj Gen (US Army, Army War College)

7
embarkation
   11, 41, 45, 54, 87
employment
   5, 7, 10, 36–38, 70, 105, 157, 159, 170, 209, 234, 238, 239, 249
enemy
   2, 11, 30, 33–35, 42, 45–50, 68, 71, 79–81, 85, 89, 91, 95–97, 99–102, 104, 105, 107, 108, 111, 113, 116, 119–21, 123, 125–27, 130, 131, 136–38, 141, 154, 155, 157, 163, 168, 169, 171, 174, 176, 180, 182–90, 194–96, 207, 216, 217, 228, 234, 238
engineers
   40, 47, 66, 92, 99, 123, 124, 126, 158, 169, 173
England
   29–31, 33, 34, 42, 43, 46, 53, 68, 77, 84, 87–89, 112, 136, 137, 144, 164, 167, 168, 170, 175, 177, 178, 208, 209, 219, 220, 225, 229, 230, 232, 233, 242, 250
enlist
   2, 6, 10, 15, 16, 32, 40, 43, 71, 74, 75, 129, 130, 135, 157, 185, 194, 210, 211, 214, 218, 219, 237, 251
Enns River, Austria
   134
entertainment
   42, 87, 132, 175, 218
equality
   9, 11–13, 33, 67, 78, 88, 122, 140, 143, 159, 185, 186, 211, 216, 238
equipment
   11–13, 31, 33, 40, 41, 43, 54, 66, 71, 73, 74, 78–80, 84, 87–89, 92, 93, 112, 120, 122, 126, 131, 136, 174, 178, 183, 184, 189, 217, 230
Erlenbach, Germany
   97
escape
   16, 71, 80, 87, 101, 125, 183, 186, 187, 191, 197
Eupen-Malmedy Region, Belgium
   187
Europe
   2, 3, 5, 12, 18, 20, 21, 30, 31, 34, 35, 41, 42, 45, 49, 50, 59, 68, 72–74, 76, 84, 86, 108, 109, 115, 116, 119, 126, 135, 137, 138, 140–42, 144, 154, 155, 161, 165, 178, 179, 181, 192, 194, 207–9, 214, 216, 218, 219, 221, 225–27, 229, 231, 233–36, 245–51
evacuation
   31, 51, 97, 98, 100–102, 183
Evangeline, Camp (Claiborne; US Army)
   73
executive
   74, 98, 160, 218, 235, 250
explosive
   29, 30, 163, 174, 189
exterminate
   96, 131, 132

F

facility
   15, 16, 37, 39, 44, 97, 132, 170, 185, 207, 216, 217, 220, 223
family
   7, 14, 16, 38, 102, 109, 164, 187–91, 193, 195, 205–7, 212, 232, 234
famous
   87, 129, 134, 157, 175, 178
fatality
   35, 113, 120, 169, 196
Fatherland (Germany)
   12, 109, 124, 132, 155, 182, 186, 188
FBI (Federal Bureau of Investigation)
   159
federal
   2, 159, 237
female
   71, 94, 211–15, 217, 219, 227, 230, 231, 236, 238, 250, 251
fire
   17, 35, 47, 48, 50, 80, 81, 83–85, 88, 91, 93, 95, 98–102, 104, 111, 113, 119–23, 125, 129–31, 134, 136, 137, 141, 143, 157, 162, 168, 169, 172–74, 176, 179, 182–85, 189, 194, 197, 207, 216, 238, 247
fitness
   6, 220
five-star general (US Army)
   74
flag
   58, 130, 170, 187, 205
fleet
   29, 46, 67, 167, 170
flight
   27, 33, 218, 219
Florida, US
   77

fly
　35, 39, 42, 43, 46, 49, 53, 58, 68, 157, 177
food
　11, 33, 92, 109, 126, 136, 154, 185, 208, 226
football
　73, 75, 76, 94
force
　11, 12, 16, 19, 23, 27, 31, 33, 34, 37, 42, 45–47, 49, 50, 52, 53, 55, 68, 71, 73, 79, 84–87, 91, 92, 96, 104–6, 110, 112, 115–17, 124–26, 128, 130, 135, 138, 167, 170–72, 174, 178, 184, 186, 188, 189, 194, 195, 207, 210, 214, 216, 227, 238, 246, 247
forest
　108, 123, 131, 178, 180–82, 185, 187
formation
　67, 176, 228, 233
Forts (various US military)
　34, 39, 54, 76, 77, 79, 142, 143, 202, 215, 216, 236, 239, 241, 250, 252
France
　5, 6, 11, 12, 19, 22, 24, 30, 33, 34, 42, 44, 46, 52–54, 68, 69, 84, 85, 89, 91, 92, 99–101, 104–6, 112, 113, 122, 124, 126, 128, 129, 135, 136, 147, 150, 167, 170–72, 176–78, 183, 195, 217, 220, 221, 231–35, 242–44, 246, 247, 250
freedom
　119, 125, 130–32, 141, 192, 240, 250
friendly (fire, weapon, etc.)
　95, 125, 163, 169, 170, 179, 184, 216
frigates
　167, 245
front (European fronts, front lines, etc.)
　6, 45, 68, 89, 99, 103–5, 107, 108, 111, 116, 117, 119, 124, 135, 143, 162, 178, 180, 182, 183, 221
frostbite
　120, 121, 162, 188
führer
　111, 173, 182
funds
　13, 192
funerals
　224

G

Garrison, Willie MN3 (US Navy)
　252

Geimont, France
　97
general (US Army)
　3, 5, 7, 10, 13, 17, 31, 34, 37, 41, 51, 52, 55, 59, 62, 63, 65, 67, 68, 74, 76, 82, 83, 86, 92–95, 97, 102, 103, 105–10, 113–19, 124, 128, 129, 131, 132, 135, 137–39, 143, 153, 157, 159, 161, 167, 169, 170, 173, 174, 179–82, 192, 194, 208–10, 213, 219–22, 228, 229, 240, 241, 243, 245, 249, 251, 252
Geneva Convention
　98, 108, 154, 155, 162, 185, 186, 188, 196
Georgia, US
　39, 54, 77, 193, 215, 237
Germany
　11–13, 18, 19, 29–31, 33–35, 45–47, 49, 50, 53, 55, 67–69, 73, 81, 85, 86, 89, 91, 94, 98–102, 104–13, 115, 119–21, 123–32, 135–38, 140, 142, 146, 154, 155, 157, 165, 168–75, 177–86, 188–91, 194, 195, 197, 199, 210, 211, 216, 217, 231, 233, 234, 238, 245, 246, 248, 249, 252
Gerow, Leonard T. Maj Gen (US Army)
　5, 52
GFRC (Ground Force Replacement Command; US Army)
　115, 116
Ghost Front (Belgium, Schnee Eifel sector)
　180, 183
GI
　67, 78, 140, 166, 188, 191, 193, 239
Gilmore, Morris Barton, Sgt (US Marine Corps)
　252
Glasgow, Scotland
　217, 219–21
Gold Beach, Ver-sur-Mer, France
　46, 167
Goodyear (blimp)
　29, 34
government
　13, 38, 72, 109, 140, 155, 157, 160, 174, 178, 196, 206, 209, 237
governor
　2, 15, 73, 211
graduate
　40, 75, 76, 98, 153, 162, 214, 215, 237, 238

grave
  50, 115, 158, 190
Gravett, Clarence Sr. PFC (U.S. Army Air Forces; Tuskegee Airman; Author's father)
  4, 16, 28, 252
Gravett, Peter Maj Gen Retired (US Army)
  4, 28
Greenock, Scotland
  42
Gregg, Arthur J. Gen (US Army)
  241
Gregg-Adams, Fort (US military fort, Virginia; formerly Fort Lee)
  241
ground (ground forces, combat, etc.)
  31, 41, 45, 55, 84, 115, 120, 162, 171, 172, 206, 235
group (Army, Armored, Artillery)
  31, 92, 97, 124, 160, 161, 164, 168
Gruber, Camp (US military camp, Oklahoma)
  161, 162, 164
Gruflange, Germany
  119
Guébling, France
  99, 100
Gullahs (Black Muslims)
  77
gun
  12, 46–49, 66, 67, 79–82, 85, 90, 91, 93, 101, 102, 111, 119, 120, 123, 125, 130, 134, 136, 141, 143, 146, 163, 164, 167, 169, 179, 183, 186, 188, 190, 246

H

Hague Convention/Regulation on War
  98
Haislip, Wade H. Gen (US Army)
  5
Hamilton, Eugene PVT (US Army 761st Tank Battalion)
  146
hand-to-hand combat
  79, 162, 216
Harlem, New York, US
  42, 87
Harlem Hellfighters (369th Infantry, US Army National Guard)
  150
Harris, James PO2 (US Navy)
  252
Harris, Robert L. PFC (Gen Patton Third Army; US Army Constabulary)
  252
Harrison, Ivan Capt (US Army 761st Tank Battalion)
  145
Hartman, R.W. Lt Col (US Army)
  139
Hawaii (US)
  54, 161, 210
Haye-du-Puits, France
  169
headquarters
  31, 40, 87, 97, 106, 129, 138, 161, 168, 169, 183, 184, 206, 209, 214, 219, 222, 228, 229, 233
hedgerow
  84–86, 169
Henri-Chappelle American Military Cemetery (Belgium)
  193
Hermès, Belgium
  123
heroic
  3, 25, 50–52, 65, 97, 100, 101, 118, 137, 138, 191–94, 240, 248
Herresbach, Germany
  123
Herrington, Aaron Maj (Tuskegee Airman, US Army Air Force)
  252
high school
  78, 162
Hindenburg (German airship)
  35, 36
Hiroshima, Japan
  54
Hispanics
  1
Hitler, Adolf
  3, 11, 12, 68, 111, 112, 124, 157, 158, 168, 172–74, 181, 199, 208, 210, 215, 238, 240
HMS Aquitania, HMS Queen Mary
  42, 224
Hobby, Oveta Culp (US Secretary of Health, Education, and Welfare; WAAC Director)
  211, 212, 216, 221
Hobby, William P. Gov (Texas, US)
  211
Hodges, Courtney Hicks Gen (US Army)

5, 52
Holland (Netherlands)
   68, 119, 123, 136
homecoming
   1, 71, 140
honor
   1, 6, 8, 41, 51, 52, 76, 94, 100, 121, 122, 138, 140, 142, 159, 173, 191–94, 197, 224, 237, 240, 241, 249, 250
Honskirch, France
   97, 104, 105
Hoover, J. Edgar (Director of the Federal Bureau of Investigation)
   159
horse
   33, 73, 90, 126, 157, 158, 232, 252
hospital
   37, 51, 102, 174, 189, 190, 213, 226
Houffalize, Belgium
   178
housing
   6, 38, 140, 174, 185, 223
howitzer (artillery weapon)
   162, 163, 169, 198
Huachuca, Fort (US military, Arizona)
   252
Huem, Holland
   119, 123
Hunt, Hollis Lt Col (US Army)
   98, 99, 121, 122

I

Iceland
   10
immigrants
   109
imprisoned
   168, 185
incursion
   91, 106, 108, 119, 124, 167, 173, 194
induction
   1, 2, 15, 70, 71, 78, 156
infantry
   3, 4, 6, 40, 44, 47, 52, 67, 80, 85, 86, 91–93, 95, 97, 99, 101, 102, 104–9, 111, 115–19, 123, 124, 129–31, 133, 136–38, 141, 150, 151, 153, 159, 168, 171–74, 177, 179, 180, 184, 185, 189, 194, 251
injury
   17, 76, 86, 98, 99, 113, 121, 123, 162, 163, 168, 186

injustice
   16, 212, 248
inspection
   40, 80, 82, 101, 218, 220, 228
insubordination
   76, 213
integration
   1, 2, 14, 75, 86, 113, 186, 238
Intelligence (Army)
   29, 108, 206, 227
international
   98, 108, 154, 172, 186, 216, 233
interview
   118, 133
invade
   11–13, 19, 31, 42–44, 47, 54, 68, 85, 154, 157, 167, 171, 178, 210, 245, 246
investigation
   29, 155, 190, 191, 195, 196, 213, 248
Iowa, US
   202, 215
Iraq
   36, 71, 207
isolationists
   11, 12
Italy
   159, 210, 246

J

Jabeek, Holland
   123
Jackson, Joseph PFC (US Army 333rd Field Artillery Battalion; 969th Field Artillery Battalion)
   199
Jackson, L.D. PFC (General Patton's Third Army, Red Ball Express)
   252
James, C.L.R. (African American writer)
   156
James, Ruth L. PVT (US Army 6888th Central Postal Directory Battalion)
   243, 244
Japan
   2, 12, 29, 54, 141, 157, 158, 210, 245, 246
jeep
   48, 93, 224
Jernigan, Patricia Maj (US Army 6888th Central Postal Directory Battalion)
   222
Jersey, Dr. Paul D. (Selective Service

Assistant Director)
15
Jewish
2, 17, 131, 132, 157
Jim Crow (era, laws)
1, 17, 67, 137, 156, 165
job
16, 37, 38, 47, 71, 95, 115, 118, 122, 128, 138, 140, 156, 157, 212, 213, 223, 226, 236, 249, 250
Jodl, Alfred Gen (Germany)
135
Jones, Fred Douglas TPR (Buffalo Soldier, US Army)
252
junket
218
Juno Beach, Normandy, France
46, 167

K

Kansas, US
76
Kaserne Tallandier (former French military headquarters; Napoleon)
233
Kelsey, Harmon Lt Col (US Army 333rd Field Artillery Battalion)
160, 163, 169, 175, 176, 179, 183
Kentucky, US
77, 79
Kerprich, France
101
KIA (killed in action)
114, 129
killed
6, 35, 46, 86, 94, 98, 100, 101, 104, 105, 108, 111, 112, 114, 118, 120, 121, 125, 126, 130, 131, 141, 163, 168, 169, 174, 179, 181, 183, 185, 188, 194, 197, 226, 247
Killeen, Texas, US
143, 250
Kilmer, Camp (Army; New Jersey, US)
53
Klingenmunster, Germany
125
Knittel, Gustav Maj (German commander)
190, 249
Korean War
2, 153, 241

KP (kitchen police unit)
158
K-rations
188
Kriegberg, Germany
119
Krueger, Walter Gen (US Army)
5
Kulmbach, Bavaria
130
Kutonase (German cable cutter)
49

L

labor
7, 14, 37, 154, 157, 158, 186, 213
la Compagnie d'aérostiers (French Aerostatic Corps)
33, 168
Lakehurst Naval Station (New Jersey, US)
35
landing
24, 25, 29–32, 35, 43, 44, 46–54, 67, 68, 88–91, 124, 125, 135, 137, 154, 157, 167, 168, 171–73, 179, 180, 182, 219, 221, 224
Langer, Maria and Mathias (Belgium)
187–91
language
38, 229
launched
12, 29–31, 33, 49, 179, 217
laundry
37, 38, 158, 237
LaVigne, Gertrude 1LT (US Army 6888th Central Postal Directory Battalion)
203
Lawson, Thomas O. Brig Gen (US Army)
252
Lawton, Fort (US military, Washington)
54
leadership
2, 3, 5–7, 9, 10, 12, 13, 15, 32, 38, 40, 43, 44, 66, 67, 72, 74–76, 89, 98, 100, 101, 109, 113, 121, 139, 141, 155–60, 165, 176, 185, 195, 214–16, 222, 227, 229, 230, 233–36, 245–47, 249
Lear, Ben Gen (Commander, US Second Army)
82
Leatherwood, James PFC (US Army 333rd

Field Artillery Battalion)
  193
Lee, Fort (US military fort, Virginia; now Fort Gregg-Adams)
  239, 241
Lee, John C.H. Gen (US Army)
  51, 116, 219–22, 228, 229
legal
  70, 76, 77, 84, 99, 164, 229
legislation
  13, 15
Le Havre, France
  232
Leigh-Mallory, Trafford Sir ACM (British Royal Air Force)
  31
Lend-Lease Act, 1941
  12
Lesneven, France
  173, 174
Les Pieux, France
  89, 91, 92
letters
  11, 15, 86, 164, 206–9, 213, 226, 229, 234, 240, 249
liberated
  30, 96, 101, 121, 125, 131, 133, 134, 141, 173, 174, 177, 194, 219, 246
Liege, Belgium
  193
lieutenant
  4, 39, 52, 62, 74–76, 80, 89, 93, 97–99, 106, 108, 113, 115, 121–25, 135, 139, 145, 147, 160, 161, 163, 167, 169, 170, 175, 176, 179, 194–96, 212, 214, 219, 221, 228, 235, 236, 240, 241, 244, 250–52
logistical
  33, 40, 84, 92, 126, 164, 177, 178, 180, 181, 211, 219, 220, 248
London, England
  29, 34, 68, 165, 175, 219, 221, 224
Long Beach, California, US
  177, 224
Long Island, New York, US
  146
long-range
  123, 163, 167
Long Tom (155-mm field gun)
  131, 143, 162, 163
Lorraine, France
  93
Los Angeles, California, US
  29, 69, 75, 76, 177
Losheim Gap, Belgium
  179, 181
losses
  36, 48, 58, 85, 86, 100, 101, 105, 108, 111–13, 115, 117, 121, 125, 126, 132, 135, 141, 155, 162, 168, 169, 178, 179, 184, 192, 193, 195, 197, 205, 247
Louis, Joe SGT (US Army; Professional Boxer)
  42
Louisiana (US state; Louisiana Maneuvers)
  38, 73, 77–79
LSTs (landing ship tanks)
  88
Luftwaffe (German Air Force)
  31, 49, 50, 53, 67, 131, 172, 189
Lumpkin, Theodore "Ted" Jr. Lt Col (US Army Air Forces; Tuskegee Airman)
  252
Luxembourg, Europe
  68, 69, 113, 119, 122, 136, 178, 183

M

machine gun
  12, 35, 47, 49, 66, 82, 85, 93, 119, 123, 125, 130, 134, 141, 146, 169, 246
machines
  32, 35, 71, 78, 79, 85, 88, 111, 120, 245
magazine (ammunition; publications)
  17, 84, 97, 176, 206
Magee, John Gillespie Jr. (fighter pilot, Canadian Royal Air Force)
  27
Maginot Line, France
  91, 105, 171
mail
  11, 175, 200, 208, 209, 214, 225–28, 230, 232–35, 243
maintenance
  66, 79, 80, 93, 115, 121, 122, 134, 136, 158, 174
major (military rank)
  7, 31, 41, 52, 95, 97–100, 102, 107, 122, 128, 129, 137, 161, 167, 173, 190, 214, 215, 218–22, 225, 228–31, 235, 236, 242, 249, 251, 252
Malmedy, Belgium

108, 109, 155, 186, 195, 199, 249
maneuvers
   43, 73, 81, 82, 172
Manhattan, New York, US
   84
Marine (US Marine Corps; merchant marine)
   3, 70, 157, 170, 206, 208, 210, 252
marksmanship
   79, 162
marshal
   31, 43, 182
Marshall, George Gen (US Army; Chief of Staff)
   5, 10, 74
Maryland, US
   39
Mason-Dixon Line, US
   78, 140
massacre
   5, 46, 155, 190–92, 195, 196, 249
Matchett, Henry Brig Gen (Ground Force Reinforcement Command)
   116
McAuliffe, Anthony Brig Gen (US Army)
   110, 129, 138
McClure, Donald HM2 (US Navy)
   252
McHenry, Irvin Capt (US Army 761st Tank Battalion)
   145
McLeod, William Capt (US Army)
   160, 183, 186
McLeod-Bethune, Mary (US educator, activist, humanitarian)
   72, 159, 212, 215
Meade, Fort (US military fort, Maryland)
   39
mechanical
   4, 13, 40, 65–67, 71, 73, 79, 80, 120, 251
medal
   6, 51, 52, 54, 100, 113, 118, 122, 142, 179, 196, 248, 250
Medal of Honor
   6, 51, 52, 122, 142, 250
media
   11, 14, 72, 97, 109, 155, 191, 206, 230, 248
medical
   6, 16, 47, 50, 51, 70, 84, 97, 98, 100, 102, 109, 121, 136, 154, 164, 185, 190, 239
102
Memorandum of the Chief of Staff Regarding Negro Manpower in WWII (US; Nov. 10, 1925)
   7, 10
memorial
   101, 143, 191–93, 205, 230, 239, 240
meteorology
   30, 40, 66, 108
Metz, France
   124
Meuse River, Europe
   181
Mexican-American
   16
Middleton, Troy Maj Gen (US Army Eighth Corps)
   167, 173, 174, 180
military
   1–3, 6, 7, 10–13, 16–21, 29, 32, 33, 37–39, 41, 42, 51, 65, 66, 68, 70–74, 76, 86, 93, 101, 102, 122, 140, 142, 153, 155–57, 159, 160, 165, 168, 169, 173, 175, 176, 178, 179, 183, 185, 188, 191, 193, 195–97, 205–9, 213–29, 231–34, 236–40, 245, 247–49, 252
minefields
   22, 79, 91, 100, 124, 136, 141, 169, 173, 252
minister
   157, 213, 214
minorities
   11, 15, 71, 165, 220, 239, 245
mission
   41–43, 46, 51, 54, 55, 66, 69, 75, 91, 93, 95, 96, 104, 109, 112, 119, 128, 130, 131, 138, 158, 168–70, 172, 179, 205, 206, 215, 216, 220, 225, 227, 229, 230, 232, 233, 236, 240, 248, 250
Mississippi, US
   79, 193
Montfort Point Marines (US Marine Corps)
   3, 252
Montgomery, Bernard Law Gen (British commander, 21st Army Group)
   31
monument
   143, 192, 197, 223, 249, 250
Moore, Brenda Dr. PhD (US military

Meharry Medical School, Tennessee (US)

sociologist)
    238, 240, 241
morale
    123, 127, 175, 208, 209, 220, 227, 229, 234, 236, 237
mortar
    47, 82, 102, 245
Morville-lès-Vic, France
    97, 101, 107
Moss, Nathaniel PVT (US Army 333rd Field Artillery Battalion)
    193
Moten, George PFC (US Army 333rd Field Artillery Battalion)
    193
Moyenvic, France
    97
MP (military police)
    93
murder
    108, 109, 154, 155, 186, 188, 189, 196, 197, 248, 249
Myers, Fort (US military fort, Virginia)
    142

N

NAACP (US National Association for the Advancement of Colored People)
    71, 159
Nagasaki, Japan
    54
National Archives (US)
    22, 24, 56–60, 110, 142, 144–48, 198, 199, 202, 239, 242–44
National Guard (US Army National Guard)
    2, 65
National Negro Council; National Council of Negro Women (US)
    157, 212
Navy (US, Britain)
    12, 70, 89, 157, 208, 210, 252
Nazi
    11, 45, 47, 49, 50, 68, 81, 96, 113, 132, 144, 146, 155, 168–70, 172–74, 180–82, 185–90, 192, 194, 210
Nebraska, US
    34, 39
Negro
    2, 3, 5–11, 13–17, 38, 46, 71, 72, 74, 75, 81, 88, 93, 97, 100, 101, 105, 112, 113, 115–17, 119, 121, 122, 128, 132, 140, 142, 151, 156–61, 163, 165, 169, 175, 176, 187, 211, 212, 215, 216, 221, 227, 229, 230, 232, 237, 238, 247
Neider-Schlettenbach, Germany
    97
Netherlands (Holland)
    91
Neuhaus, Germany
    131
news
    10, 11, 46, 51, 93, 97, 102, 190, 205, 206, 224, 227, 232
non-combat
    102, 105, 121, 141, 158
non-commissioned officer (NCO)
    6, 8, 17, 40, 86, 113, 116, 117
Normandy, France
    24, 29, 30, 32, 34, 41, 47, 48, 50, 52, 53, 55, 67, 68, 84, 89, 167–69, 171, 198, 247, 250
nurse (military)
    51, 98, 130, 196, 213, 219, 238

O

Oahu, Hawaii (US)
    54
Obama, Barack (US President)
    52, 250
objective
    74, 89, 102, 112, 124, 125, 128, 170, 177, 181
occupied
    11, 12, 77, 96, 102, 124, 137, 140, 171, 173, 178–80, 216, 218, 227
ocean
    47, 53, 137, 170
offensive
    18, 45, 66, 67, 85, 113, 171
officer
    5–10, 12, 17, 32, 35, 39, 40, 43, 50, 51, 66, 74–76, 82, 86, 95, 98, 99, 102, 105, 107, 113, 116, 117, 121, 122, 127–30, 135–37, 153, 157, 158, 160, 173, 176, 179, 185, 186, 194, 209, 211, 213–15, 218, 219, 222, 227, 228, 230, 234, 235, 240, 241, 250–52
Officer Candidate School (OCS)
    153
Oglethorpe, Fort (US military fort, Georgia)
    215, 216
Ohio, US
    237, 239

Oklahoma, US
77, 161, 162
Omaha, Nebraska, US
24, 34, 41, 46–50, 53, 58, 68, 89, 167, 168, 247
operation
1, 2, 5, 9, 11–13, 20, 31, 33, 40–44, 48, 54, 66, 67, 71, 78, 81, 86, 87, 92, 96, 97, 99, 112, 122, 123, 125, 126, 129, 134, 138, 142, 143, 153, 161, 163, 167, 169–71, 181, 184, 194, 206–8, 219, 224–26, 228, 229
oppression
45, 107
OPSEC (operational security)
207
orders
15, 33, 53, 77, 80, 81, 84, 93, 109, 112, 117, 124, 134, 168, 170, 183, 218, 220, 222, 228, 230, 231
Oregon, US
68
organization
10, 11, 32, 40, 43, 70, 87, 92, 93, 129, 155, 159, 174, 195, 205, 210–15, 222, 225, 227, 229
Overlord, Operation
18, 31
overseas
12, 32, 41, 82, 84, 88, 89, 120, 130, 135, 165, 205, 206, 208, 209, 211, 214, 216–18, 223, 224, 230, 234, 237, 241, 248

P

Pacific Fleet (US)
29
panzer tank (German)
105, 109, 123, 124, 127, 130, 136, 141, 180, 181, 185, 190
Paris, France
37, 52, 177, 219, 230, 231, 234, 250
patriotic
11, 16, 94, 196, 205, 208, 229, 236, 245
patrol
9, 167, 182, 223
Patton, George S. Gen (US Army)
3, 5, 55, 62, 63, 65, 67, 72, 74, 76, 86, 87, 89, 91–95, 99, 105–9, 118, 122, 124, 128, 129, 131, 132, 138, 139, 141, 143, 153, 161, 170, 173, 180, 194, 226, 240, 245, 248–50, 252
Paul, Willard S. Maj Gen (US Army)
95, 102, 107, 128, 138

peace
13, 133, 181, 208, 233, 237
Pearl Harbor, Hawaii, US
12, 29, 158, 161, 171, 210, 245
Peiper, Joachim SS Lt Col (German Schutzstaffel)
195, 196
peninsula
53, 168, 172
Pennsylvania, US
164
Pentagon, US
215
performance (combat, unit, etc.)
8, 50, 113, 122, 128, 175, 222, 250
Pershing, John J. "Blackjack" Gen (Commander, American Expeditionary Forces)
34
personnel
39–41, 43, 74, 84, 86, 98, 116, 136, 193, 206, 208, 225, 229
Philadelphia, Pennsylvania, US
33, 50, 77
Photographs (by US Army battalion)
4, 19, 22, 24, 28, 56–60, 110, 144–47, 150, 198–200, 202, 242–44
pillboxes
91, 125, 141, 173
pilot
1, 27, 50, 210, 219
pistols
76, 85, 93, 126
plane
8, 35, 42, 49, 50, 112, 136, 143, 167, 169, 218, 219
platoon
47, 76, 79, 92, 93, 99, 118, 124, 129, 131
police
93, 153, 156, 158, 168, 223
policy
5, 7, 65, 72, 76, 79, 88, 105, 106, 117, 153, 175, 196, 206, 211, 212
Polish
132
politics
136, 154, 211, 212
Pont-L'Abbe, France
168
port
12, 30, 41, 53, 170, 173, 177, 178, 181
positions

6, 37, 38, 50, 66, 80, 85, 100, 102, 108, 115, 138, 163, 168, 171, 179, 182, 189, 206, 211, 212, 215, 223, 227
post
17, 37, 38, 96, 123, 131, 168, 189, 205, 207, 208, 222
postal
3, 17, 42, 175, 201, 207–9, 214–16, 222, 225–28, 230–36, 238, 239, 242, 245, 248, 250, 252
posthumously
250
POW (prisoner of war)
44, 81, 130, 131, 154, 168, 185, 186, 233
prejudice
98, 100, 157
preparation
7, 11, 40–44, 66, 74, 84, 89, 96, 115, 136, 163, 164, 167, 182, 199, 233
president
2, 12–15, 52, 100, 138, 141, 142, 157, 194, 212, 218, 230, 238, 245, 250–52
press
2, 51, 102, 106, 158, 159, 191, 206, 213, 240, 248
Prestwick, Scotland
217, 219, 238
prison
44, 81, 108, 126, 129, 130, 132, 133, 144, 154, 168, 185–88, 195, 233, 234, 249
Pritchett, William TSgt (US Army 333rd Field Artillery Battalion)
193
private (rank)
1, 6, 22, 98, 115–18, 146, 193, 199, 243, 244, 251, 252
procedures
1, 7, 66, 80, 82, 84, 100, 129, 134, 140, 154, 163, 164, 168, 185, 208, 209, 213, 214, 225, 226, 228, 233
professor
137, 240
program
15, 32, 115, 118, 205, 239, 240, 250
promoted
74, 88, 122, 212, 215, 222, 236, 250
propaganda
112
protest
211, 213
Protestant
17, 157, 163

protocol
40, 162, 228, 229, 249
provisions
11, 38, 177, 224
psychological
5, 8, 9, 112
published
107, 122, 128, 132, 176, 190, 222, 240, 241, 249
PX (postal exchange)
17, 37

Q

qualification (tests, exams)
14, 50
quarters
38, 41, 79, 92, 94, 118, 174, 219, 222, 233
quotas
72, 212, 238

R

race
5, 7, 11, 13, 14, 38, 39, 42, 50–52, 54, 65, 67, 74, 75, 77–79, 86, 88, 94, 98, 116, 117, 119, 137, 140–42, 156, 175, 186, 196, 211–13, 215, 229, 230, 233, 236–38, 241, 248
radio
48, 66, 88, 136, 183, 206
RAF (Royal Air Force)
42, 172
Ragland, Mary T/5 (US Army 6888th Central Postal Directory Battalion)
240
Ramcke, Herman Gen (Chief Officer, Adolf Hitler's Palace Guard Unit)
173, 174
Ramsay, Sir Bertram Adm (British Naval Commander)
31
Randolph, Phillip (American labor unionist, activist, politician)
157
rank
9, 12, 65, 86, 113, 117, 123, 156, 157, 167, 212, 215, 220, 228, 250, 251
recognition
8, 32, 52, 79, 100, 137, 141–43, 191, 192, 196, 236, 240, 248, 250, 251
recommendation
51, 100, 106, 122, 241
reconnaissance

36, 104, 124, 182, 190
recreation
   33, 35, 229
recruit
   13–15, 17, 74, 81, 108, 115, 162, 180, 203, 211, 212, 215, 223, 224, 233, 246
Reed, Leon Lt Col (US Army)
   39
Regensburg, Bavaria
   131
regime
   126, 216
regiment
   4, 14, 87, 92, 104, 105, 119, 124, 130, 131, 141, 151, 179, 184, 185, 252
regulations
   98, 229
Reims, France
   135
Reisdorf, Bavaria
   124, 125
religion
   17, 70, 98, 205
Rennes, France
   172
repair
   39, 40, 66, 80, 105, 115, 121, 136, 169, 174
rescue
   51, 104, 111, 183, 210
research
   7, 13, 142, 241
reserve
   119, 157, 184, 210
rest and recuperation (R&R)
   108, 119, 131, 134, 174, 178, 179
retired
   35, 251
Rhine, Rhineland, Rhine River
   112, 124, 125, 128, 129, 132, 135, 137
Richardson, William L. Brig Gen (IX Air Defense command)
   52
Ridgeway, Matthew Gen (US Army; Supreme Allied Commander Europe; Chief of Staff))
   5
rifle
   12, 41, 48, 79, 84–86, 115, 116, 118, 126, 162, 189
Riley, Fort (US fort, Kansas)
   76
riot
   42, 112
river (various)
   41, 106, 124, 125, 128, 131, 134, 181
Rivers, Ruben SSG (US Army)
   100, 101, 121, 122, 250
Robinson, Jackie 2nd Lt (US Army 761st Tank Battalion; professional baseball player)
   74, 76, 77, 147, 244
role
   13, 29, 31, 38, 42, 52, 109, 115, 120, 158, 170, 181, 210, 222, 226, 230, 237, 238, 247, 252
Roosevelt, Theodore (US president)
   12, 13, 15, 72, 76, 156, 157, 159, 212, 215, 230
ROTC (Reserve Officers Training Corps)
   157
Rouen, France
   232–34, 242–44
route
   12, 16, 17, 38, 68, 121, 164, 169, 176, 177, 180, 184, 219, 232
rural
   14, 37, 78, 162
Russia
   68, 111, 129, 130, 132, 134, 135, 137
Rutgers University (New Jersey, US)
   75

S

sailors
   3
Saint Aubin, France
   177
Saint Lawrence, Canada
   12
Saint Quintin, France
   177
Saint-Sauveur-Lendelin, France
   172
Saint Vith, Belgium
   121
salute
   93, 136, 219, 221, 240, 250
Sarre Union, France
   105
Sauer River, Europe
   182
Schnee Eifel sector, Belgium
   180, 181

INDEX | 295

Schönberg, Germany
 109, 123, 179, 187
school
 1, 14, 29, 34, 76, 102, 105, 120, 153, 162, 205, 214, 215, 221, 223, 232, 237, 239
Schuster, Gladys PVT (US Army 6888th Central Postal Directory Battalion)
 240
Schuyler, George (American columnist, Pittsburgh Courier)
 156
Scotland
 42, 217, 219, 220, 224, 238
sea
 48, 135, 179, 208, 220
secretary
 142, 240, 241
security
 10, 30, 44, 45, 134, 164, 207, 218, 223, 233
segregated
 1–3, 5, 6, 9–11, 13–17, 37, 39, 65, 73–79, 88, 100, 103, 109, 117–19, 129, 137, 140, 155, 156, 164, 165, 168, 176, 179, 185, 186, 192, 215–17, 227, 229, 230, 236–38, 245, 251
senate
 190, 192
Senegal, Africa
 126
sergeant
 50, 54, 78, 82, 100, 101, 117, 121, 193, 203, 250–52
Serre, France
 97
service
 1–3, 5, 8, 11, 13, 15–17, 32, 33, 35, 37, 40, 41, 50–52, 65–67, 70, 71, 74, 76, 83, 84, 95, 100, 101, 104, 111, 112, 115, 117, 118, 121–24, 134, 137, 140, 143, 147, 155–59, 162, 165, 168, 173, 174, 178, 180, 183, 188, 190, 192, 194–96, 205, 206, 209–15, 221, 226, 229–31, 233, 237–41, 244–46, 251
sexism
 238
SHAEF (Supreme Headquarters Allied Expeditionary Forces)
 106
Shanks, Camp (US military camp, New York)
 41, 42, 77, 84, 164, 216
Shaw, Arko PFC (US Army 320th Barrage Balloon Battalion)
 22
shells
 47, 98, 106, 163, 174
shelter
 8, 154, 174
Sherman tank
 79, 82, 85, 86, 88, 92, 99, 104, 119, 123, 184
ship
 12, 29, 31, 35, 46, 51, 53, 54, 79, 87, 88, 105, 144, 167, 170, 173, 177, 216, 217
shoot
 81, 83, 94, 99, 122, 123, 133, 168, 169, 171, 176, 179, 183, 188, 189
shore
 46–49, 89
Shropshire, James Pvt (US Army 320th Barrage Balloon Battalion)
 22
Sicily, Italy
 246
Siegfried Line (German defense)
 86, 91, 99, 112, 124, 125, 128, 129, 141, 171, 173, 178, 179
Signal Company, 103rd (US Army 103rd Infantry Division)
 124
signed (documents, acts, awards, etc.)
 11, 12, 135, 139, 142, 186, 231, 238, 240, 250
Silver Star Medal
 100, 102, 118, 142, 196, 248
Simpson, William H. Gen (Fourth US Amy)
 5
sister (unit, battalion)
 161, 164, 173, 194
Six-Triple-Eight (nickname for 6888th Central Postal Directory Battalion)
 214, 218, 230
skirmishes
 120, 248
sky
 27, 29, 31, 32, 40, 50, 53, 55, 119, 157, 172, 177, 184, 218
slain
 47, 49, 90, 109, 113, 126, 169, 184, 188, 248
slavery

8, 14, 15
Smith, Alvin PFC (US Army 320th Barrage Balloon Battalion)
22
Smith, Walter Bedell "Beetle" Lt Gen (US Army)
5, 31
snipers
85, 102, 168
snow
97, 108, 178, 180, 184, 185, 187–90, 193
society
88, 235, 238, 240, 245
soldier
1–3, 5, 6, 8–17, 25, 28, 31–34, 37–54, 58, 63, 65–67, 69–81, 83–95, 98–105, 107–9, 111–13, 115–37, 140–42, 144, 153, 155–60, 162–65, 167–70, 172, 174–92, 195–97, 199, 200, 203, 205–8, 211, 213, 216–30, 232–34, 236, 237, 247–49, 251, 252
son
13, 157, 164, 205, 210, 251
south
1, 2, 6, 9, 13–17, 34, 37, 39, 42, 43, 54, 65, 67, 70–72, 75, 77–79, 88, 109, 124, 125, 129, 140, 156, 162, 165, 167, 172, 178, 193, 194, 207, 211, 213, 215, 218, 219, 230, 237
Southwick House, England (Gen Eisenhower command headquarters)
31
Soviet
135, 154
speech
83, 222, 236, 240
sports
78, 229, 232
spouse
70, 206, 209
Springarn, Dr. J.E. (NAACP Chairman)
71
squad
13, 39, 43, 44, 92, 167, 180, 252
SS (Schutzstaffel; German paramilitary organization under Adolf Hitler)
133, 185, 190, 195
St. Aubin-d'ubigné, Brittany, France
172, 177
St. Malo, Brittany, France
173

St. Nicolas-de-Port, Lorraine, France
92, 95, 96
St. Vith, Belgium
178, 179, 181, 185
staff
7, 10, 31, 39, 50, 54, 74, 92, 100, 101, 104, 118, 121, 130, 134, 137, 158, 169, 190, 193, 209, 219, 221, 223, 228, 240, 250, 251
standard
6, 8, 14, 15, 43, 78, 82, 102, 154, 163
stars (medals)
52, 54, 100, 102, 113, 142, 179, 196, 248
Stars and Stripes Newspaper (military paper)
51, 102, 128
state (US states)
2, 14, 39, 69, 73, 84, 88, 140, 159, 165, 211, 240, 245, 247, 249, 251
station
14, 17, 29, 33, 35, 76, 77, 84, 98, 102, 130, 164, 181, 206, 215, 224, 226, 234, 241
stereotype
86, 122, 230
stevedore (US Army)
6, 115, 177
Stevens, Johnny SSG (US Army 761st Tank Battalion)
133
Steward, Camp (US military camp, Georgia)
39
Stewart, Camp (US military camp, Georgia)
54
Stewart, James TSgt (US Army 333rd Field Artillery Battalion)
54, 193
Steyer, Austria
134
strategy
11, 46, 48, 68, 96, 108, 119, 163, 177, 178, 249
strike
47, 73, 75, 104, 108, 189
structures
37, 91, 120, 125, 171
Stuart tank
79, 123
submarine

170
subordinate
　139, 167, 168, 173, 228, 249
success
　3, 9, 11, 13, 29, 32, 33, 49, 55, 66–68, 82, 86, 93, 94, 101, 106–8, 112, 115, 120, 122–25, 128, 129, 136, 159, 169–71, 179, 181, 214, 222, 225, 227, 233, 236, 246, 250
Sumlin, Jessie CPL (US Army 320th Barrage Balloon Battalion)
　22
supplies
　17, 33, 47–49, 96, 109, 115, 126, 136, 141, 158, 169, 170, 184, 223
support
　2, 12, 15, 16, 38, 44, 46, 47, 51, 54, 71, 72, 85, 86, 92, 97, 99–101, 106, 107, 109, 111, 112, 119, 124, 125, 128–31, 143, 156–58, 160, 168, 171–75, 177, 179, 181, 184, 194, 211–14, 219, 224, 236, 238, 245, 248
Supreme Commander of Allied Forces (Gen Dwight D. Eisenhower)
　31, 52, 59, 74, 106, 109, 116, 135, 229
surprise attack
　12, 158, 169, 183
surrender
　54, 109–11, 125, 126, 130, 131, 135, 174, 178, 183, 185–88, 195, 231, 245
survive
　50, 52, 79, 104, 133, 142, 143, 171, 174, 184–86, 188, 194, 196, 199, 217, 240, 250, 252
Switzerland
　91, 106, 154
Sword Beach, Normandy, France
　46, 167
system
　39, 66, 70, 80, 174, 207–9, 225, 226, 234, 238, 239

T

tactical
　5, 11, 33, 40, 41, 44, 46–48, 50, 53, 66–68, 73, 74, 79, 80, 85–87, 105, 125, 126, 161, 162, 206
tank
　3, 11, 13, 42, 47, 55, 60, 61, 65–68, 71–74, 76–82, 84–93, 95, 98–102, 104–7, 109, 111–14, 117, 119–37, 139–47, 153, 158, 160, 164, 167, 169–71, 173, 174, 177, 180, 183, 184, 240, 245, 247, 250
target
　6, 12, 47, 66, 79–81, 84, 88, 162, 163, 172, 179, 182
task
　31, 45, 47, 112, 124, 128, 130, 138, 211, 213, 219, 228, 236
Taylor, James T. (Dean of Men, North Carolina College for Negroes)
　157
team
　44, 47, 73, 94, 113, 129, 139, 141, 143, 168, 178, 219, 225, 229, 235, 240, 250
technical
　7, 11, 13, 32–34, 36, 40, 66, 67, 70, 71, 73, 80, 120, 123, 153, 160, 163, 193, 206, 207, 211, 247
Teddy, Arthur (British Air Chief)
　31
Teisendorf, Germany
　140
telegram
　157
telephone
　40, 90, 183, 206
television
　205, 206
temperatures
　97, 108, 120, 137, 180, 187
Tennessee, US
　15, 32, 37–39, 41, 57, 79, 102
tennis
　229, 233
tent
　41, 73, 79, 180
terrain
　46, 73, 79, 85, 86, 105, 107, 128, 138, 163, 171
territory
　12, 34, 73, 105, 106, 180
test
　6, 8, 14, 33, 41, 50, 73, 233
Texas, US
　39, 73, 77, 81, 143, 193, 211, 250
Thanksgiving
　104
Theater, European (European Theater of War)
　2, 3, 5, 17, 31, 52, 86, 91, 115–17, 119, 138, 141, 142, 175, 179, 194, 208, 209, 214, 219–22, 234, 245, 248, 250
three-star general (US Army)

74, 94, 161, 167
Tiger tanks (German)
  180
Tillet, France
  97, 109, 111, 112
Timberlake, E.W. Brig Gen (49th Anti-Aircraft Artillery Brigade)
  52
Tommies (British soldiers)
  50
Torchville, France
  102
torture
  189, 190
tournaments
  229, 233
town
  17, 37, 38, 69, 89–92, 96, 97, 99, 101, 102, 104, 105, 108, 109, 112, 121, 125, 126, 130, 141, 155, 168, 169, 171, 173, 177, 178, 207
tradition
  17, 73, 101, 104, 132, 180, 216, 220, 221
tragedy
  3, 35, 36, 85, 155, 191, 249
trains
  17, 41, 44, 77, 79, 132, 164, 216, 221, 232
transferred
  17, 46, 76, 226, 232
transportation
  14, 33, 44, 48, 51, 53, 115, 126, 132, 165, 170, 185, 187, 217, 220, 245
travel
  33, 35, 68, 77, 123, 163, 173, 177, 215, 216, 218, 232
Traves Haute-Saome, France
  195
treaty
  11, 98, 154
trek
  90, 92, 128, 177, 234
trenches
  85, 91, 150, 182
tribute
  138, 143
troops
  10, 11, 31, 33, 41, 42, 47–49, 66–68, 75, 78–85, 87, 106, 107, 113, 116, 117, 121, 126, 143, 151, 168, 171, 174, 177, 178, 182, 189–91, 198, 217, 218, 220, 221, 226, 229, 242, 249, 252
trucks
  90, 115, 118, 132, 136, 163, 170, 183, 187, 188, 245
Truman, Harry (US President)
  14, 238
Truscott, Lucian Gen (US Army)
  5
turret
  82
Tuskegee Airmen (US Army Air Forces)
  1, 3, 13, 157, 252
two-star general (US Army)
  67, 102, 161
Tyson, Camp (US military camp, Tennessee)
  32, 37–41, 57
Tzu, Sun Gen (China)
  105

U

U-boat
  53, 216
UCLA (University of California at Los Angeles)
  76
Ukrainian
  135
uniform
  1, 6, 8, 17, 75, 140, 143, 150, 154, 180, 210, 221, 231, 245, 246
Union
  33, 97, 105, 131, 132, 154
unit
  1–3, 5, 6, 8, 11, 14, 30, 32, 34, 35, 39–44, 48, 50–55, 65–68, 71–79, 81, 82, 84–88, 90, 92–97, 100–102, 105, 106, 109, 111, 115–20, 122–29, 131, 134–36, 138–43, 153, 155–61, 163, 164, 167–73, 175–77, 179–81, 184, 185, 190, 192, 194, 205–9, 211, 213–16, 220–30, 232–36, 238, 240, 241, 245, 247–52
United Kingdom (UK)
  165, 219, 230
United States of America
  2, 3, 5, 7, 10–16, 18, 20, 21, 29–32, 34, 35, 37–39, 41, 43, 45, 47, 49–52, 54, 63, 65, 67, 68, 70, 71, 73–75, 77, 81–86, 88, 89, 101, 102, 104, 106–8, 111–13, 115, 117, 119, 121, 124, 125,

128–31, 134–36, 138–43, 145, 147, 153–57, 167, 168, 170–73, 175–84, 187–89, 191–96, 200, 206, 208, 210–15, 223–25, 229, 232–34, 236–41, 244, 245, 247–52
university (various)
50, 75, 76, 98, 137, 140, 237, 241
USMC (United States Marine Corps)
252
USO (United Services Organization)
174, 175
Utah Beach, Normandy, France
30, 46, 49, 53, 167

V
valor
51, 95, 113, 121, 169, 191, 196, 248, 250
Vandenberg, Hoyt S. Maj Gen (Ninth Air Force commander)
52
V-Bombs
136
VE Day (Victory in Europe Day)
135, 231
vehicle
13, 33, 35, 48, 66, 74, 78–80, 89, 90, 93, 122, 126, 130, 136, 141, 145, 163, 167, 173, 177, 183, 187, 190, 232, 246
Velden, Germany
131
Veldenstein Castle, Germany
131
veteran
2, 82, 104, 107, 115–17, 138, 143, 170, 173, 195, 237–40, 251, 252
VHA (Very High Altitude Balloon)
39
Vic-sur-Seille, France
97, 98, 113, 147
victory
3, 45, 49, 67, 68, 97, 107, 108, 112, 116, 124, 135, 136, 139, 194, 197, 231, 234, 242
Vietnam War
153, 205–7, 241, 245, 251
village
69, 108, 109, 112, 121, 125, 126, 171
Virginia, US
39, 142, 193, 239, 241
VLA (Very Low Altitude Balloon)
39

Volkswagen
188, 195, 249
volleyball
229, 233
volunteer
2, 16, 71, 75, 86, 116–18, 210, 212, 214, 216, 237
von Clausewitz, Carl Gen (Prussian)
105, 110, 135, 182
von Friedburg, Hans Adm (Germany)
135
von Lüttwitz, Heinrich Freiherr Gen (Panzertruppe; Germany)
110
von Rundstedt, Karl Rudolf Gerd Generalfeldmarschall (German Field Marshal)
182
vote
10, 13, 140, 230

W
WAAC (Women's Army Auxiliary Corps)
158, 202, 210–12, 215, 239
WAC (Women's Army Corps)
158, 205, 210, 212–16, 219–23, 229, 230, 233, 235, 239–41
Waffen SS (combat branch of Nazi paramilitary organization)
190
wagons
33, 232
Wales, Great Britain
42, 43
war
1–3, 5–7, 9–13, 15, 17, 25, 28–36, 39–41, 44–46, 50–52, 54, 65, 66, 68, 69, 71–74, 76, 79, 81–83, 86–88, 90, 91, 93–95, 97, 98, 100, 101, 103, 105, 106, 108, 109, 111, 112, 117–19, 121, 122, 124–26, 129, 130, 132, 134, 135, 137, 139–43, 147, 151, 153–59, 161, 162, 164, 167, 168, 170, 173, 174, 177, 178, 180, 181, 185–88, 190–97, 205–8, 210, 211, 213–20, 223–25, 228, 232–41, 244, 245, 247–52
Washington (DC, state)
15, 54, 68, 82, 215, 216, 239
WASPS (Women Air Force Service Pilots)
210
water

30, 41, 48, 51, 53, 89, 158, 162, 170, 174, 188, 216, 223
weapon
   12-14, 17, 39, 41, 45, 48, 66, 71, 74, 75, 79, 81, 85, 88, 116, 124, 126, 136, 161-64, 169, 174, 177, 183, 185, 189, 195, 197, 216, 217, 223, 247
weather
   30, 39, 41, 53, 89, 97, 107, 108, 111, 112, 119, 120, 128, 138, 162, 163, 178, 184, 188, 189, 207
Weems, Mary Maj (US Army WAC Director)
   219
Weinstein, Lewis TSgt (US Army Chief of the Liaison)
   118
Wereth, Belgium
   108, 109, 186-92, 194, 196, 197, 249
white
   1, 2, 5-11, 14-17, 32, 37-39, 42, 52, 54, 65, 67, 71-76, 78, 79, 81, 82, 86, 88, 90, 92, 95, 98, 101-3, 109, 112, 113, 116-18, 121, 122, 130, 138, 140, 141, 153, 155-63, 165, 166, 170, 175, 176, 185-87, 195, 196, 211-14, 216, 217, 219-21, 225, 227-30, 233, 234, 236-39, 247-49, 251
Whitelaw, John Brig Gen (US Army Assistant Division Commander 17th Airborne)
   113
WIA (wounded in action)
   129
Wiesel, Elie (American writer, activist, Nobel Laureate in Peace)
   133
wife
   1, 16, 94, 211, 249
Williams, D.J. Capt (US Army)
   74, 75, 98, 99, 101, 113
win
   55, 67, 74, 118, 132, 135, 157, 168, 174, 197, 210, 212, 230, 233, 246, 249
winch operations
   40, 43, 48
Wingo, Charles Maj (US Army)
   98-100
withdraw
   101, 105, 183, 185

woman
   3, 6, 8, 11, 13, 37, 38, 65, 70, 88, 90, 111, 132-35, 158, 165, 175, 190, 203, 205, 208-19, 221-27, 229, 230, 232-41, 245, 246, 248, 250, 252
Women Air Force Service Pilots (WASPS)
   210
Woodson, Waverly "Woody" Jr. SSG (US Army)
   50-52, 54, 250
Woodward, Edna Capt (US Women's Army Corps)
   252
work
   6, 11, 13, 37-39, 41, 49, 51, 75, 78, 79, 81, 85, 92, 129, 135-37, 156-58, 160, 162, 163, 195, 209, 211, 220, 223, 226-28, 233-35, 237, 249
wounded
   46, 50, 51, 80, 89, 97, 98, 100-105, 108, 111, 113, 120, 121, 125, 130, 131, 141, 174, 179, 181, 183, 185, 186, 190, 194, 196, 206, 226
writer
   156, 205
Wuisse, Germany
   99
WWI
   5-7, 34, 35, 91, 150, 159, 171
WWII
   3, 10, 11, 13, 14, 27, 40, 49, 54, 55, 63, 65, 67, 71, 76, 81, 92, 131, 132, 143, 144, 155, 161, 162, 164, 170, 175-77, 179, 194, 198, 205, 207, 209, 210, 218, 220-23, 227, 233, 234, 236-40
Wyman, Willard G. Maj Gen (US Army)
   137, 138

X

XII Corps (Patton's Third Army)
   87, 91, 92, 106, 128
XLVII German Panzer Corps
   109
XVIII Corps
   121
XX Corps (Patton's Third Army)
   87, 92

Y

Yale University (Connecticut, US)

98
Yank Magazine (WWII publication)
176

Z
zeppelins (blimps)
    35
zone
    42, 51, 91, 116, 147, 17

www.ingramcontent.com/pod-product-compliance
Lightning Source LLC
LaVergne TN
LVHW041748060526
838201LV00046B/945